Spiritual Direction

Spiritual Direction

A Beginner's Guide

by

Richard G. Malloy, S.J.

ORBIS BOOKS

Maryknoll, New York 10545

ORBIS BOOKS
Maryknoll, New York 10545

Fathers and Brothers
MARYKNOLL™

Founded in 1970, Orbis Books endeavors to publish works that enlighten the mind, nourish the spirit, and challenge the conscience. The publishing arm of the Maryknoll Fathers and Brothers, Orbis seeks to explore the global dimensions of the Christian faith and mission, to invite dialogue with diverse cultures and religious traditions, and to serve the cause of reconciliation and peace. The books published reflect the views of their authors and do not represent the official position of the Maryknoll Society. To learn more about Maryknoll and Orbis Books, please visit our website at www.maryknollsociety.org.

Library of Congress Cataloging-in-Publication Data

Names: Malloy, Richard G., author.
Title: Spiritual direction : a beginner's guide / Richard G. Malloy.
Description: Maryknoll : Orbis Books, 2017. | Includes bibliographical
   references and index.
Identifiers: LCCN 2017010525 (print) | LCCN 2017027164 (ebook) | ISBN
   9781608337187 (e-book) | ISBN 9781626982536 (pbk.)
Subjects: LCSH: Spiritual direction--Catholic Church. | Spiritual
   life--Christianity.
Classification: LCC BX2350.7 (ebook) | LCC BX2350.7 .M35 2017 (print) | DDC
   253.5/3--dc23
LC record available at https://lccn.loc.gov/2017010525

Contents

Preface

The twenty-first century will be religious or spiritual, or not at all.
—Andre Malraux

The treasure is hidden within you. . . . The treasure is hidden within the field of our inner experience. As we reach adulthood, we become more aware not only of the field's mystery and complexity, but also its dangers and so the temptation is to ignore it. We may succeed, but our inner life will remain alive, influencing our behavior and often kicking vigorously.
—Gerard W. Hughes, S.J., *God of Surprises*

Mother Teresa diagnosed the world's ills in this way: we've just "forgotten that we belong to one another." Kinship is what happens to us when we refuse to let that happen. With kinship as the goal, other essential things fall into place; without it, no justice, no peace. I suspect that were kinship our goal, we would no longer be promoting justice—we would be celebrating it.
—Greg Boyle, S.J., *Tattoos on the Heart*

"We have just enough religion to make us hate one another," Jonathan Swift once observed, *"but not enough to make us love one another."*
—Pastor Barbara Taylor, *An Altar in the World*

Spiritual direction is all about finding the treasure within us, there in our inner experience. All we need do is pay attention to our inner selves and how we relate to reality. Such attention will help us live happy and healthy and holy and free.

I'm visiting friends. Great News! They have just become grandparents! My mother used to say, "Grandchildren are what you get for not killing your own kids." This couple is overjoyed that their little grandson (7 lbs., 10 ozs.!) has been born healthy and whole. But they share they feel a little estranged from their adult children. Their four kids, they think, are holding them at arm's length. I've known this family for over twenty-five years. I suggest that maybe the kids are just "in their twenties." What were we like when we were twenty-somethings back in the 1970s? A good spiritual director will try to tease out in informal and more scheduled settings what is moving in our minds and hearts. Which thoughts, feelings, worries, hopes, dreams, fears are getting us to where were are happy, holy, healthy, and free? And which are moving us away from being our deepest, truest selves? This couple really wants to be relishing and enjoying the wonder of a grandchild in their lives, not wallowing in worries about whether or not their own kids love them. And we all have to learn how to really let go and trust at times. Their kids are fine. Parents can sometimes feel adrift in the empty nest. This is friendship-level "spiritual direction."

At an Ignatian silent retreat in a Jesuit retreat center, a woman photographer shares that her banker husband is not as communicative and loving as she would like. She feels love starved. She wants much more for and from her marriage of over twenty years. Over several days of prayer and conversation about what she's hearing from a God in whom she's not sure she really believes, she discerns and decides she has to go and tell her husband and their son what she really needs and wants from them. She is noticeably more relaxed and comfortable after taking a few days to wrestle with these matters. There's a smile on her face and a bounce in her step. She's had a good retreat.

A few months later she calls me. I'm in an airport. We take up where we left off. She followed up. Really laid it on the line for her family. There was some positive response from her husband and son. Her son is noticeably better in the way he deals with her. But her husband is still too distant, too unable to relate to her the way she wants. Now there's a guy at work who is into "polyamory." Why shouldn't she go and get from him what her husband can't or won't give her? She wants to "keep commitments made," but this is a difficult discernment for her.

We talk for an hour on the phone. (My plane is delayed. Divine intervention?) I offer various ways of thinking and praying about what she's facing. Starting a new relationship often just means that both people bring along all the baggage and unresolved issues from previous relationships. Is this option really better? Will it fulfill her and make her happy, or will it just throw her life into chaos? A friend once told me he asked a buddy of ours how his second marriage was. (The guy had divorced his first wife.) The guy said, "Well, it's about 2 percent better." Is ending a marriage, or living in "polyamory" (whatever that is), worth it? For "2 percent better"? Still, she has to make the decision. Spiritual direction is much like coaching. A director is on the sidelines, while the directee is out on the field with her/himself, others, and God. The phone connection clicks off.

I sit in the bustling airport and pray. I ask God to help this woman. Spiritual direction often extends beyond the formal time of silent retreat, and good direction is rooted in prayer beyond the scheduled sessions. God works in mysterious and often opaque ways. We were always told at the Jesuit Center in Wernersville, Pennsylvania, to suggest to people that they wait a few months before evaluating what actually happens in a retreat. What is God's desire here? God wants the woman to know and feel love in her life. Should she wait for her husband to change in ways he may never change? Can she change in ways I've suggested she might think about doing? Can she accept her life as it basically is, and find joy and peace? Is the commitment of marriage worth it? Does the sacrament hold? Spiritual direction is no power trip. I have no way of making her do anything one way or the other. As St. Ignatius said, the Holy Spirit is the real director. We must trust the slow and sometimes confusing work of God in people's hearts, minds, and lives.

It's 11:30. I've been listening to confessions for three hours on a Saturday night SEARCH retreat at the University of Scranton Chapman Lake Retreat Center. A sophomore woman enters the small meeting room where I'm sitting clothed in Catholic alb and stole. She sits in the chair adjacent to mine. A candle is lit next to the Bible on the small table in front of us. I welcome her and begin to explain gently what the sacrament of reconciliation is all about. Many college students haven't been to confession in years. "Naming what is messing up our lives, that's what sin is. Sin messes up our lives. Naming what is hurting us gives us the power, the ability, to begin letting God help us no longer allow sin to mess up our lives."

Her eyes well with tears. "I just want to talk. I don't really know if I need to confess anything." She sits. I wait. In a minute she sighs, and with stunning sadness says, "I hate myself. I hate everything about myself." A long conversation ensues. Trying to get her to really know that God loves her, and that a relationship with God can be a basis for her learning how to love herself, will involve resolving her relationship with her father, and coming to believe she is lovable and of supreme value and worth, just as she is. But this won't happen in one, long conversation. It will take lots of listening and offering back to her ways she can begin to imagine herself and her life in more loving and life-giving ways. Ongoing spiritual direction can be a lifeline for her.

What do you want out of life? If you're lucky, you will live eighty years, some 29,200 days. What will you do with all those hours? How will you choose? What method will guide you in creating this one, wonderful life you've been given? Are there lifelines that can help you? Spiritual direction in the Ignatian tradition can be a relationship that can assist you on your journey. And at root and route, at heart and mind and soul, our lives' journeys are all about love. We are made by love, for love, to love, unto love.[1] Spiritual direction helps us to live our lives in loving relationship to God, to become our deepest, truest selves, and to form a just and peaceful world.

Adele and Garth Brooks have both sung the beautiful lyrics of Bob Dylan's "Make Me Feel Your Love": "I'd go hungry; I'd go black and blue, I'd go crawling down the avenue. There ain't nothing I wouldn't do, to make you feel my love." Who loves you? Who do you love? God is love and God wants to make you feel God's love: personally, communally, deeply, really. You can experience God. You can communicate with God. You can learn God's language of love. Now, caution. The great comedian Lily Tomlin once said, "How come when we talk to God, we call it prayer. But when God talks to us, we call it schizophrenia?" Learning how to name and claim our experiences of God is challenging. This book is all about how to meet that challenge, and meet it holding close the guidance and wisdom of ancient traditions. The good news is that people have spent centuries trying to figure out how to relate to God, how to communicate with God, how to live our lives rooted in and following the route of that central relationship in our lives.

More, such a centering of ourselves in our relationship with God opens us to both the deepest depths of the final frontier, our deepest, truest selves, and to the deepest depths of our relationships with others. The more we are connected to, in contact with, and aware of God in our lives, the more we are called to pay attention to those who need our love. And real love is best expressed in deeds of service.

Disney's animated film *The Hunchback of Notre Dame* is a spectacular lesson aimed at children, but merits adult attention, too. The gypsy girl Esmeralda courageously defends the Hunchback as he is ridiculed and pelted with garbage on the town square. The town powers chase her

---

1. Cf. Richard G. Malloy, *A Faith That Frees: Catholic Matters for the 21st Century* (Maryknoll, NY: Orbis Books, 2008), 103.

into the cathedral, where she seeks sanctuary. She sings before a statue of Mary "God Help the Outcasts":

"I don't know if You can hear me, or if You're even there. I don't know if You would listen to a gypsy's prayer. Yes, I know I'm just an outcast. I shouldn't speak to You. Still I see Your face and wonder, were You once an outcast too? God help the outcasts, hungry from birth. Show them the mercy they don't find on earth. God help my people. We look to You still, God help the outcasts, or nobody will."

People of the church are heard singing, asking for favors from God—self-centered, self-seeking favors. "I ask for wealth, I ask for fame, I ask for glory to shine on my name. I ask for love, I can possess. I ask for God and his angels to bless me."

Esmeralda sings in response, "I ask for nothing. I can get by. But I know so many less lucky than I. Please help my people, the poor and down trod. I thought we all were the children of God. God help the outcast, children of God."

Spiritual direction can help us begin to hear the cry of the poor, especially when we've been able to listen to our own pain. As we realize God transforming us, we can glimpse how to generously cooperate in God's transformation of our world. Spiritual direction can also help us know the joy in our lives, the joy that is rooted in God's love for us. Out of pain and joy, we can again hope the fires of God's love can transform us and our world.

INTRODUCTION

Spiritual Direction: Puzzle to Promise to Purpose

Most people do not see things as they are; rather they see things as they are.

—Richard Rohr, *Falling Upward*

"Tell me one last thing," said Harry. "Is this real? Or has this been happening inside my head?" Dumbledore beamed at him . . . , "Of course it's happening inside your head, Harry, but why on earth should that mean that it is not real?"

—J. K. Rowling, *Harry Potter and the Deathly Hollows*

Life does not consist mainly—or even largely—of facts and happenings. Life consists mainly of the storm of thoughts that is forever blowing through one's head.

— Mark Twain

Be Yourself. Everyone else is taken. (No one's really sure who said this).

There's an old story of a man walking up to a construction site and engaging the workers in conversation. He asks what they are doing. The first man says, "I'm mixing cement." The second says, "I'm laying bricks." The third replies, "I'm building a cathedral."

Life is often a puzzle. Sometimes it is hard to see the cathedral in the cement and bricks of our days. The power of our faith provides promise. The practice of spiritual direction can help us identify and fit together the pieces of the puzzle, release the power of the Holy Spirit in our minds, hearts, and souls, and make the promise of our purpose more evident in the living of our lives of service and praise.

Spiritual direction helps us realize our lives and actions in larger contexts, more and more related to and connected with everything that is. It is a relational process within which a person is listened to and heard, and she or he in turn listens to a coach/companion/director who strives to help the directee recognize, discern, and live out the graced and gifted patterns God weaves in the tapestry of our lives. In spiritual direction, followers of Jesus come to know and become their deepest, truest selves in community. Frank and open dialogue forms the fulcrum by which God enters into the graced conversations. Prayer practice and loving service test the insights and inspirations shared by two disciples trying to find God, and for Christians, trying to live as Jesus would in our complex, confusing, and often contradictory contemporary world. Our faith seeks understanding. Philosopher Hans Georg Gadamer writes: "To understand means to come to an understanding with each other. Understanding is primarily agreement." Furthermore, "To reach an understanding in a dialogue is not merely a matter of putting oneself forward and successfully asserting one's own point of view, but being transformed into a communion in which we do not remain what we were."[1]

Spiritual direction helps us "come to an understanding" so we can better understand ourselves, our communities, our God, and the relationship between the three. In spiritual direction we discern and discover the community currents and commitments that contour the choices and prayerful patterns of our lives. We see deeper into the social structures that make up our societies.

When I entered the Society of Jesus, the message mediated to me by my novice director and spiritual directors was "Be yourself. That's the person God has called to the work of faith and justice and reconciliation as a Jesuit today." When I once said to an older, wiser Jesuit that I hoped to be like some famous Jesuits, like a Horace McKenna or a Dan Berrigan, he said something I've never forgotten: "Why don't you just be the first Rick Malloy?" Years of regular spiritual direction, sitting across from wise and sometimes tough old Jesuits, fed me, at times forcing me to eat and drink deeply from traditions and ways of being I needed to appropriate and fashion to become who and what I am today. At times, being directed by female spiritual directors opened new soul vistas. The ministry of lay persons, providing me with insight and direction, has grounded

---

1. Hans Georg Gadamer, *Truth and Method*, 2nd ed., trans. Joel Weinsheimer and Donald G. Marshall (New York: Crossroad, 1991), 180, 379.

me in aspects of life I may have overlooked. Reading widely from spiritual authors has revealed the beauty of our Catholic tradition's many ways of relating to God. Experiences far and wide have shown me varied apostolic paradigms. In all this God has led me, to some degree, to know who I am and what I am to do to further the Reign of God in my life and in the lives of others.

God wants us to be ourselves, the persons we deeply desire to be; as one jokester put it, to be "the person my dog thinks I am." That person, discerned and discovered by listening to and monitoring our passions and desires, that person challenged and created by our choices, that person we form and fashion constantly throughout our lives—that person is the person God needs in the world today. Our deepest, truest self is met and formed in the context of community.

To be an adult follower of Jesus the Christ in the twenty-first century means that one needs to be making a multitude of choices, often with little guidance. Our religious traditions are weak to nonexistent. Young people have "helicopter" or "lawn mower" parents, but little beyond their immediate family to form and fashion, challenge and console, who and what they are and are becoming. St. Ignatius of Loyola (1491–1556), the founder of the Society of Jesus, aka the Jesuits, developed ways to make and chart choices, based on the use of our memory, intellect, and will. Today we might summarize those three words with our "heart": "the heart is the dwelling place where I am, where I live."[2] We need to learn how to listen to the desires and promptings of our hearts. Ignatius's Spiritual Exercises are relational, based on our desires to love one another and, in so doing, choose and find our way to God. Ignatius championed the use of our imaginations in our forming of our hearts and in deciding who we will be and what we will do. Learning and practicing Ignatian Spirituality can transform our lives and our world. Spiritual direction is one help to living out our lives in relation to God and others.

Two expert spiritual directors, Jesuits Bill Barry and Bill Connolly, "define Christian spiritual direction, then, as help given by one believer to another that enables the latter to pay attention to God's personal communication to him or her, to respond to this personally communicating God, to grow in intimacy with this God, and to live out the consequences

---

2. *Catechism of the Catholic Church* (New York, NY: Doubleday, 1995), §2563 [hereafter CCC].

of the relationship."[3] Barry and Connolly go on to note that spiritual direction in the Ignatian tradition concentrates on experience, not necessarily ideas alone. Often we need to get out of our heads and stop thinking about God; we more want to relish the experience of God, an experience always mediated by our human relationships and realities. There is a great difference between kissing a girl and thinking about kissing a girl. There is a great difference between daydreaming about making the last shot to win the basketball game and actually doing so. There's a great difference in thinking about praying and actually praying.

God is mystery and promise more than answer and rule book. Barry shares that from his extensive experience as a spiritual director, he has found that God seeks us out, God wants to be in relationship with us, God wants to be with us and guide us like a loving and good parent. Those who want to deepen their friendship with God, those who want to accept the challenge of Jesus being Lord of our lives, those who want to more carefully and consciously notice and interpret the action of the Holy Spirit in our lives and world often find spiritual direction a crucial aid on their journey. Without spiritual direction, or at least guidance or mentoring, we risk making unreasonable judgments and poor decisions. Spiritual direction can help us adhere to the path of authenticity and avoid the wrong exits and pitfalls of choosing what is unauthentic.

It was said of St. Peter Canisius that, as a superior of the Jesuit community, he called forth in the men talents and abilities that existed first only in his own graced imagination. I imagine Canisius achieved success in that delicate task of calling men to become their deepest, truest selves by practicing the art of spiritual direction.

The point and purpose of spiritual direction is an ever-increasing awareness of our transformation in Christ, an ever-deepening awareness that the Holy Spirit, God, resides within us, impelling us to give ourselves to birthing forth the Kingdom of God in our lives and times. Thomas Merton, the Trappist monk and superlative spiritual writer, teaches that the Holy Spirit resides within us and that it's sad that we don't realize this transformative Spirit of joy and peace. We become our deepest, truest selves more by God's power than our power: "We become saints not by violently overcoming our own weakness, but by letting the Lord give us the strength and purity of his Spirit in exchange for our weakness and

---

3. Sean Salai, S.J., "In All Things: The Art of Spiritual Direction: Q&A with William A. Barry, S.J.," *America,* November 23, 2016.

misery. Let us not then complicate our lives and frustrate ourselves by fixing too much attention on ourselves, thereby forgetting the power of God."[4]

And the more we come to know and appreciate who and what we are in relation to God, the more we come to awareness of the other in our lives, the other who is God and the other who we may think are strangers in our lives, but who in reality are our sisters and brothers. Pastor Barbara Taylor writes: "The Hebrew Bible in one verse commands, 'You shall love your neighbor as yourself,' but in no fewer than 36 places commands us to 'love the stranger.' Why should we love the stranger? Because God does."[5]

Spiritual direction can help us know and relish the more transcendent aspect of our lives and being. It can help us know ourselves, others, and God. In this life, we are not just mixing cement, or laying bricks. We are building cathedrals. *Ad Majorem Dei Gloriam*, to the Greater Glory of God.

---

4. Thomas Merton, *Life and Holiness* (New York: Herder and Herder, 1963), 30–32.

5. Barbara Taylor, *An Altar in the World: A Geography of Faith* (New York: Harper-One, 2009), 97.

CHAPTER 1

What Is the "Spiritual" Life?

What lies beyond us and what lies before us are tiny matters when compared to what lies within us.
—Ralph Waldo Emerson

What is Spirituality? To have the answer is to have misunderstood the question.
— Ernest Kurtz and Katherine Ketcham,
The Spirituality of Imperfection

People know when their gifts are being wasted, and this knowledge can eat away at the soul like cancer. Call me a romantic, but I think most people want to be good for something. I think they want to do something that matters, to be part of something bigger than themselves, to give themselves to something that is meaningful instead of meaningless.
—Barbara Taylor, An Altar in the World

The Barna Research group reports that seventy-five million Christians go to church every Sunday. Why do they go? What are they seeking? . . . they keep coming back to church . . . despite the fact that fewer than a third of them feel they accomplish their main reason for coming: to connect with God. Eventually these people cease to expect a real encounter with God and simply settle for a pleasant experience.
—Mark Thibodeaux, S.J., Armchair Mystic

Many people today are interested in the "spiritual" life. But many of them don't feel they "really" connect with God. They often imagine an experience of God that simply doesn't exist. To connect with God means meeting God where God is, and God meeting us where we are.

God is not some six-beer feeling. God is mystery and meaning. God exists in the daily joys and struggles of our lives. You can find God both on a mountaintop or in teaching fourth graders, both in liturgies so high you get nosebleeds and in the innocent joy of tee-ball games.

When we practice and promulgate Ignatian Spirituality, we closely monitor and examine in prayer what goes on in the hearts and heads of people. In prayer, we trace the contours of meaning and revelation in our interior lives. In our overly empirical world, where what is real is understood from what can be seen and touched, spirituality can seem unreal. Yet we experience realities that we cannot sense or touch. Think of memories, for example. Or stories that move and shape us. In *Harry Potter and the Deathly Hallows*, after Dumbledore's death, Harry has an experience of his mentor's presence and asks, "Is this real, or has this just been happening inside my head?" Dumbledore replies, "Of course it's happening inside your head, Harry, but why on earth should that mean that it is not real?" The "really real" consists of the two worlds we inhabit, our inner being and the external realities with which we are in relation.

Spirituality is all about what is happening in our heads and our hearts, and how those interior realities interact with and construct the world beyond us. The spiritual aspects of our being are multiple and magnificent: our desires and dreams; hopes and hurts; fears and failings, and on and on—all the flow of consciousness we experience when we close our eyes and listen to our interior rumblings and ruminations. As Mark Twain says, "Life consists mainly of the storm of thoughts that is forever blowing through one's head."

The heart is the center of our being, "the depths of one's being," where the person decides definitively for whom, and with whom, one will live and how one will relate to God (CCC §368; cf. also §2563). Spiritual direction helps us delve into our hearts, on personal, communal, and social levels. A good director can help me become more aware of what I am choosing to do and be, what my communities are choosing to do and be, what the society in which I live chooses to do and be. I am missioned to teach at a Jesuit university. Most days I wake up, and with mug of coffee, Bible, and newspaper in hand, begin the day with prayer. I try and center my heart in God. Then I choose the daily tasks and ways of interacting with students and staff. Within the relationships that make up the school is where my heart is centered most days. A Jesuit school is a wonder to behold, serving as a locus of transformation for young adults, but I am aware of the dangerous debt many students must undertake to make the institution viable. And I am aware of the immense goodness that abounds in much of America, but my heart is torn by our being an empire that routinely kills in the name of freedom, as our drones attempt to strike at "terrorism" and too often cause collateral damage, i.e., the murders of innocents. I often mull over what's going on in my heart and feel the tugs to do more. But when I feel my heart becoming too restless and anxious about many things, I am reminded of this piece of wisdom, advice that an old Jesuit gave us for getting along in the Society of Jesus (or life in general): "One, know and realize that you are not God. Two, this is not heaven. Three, don't be an asshole."

Throughout most of human history, religions have played a large part in channeling and organizing spiritual energies and pathways. Today, religions and religious institutions are in great flux. The changes in societies and cultures in the past fifty to one hundred years have made the truth claims of religions and the religious practices of the past, suspect, if not outright rejected.

What the Spiritual Life Is Not

It is important to first realize that the spiritual life is not what some imagine it to be. It is not a spiritual Olympics where we prove how good we are before God and others (cf. the Pharisee and the Tax Collector, Lk 18:9–14). The spiritual life is not our effort to save ourselves and to make ourselves into "worthy disciples." Most of all, the spiritual life is not something we earn, have, and possess in order to show it off to others.

We have probably all met someone in the glow of the first fervor following a conversion experience who can't stop talking about how great it is to be "saved," or someone who gushes after a silent retreat, "Oh my God! Like I was like silent for like three like whole days," or someone who now knows God and wants everyone else to know how well they know God. The acerbic, but often oh so perceptive, comedian George Carlin once complained that the problem with "born again" people is that they don't shut up. "They talk too much, pure and simple. When I was born, I was so stunned that I couldn't speak for two years. If someone has a religious experience and shuts up for a couple of years, then I'll take them seriously!"[1]

---

1. Carlin is quoted in Ronald Rolheiser, *Sacred Fire: A Vision for a Deeper Human and Christian Maturity* (New York: Image, 2014), 155.

It's no accident that "silent" and "listen" are spelled with the same letters. When I was in Chile, an older American Jesuit who had been there for decades told me, "When you've been here for a month, you can write a book. After a year, you can write an article. After three years, you just remain quiet." There is something quieting and awe striking about true spiritual experience that makes it hard to talk about and articulate. I think that is why we have so much talk about sex in our culture and so little deep reflection on intimacy in marriage. It's easy to talk about sex. It's difficult to name and understand what is going on in the depths of a marital relationship. It's easy to argue about theology. It's hard to describe the prayer that changes and sustains your life. Real love is quiet, constant, and steady. So too the spiritual life.

Pastor Barbara Taylor describes the effort to stop and enter into the silence. She takes her students to a retreat center for vespers.

> We sit quietly on cushions for close to an hour, focusing all of our attention on listening to God instead of trying to get God to listen to us. This is the longest that some of us have ever intentionally remained silent, which means that it is also the first time some of us have found the entrance to the wilderness inside. Young people whose heads stay full of iTunes, Spanish homework, instant messaging, play practice, parental advice, Guitar Hero, cross-country, term papers, e-mail, romantic sagas, CSI, chorale, X Box, debate team, Second Life, baseball, the procurement of illegal substances, can be startled to hear the sound of their own heartbeats for the first time. They had no idea there was so much space inside of them. No one ever taught them how to hold still enough, long enough, for the shy deer-soul inside of them to step into the clearing and speak.[2]

The spiritual life is the attempt to live our lives in ever more growing awareness of God's love, action, and presence in our lives, and the attempt to respond to God in loving service to others. Spiritual direction and the spiritual life are schoolings in how to live with and for God in service of others. Pedro Arrupe, S.J., the legendary superior general of the Society of Jesus, quietly started a revolution in 1973 when he said that Jesuit schools must form men and women for and with others.[3] The spiritual

---

2. Barbara Taylor, *An Altar in the World: A Geography of Faith* (New York: Harper-One, 2009), 185.

3. Arrupe says, "Today our prime educational objective must be to form men-and-women-for-others; men and women who will live not for themselves but for God and

life is the living in and for the love of God and seeing the love of God order our lives and relationships, on both the personal and social levels. Getting our lives together with God leads to justice, that is, right relationships in all arenas of our lives.

The prime realities of the spiritual life consist mainly of all those immaterial aspects of our being that make up who and what we truly are. Feelings, thoughts, worries, joys, hopes, fears, angers, loyalties, commitments, insights, judgments, awarenesses, turmoils, sensations of well-being and peace, terrors, dreams, failures, fears, wonderings and worryings, passions and pursuits, on and on and on—all the wildness we sense blowing inside us when we stop and listen.

These immaterial aspects of our inner selves are intimately related to the physical aspects of our reality. Our bodies are us, and what we do with them affects and effects our spiritual selves. And what we think about, and stress and strain about, deeply affects and effects our physical well-being (or lack thereof).

This life of the Spirit is all that fills our stream of consciousness. The work of prayer and meditation, the opening of our inner selves to silence, is the work of coming to know and befriend the mystery that is me. When we slow down and stop, when we cease to pay attention to the exigent daily patterns of doing and pause to relish the reality of our simply being (which is often not so simple!), we enter the realm of the Spirit, the vast, endless, mysterious, immaterial universe wherein we know, choose, and love. In that mysterious, immaterial universe we form and fashion our eternal destiny.

Jesuit theologian Karl Rahner contemplates the relation of our life now to eternal life.[4] He notes that at death, our lives reach a culmination: we become all we could want and imagine being. Life eternal is not like switching horses and riding off into an eternal sunset. At death, all we are and have been coalesces. Ultimately, we are who and what we have chosen to be. We also are graced with the power to overcome all the limitations of this life. All the ways we have been limited by the realities of human

---

his Christ—for the God-man who lived and died for all the world; men and women who cannot even conceive of love of God which does not include love for the least of their neighbors; men and women completely convinced that love of God which does not issue in justice for others is a farce." Address to Jesuit Alumni, Valencia, 1973. For the full text of Arrupe's address, see http://onlineministries.creighton.edu.

4. Karl Rahner, S.J., *Foundations of Christian Faith: An Introduction to the Idea of Christianity* (New York: Crossroad, 1989), 436–37.

existence are transcended. We receive all the things we could not receive in our humanity. We cannot be both a Sister of Mercy in Philadelphia and a movie star in Los Angeles. We have to choose among limited possibilities in this life. But at death, all that is not of God is stripped away. We are open to receive all we could have ever wanted to be. This mysterious process of transformation in Christ culminates in our being more than we could ever have imagined, or, as the apostle Paul puts it, "What no eye has seen, nor ear heard, nor the human heart conceived, what God has prepared for those who love him" (1 Cor 2:9).

The spiritual life is the effort to be in touch with the life that is to come, and to live life now with the hope that our lives today can more closely resemble that which is to be. The spiritual life is the reversal of the way-of-life-as-self-assertion so often foisted on us by the values of what John's gospel calls the "world" and what Paul calls "flesh" (*sarx*). The reality of the spiritual life is something graced/given us. The spiritual life holds forth the promise of perfection, not in the wearying sense of making ourselves "perfect" in a never-ending chase of living morally with no errors, but in the sense of perfect as complete, like a finished work of art. Life, sex, money, and sin are all like baseball; errors are part of the game.[5] The Greek word translated "perfect" in the gospels is *telos*, from which we get teleology, the idea of something reaching the purpose and goal for which it was created. Perfection of a work of art is different from perfection as some unattainable ideal of purity.

Thomas Merton wrote in 1963 that we should remember the power of God in our lives and not spend much energy fixated on ourselves: "To be 'perfect' then is not so much a matter of seeking God with ardor and generosity, as of being found, loved and possessed by God, in such a way that his action in us makes us completely generous and helps us transcend our limitations and react against our weaknesses, but by letting the Lord give us strength and purity of Spirit in exchange for our weakness and misery."[6]

The spiritual life is not something we do; it is something God does in us. We open ourselves, position ourselves, make ourselves available, but the real action occurs when we get our ego out of the way and realize the connection that God always wants to maintain with us.

---

5. Cf. Francis Vincent, quoted in Ernest Kurtz and Katherine Ketchum, *The Spirituality of Imperfection: Storytelling and the Journey to Wholeness* (New York: Bantam Books, 1992), 1.

6. Thomas Merton, *Life and Holiness* (New York: Herder and Herder, 1963), 31–32.

How we experience and live the spiritual life depends largely on our image of God. If we see God as a stern law giver, or an implacable judge, we may imagine the spiritual life as a measuring up to rules and regulations, and the mounting of ever more demanding prayer rituals and ascetic practices. But if we see God as a God who loves us as a good parent loves a child, we will see the spiritual life as a living out of a relationship with God. Our failures, weaknesses, and needs may be better at getting us in touch with God than will an ultimately self-centered (not God-centered) need to prove to God how good we are and how much God owes us. Again, Thomas Merton:

> If we are able to believe [God] is truly our loving Father, if we can really accept the truth of his infinite and compassionate concern for us, if we believe that he loves us not because we are worthy but because we need his love, then we can advance with confidence. We will not be discouraged by our inevitable weaknesses and failures. We can do anything he asks of us. But if we believe he is a stern, cold lawgiver who has no real interest in us, who is merely a ruler, a lord, a judge and not a father, we will have great difficulty in living the Christian life. We must therefore begin by *believing* God is our Father: otherwise we cannot face the difficulties of the Christian way of perfection.[7]

Many adults, young and old, are deeply unhappy, troubled in their relationships with others and deeply dissatisfied with themselves. I've spent years on SEARCH and KAIROS kinds of retreats. Many of those who carefully prepare and present talks based on their personal experiences share stories of alcohol abuse in their families, feelings of failure, and a felt sense daily of everything from despondency to depression. Such feelings result in behaviors running from drug and alcohol abuse to cutting, to the most dangerous: a serious consideration of suicide.

If God doesn't make any difference when we are swept up in such hellish personal and societal dynamics, what good is such a God? But if God can provide us with the strength and courage, the power and ability, to confront the pain and confusion of human existence and move into an emotional and psychic space where we experience ourselves as happy and healthy and holy and free, why would we ignore God? If a relationship with God can give us serenity and sanity, peace and promise, why would

---

7. Ibid., 32.

we avoid, question, or deprecate God? The way to know God exists is to discover and name our experiences of God. We know God when we know God loves us and saves us. Spiritual direction is a process that helps us to know God and ourselves, and thus to discover and choose promise and purpose over endless puzzlement.

As a high school and college student, I was definitely the least likely to ever become a Jesuit priest. I'd stopped going to Mass when I was thirteen, not because I'd made some conscious decision about the matter; I just found Mass boring and too time consuming. The 1970s were good times and our partying wasn't to ease our pain. But it did raise the roof.

When I was a sophomore in college, I spent yet another wild night of drinking and partying in my Delta Upsilon Fraternity at Lafayette College in Easton, Pennsylvania. I ended up falling backward down a flight of stairs and spent the night in the hospital with a busted head. The look on my friends' faces as they visited me in the hospital made me realize that my wild-man persona was getting a little beyond acceptable college craziness and bordering on the dangerous. A few nights after that, with the stitches still in my skull, I walked out onto Lafayette's beautiful, peaceful quad and looked up at a full moon. I began to think about what I was doing with my life. As I gazed at the moon, I said, "OK, God. If you're there, do something." Nothing happened. I went back to my room, randomly opened a New Testament and read the first verse I saw. It was some incomprehensible line from Paul's letter to the Romans. So much for God, I figured. The truth is God moves in mysterious manners, much more intriguing than picking random lines from Scripture.

A few weeks later, over Easter break, I went back home and was looking for a summer job. My sister, a nursing student, had gotten a job as a nurse's aide at a new nursing home that had opened in our neighborhood. She was to start at the end of her spring semester. I went over looking for a job as a dishwasher, something I did three times a day in college to pay my room and board in the fraternity. Financial aid, a lot of it for football, paid the tuition. In a curious set of coincidences (or was it the workings of a mysterious God?), I was offered a job as an orderly in the nursing home. They didn't need dishwashers, but they needed orderlies. It was a minimum wage job, so I said sure.

When I returned home, my sister almost bust a gut laughing. "You? An orderly? Do you know what orderlies do?" A few weeks later, semester finished, I went home. My sister was mad as hell. The nursing home told her they had no record of her application. But they asked her if she knew me and when I was going to start working. She said, "Look, I'm the nursing student. He's just a goddam jock. Why are you holding a job for him, and forgetting about me?"

Things worked out, and we both started our summer jobs in the nursing home. I really didn't have a clue what orderlies did, but I quickly found out. Orderlies care for old people and wash every area of their bodies. They give enemas, clean up after people, and change diapers—big diapers—on old folks' bodies. The closest thing to washing feet that we have in our society is the care nurses' aides and orderlies provide for our elderly in nursing homes.

I was utterly surprised to realize how much I loved working with the old folks, how much joy and peace filled me as I was working there for minimum wage. Service in that nursing home slowly reawakened in me a vocation to the priesthood. I remember when I was nine or ten looking up at the priest presiding at a daily Mass during Lent to which the whole grade school student body was taken and thinking, "Someday, I'm going to do that." But wild, good times in high school and college—playing football, rugby, and lacrosse, enjoying the *Animal House* frat life, chasing girls, and running from God—pushed any considerations of priesthood, or even faith, far from my mind.

It was taking care of those old people that changed me. Helping them, and being with them as they were dying, made me wonder. What is life all about? Why am I here? What am I going to do with my life? It was clear to me that, if I was lucky, I had some sixty more years. And death would come to me as it does to us all. What's next? Is there anything after that?

The only one who ever claimed to have come back from the dead was Jesus. I began to think again about Jesus. I read the gospels. I read Thomas Merton's autobiography *The Seven Storey Mountain* and realized that one could be a priest even if one had been much less than a saint. The idea of priesthood came gently and insistently back. I started going to daily Mass, sitting way in the back. One day, the new, young priest in the parish saw me walking with my mother in the ACME parking lot across from the church. He came running over to us and said he wanted to meet me. My mother is looking at the priest and looking at me, wondering, she later told me, what the hell had I done and what kind of trouble was I in now.

The summer in the nursing home was a revelation. Helping the elderly filled me with purpose and revealed to me the energy of doing meaningful work. And, as I said, the work filled me with joy. Being an orderly was much better than tearing up the bars in Margate, New Jersey, or the frat houses at Lafayette College. I loved those old folks. And being young and strong, I could do things for them the female aides couldn't do as easily. I lifted people, out of bed into chairs, and out of chairs back into bed. One little bald Jewish guy, who always wore a wool cap and large coke-bottle glasses, would always yell in his thick, European accent, "Get me Ricky. He'll lift me without hurting me." He was all skin and bones, and the gals' lifting him under his arms hurt him. I'd come into his room, put one hand under his thighs and the other under his upper back and just lift his 110 pounds right out of his chair and into bed. He'd smile and thank me. One night, I put him to bed and tucked him in, patted him on his bald head and said good night. He said, "Goodnight, Ricky. You're a good boy." That was around 8:30 p.m. The old folks always wanted to go to bed early. At 10:45 p.m., near the end of my shift, I checked on him. He had died. It amazed me that I was the last person he spoke to before he entered the next life.

Experiences like this made me realize that life is short. Death didn't scare me. It seemed natural and, at a certain stage of life, welcomed. But what did the fact of death mean? I found myself asking, what was the reality of old age and death teaching me?

Margaret, some seventy years young, suffered horribly from severe rheumatoid arthritis. Yet she was one of the nicest and happiest people I had ever met. Despite being in almost constant pain, she was always upbeat and interested in how others were doing. She also was one of the most dedicated Phillies fans in the history of the city of brotherly "shove." Her attitude toward her condition taught me much about how to accept suffering.

One day I walked into the room of a man who had just arrived at the nursing home. These were always tender times for the elderly. The reality of being in the home could be sad and painful. In those days, people went to the nursing homes to die, not live for ten or fifteen years. This guy was suffering from throat cancer and had had a tracheotomy. He spoke in a funny sounding wheeze. He knew how to use his "voice" to effect humor and had the ready wit to go with it. I smiled and asked him if he'd like me to fill his water jug. He put his finger on the trach hole, winked at me, and said, "Water? No thanks. Never touch the stuff. Fish fuck in it you know." I rolled on the floor laughing for five minutes. He prepared for his impending death with great humor and gratitude for his life.

Through that summer, I pondered over what life was all about. I began to pray. I asked God to let me know what he wanted me to do. Nothing startling happened. I didn't see lights in the night or hear voices. I didn't have some extraordinary experience. Reading the gospels moved me in ways I dimly comprehended. Mark 10:21 just kept recurring in my daydreams. "Jesus looking at him, loved him . . . Come, follow me." Still, I gradually realized how fascinating God is and I wanted to live my life the way Jesus lived his. I began to investigate life as a Jesuit. From Jesuits, I learned that Ignatian Spirituality is based on our freely choosing to serve. We can learn what God's will is by sifting through our different desires and discovering which desire is the deepest and longest lasting.

What Does God Want?

There's an old *Peanuts* cartoon with Charlie Brown and Linus speaking to one another. In the first panel, Linus, holding his security blanket, announces, "I think the world is much better today than it was, say, five years ago." Charlie Brown reacts and yells at Linus, "How can you say that? Don't you listen to the radio? Read the newspapers?" Charlie Brown continues, "How can you stand there and tell me this is a better world?" Linus replies, "I'm in it now." We are here now. The world is better because we're in it. God will use us to help heal our planet and save people from lives of boredom, meaninglessness, and despair. God needs us to help make a world of peace and prosperity, joy and justice, faith and freedom, hope and healing, life and love. As Jesus says to Peter in the movie *Son of God*, "Come on. We're going to change the world."

As a young man, I realized God loves us like a good parent and wants the best for us. In another old *Peanuts* cartoon, Charlie Brown and Linus are leaning their elbows on a brick wall, and Charlie asks, "Do you ever think about the future, Linus?" Linus replies, "Oh yes, all the time." Charlie Brown then asks Linus, "What do you think you'd like to be when you grow up?" Linus replies, "Outrageously happy!"

God wants us to be outrageously happy. God wants us to be happy and healthy and holy and free. God wants what we want: that our lives be meaningful and transformative and true. Ignatian Spirituality is a way of living that can help us find meanings and ways to allow ourselves to be transformed and then to transform our lives and world. Spiritual direction is a way to consciously engage in such transformation.

The spiritual life is not easy. Most avoid it. Why? Because it's difficult. To stop and pray, to contemplate, to discipline your thoughts until you become aware of your truest and deepest desires, is a life-long work. After years of trying to pray, and waiting for prayer to work, waiting to get "good" at it, I finally learned (having finally read and understood a bit *The Cloud of Unknowing*) that prayer is a never-ending work. It's a lot like physical exercise. There is never a day that the dreaded treadmill (a true metaphor for our twenty-first-century lives!) or rowing machine at the gym becomes "easy." Prayer and contemplation are works to which we give ourselves and then we experience the ever-incremental improvement of our living according to the joyful exigencies of love. The bad news is that no matter how hard we work at the gym, eventually, as one female friend of mine put it, "everything sags." The good news is that no matter how poorly or well we stick with prayer, we eventually become a bit more present to the present moment, more compassionate with ourselves and others, more concerned for justice and truth, more joyful, playful, and just plain happy.

Gerald May in his wonderful book *The Awakened Heart* writes: "When people tell me they have trouble taking time for prayer or meditation, I often ask them what unpleasant things they might be wanting to avoid. I often ask myself the same question."[8] Trying to live a disciplined, conscious spiritual life will rather quickly reveal to us our shortcomings and inabilities to be routinely and consistently considerate of others, compassionate, kind, caring, in a word, loving. Even more, we will most likely be led in our reflections and prayer to remember, relive, and attempt to integrate the pain and difficulties of our lives. No one is perfect and no one has a perfect life. We often prefer to put the pain out of our awareness and live as if "we're done with that," whatever "that" is.

Prayer is not to lift us out of life to heaven. Prayer connects the realities of daily life with the awareness of heaven, the deepest dimension of reality. Heaven isn't off "somewhere in a galaxy far, far away." Heaven is as close as our skin, as our breath, as our spouse, family, and community. If you can't find God at the breakfast table, you can't find God in your prayer corner.

Matthew Fox prophetically preaches that prayer is not an exceptional experience. Prayer is not about mumbling words mindlessly, nor is it with-

---

8. Gerald G. May, M.D., *The Awakened Heart: Opening Yourself to the Love You Need* (San Francisco: HarperSanFrancisco, 1991), 99.

drawing from one's culture and times or giving in to the cultural idols of our times. Prayer is not about changing God. And, Fox adds, prayer is not "talking to God," which inverts real prayer and reduces prayer to our talking to ourselves.[9] For him, prayer is a radical response to life.[10]

God is not a thing among other things. God is not some larger version of Santa Claus and the Easter bunny. Our praying does not make God different; it makes us different. Prayer is about transformation, transformation of ourselves and of our culture and society. More than just our contacting or manipulating God, prayer is about God mysteriously and captivatingly becoming the center of our lives and the life of our world. There are many ways to pray, and all are good and useful. The "use" of prayer is more evident in the way one lives one's life. St. Teresa of Avila said prayer is like water for the flowers.[11] You know the water is present and flowing when you see the flowers bloom.

In *The Cloud of Unknowing,* the anonymous fourteenth-century author describes the prayer of simply sitting in silence and opening up ourselves to the presence of God. Today, Trappist monks Thomas Keating and Basil Pennington have taught this way of praying as Centering Prayer, the sitting in silence for twenty minutes once or twice a day and simply repeating a word or prayer phrase.[12] I would suggest that any form of prayer can lead us to the point of the spiritual life: the experience of connection, communion, and intimacy with God. Daily Eucharist, Scripture reading and spiritual reading, the rosary, Ignatian contemplation: there are many ways to pray. Yet most who get serious about the practice of prayer often come to desire ever simpler forms of prayer. Simply wanting to be present and silent before God opens the most direct route to the hope of the spiritual life. The author of *The Cloud of Unknowing* teaches:

> And so diligently persevere until you feel joy in it. For in the beginning it is usual to feel nothing but a kind of darkness about your mind, or as it were *a cloud of unknowing*. You will seem to know nothing and to feel nothing except a naked intent toward God in

---

9. Matthew Fox, *On Becoming a Musical Mystical Bear* (Paramus, NJ: Paulist Press, 1972), 3–26.

10. Ibid., 49.

11. See Thomas H. Greene, S.J., *When the Well Runs Dry: Prayer beyond the Beginnings* (Notre Dame, IN: Ave Maria Press, 1979), 34, 56 ff.

12. See Thomas Keating, *Intimacy with God: An Introduction to Centering Prayer,* 3rd ed. (New York: Crossroad, 2009).

the depths of your being. Try as you might, this darkness and cloud will remain between you and your God. You will feel frustrated, for your mind will be unable to grasp him, and your heart will not relish the delight of his love. But learn to be at home in this darkness. Return to it as often as you can, letting your spirit cry out to him whom you love. For if, in this life, you hope to feel and see God as he is in himself it must be within this darkness and this cloud. But if you strive to fix your love on him, forgetting all else, which is the work of contemplation I have urged you to begin, I am confident that God in his goodness will bring you to a deep experience of himself. (*The Cloud of Unknowing*, chapter 3)

One way Jesuits pray is following the Spiritual Exercises of St. Ignatius. There are several ways to experience the Exercises. Jesuits are lucky to make a thirty-day retreat where an individual goes away, usually to a retreat house set up for this occasion, and prays four or five times a day, each prayer period lasting an hour. Except for Mass and a thirty-minute or so conversation with a retreat guide, the person is alone with God. Broken into four sections of roughly seven to nine days, or "Weeks," the experience of the Full Exercises, lasting some thirty days, aims at getting one's life in order and directed toward the goal of life, which is happiness with God forever. During the First Week, the retreatant ponders in prayer who God is, how much God loves us individually and as persons connected within communities, and how we have responded to God throughout our lives. The Second Week, one prays with a contemplative, loving gaze at the life and experiences of Jesus. Ignatius encourages us to use our imaginations to bring the gospel scenes alive in our consciousness, allowing the images and messages of Scripture to root deep down in our hearts, minds, and imaginations. The Third Week, the individual accompanies Jesus through his passion and death on the cross. In the Fourth Week, one opens oneself to the reality of the resurrection and the life of the Holy Spirit in the community called "church."

Using the imagination, the retreatant enters into gospel scenes and lets unfold whatever develops. For example, Ignatius suggests picturing oneself as a little child, present in the cave in Bethlehem where Jesus is born, or as one of the fishers in the boat as Jesus walks on water. Do I find myself getting out there with Peter? Or am I sitting silently in the back of the boat, not wanting to risk getting wet, let alone drowning? In some exercises that Ignatius created such as the "Call of Christ the King" or the

"Two Standards," the person making the Exercises is impelled to imagine how he or she will choose to serve Christ and God's people.

The Exercises are rooted in the realities of our prayer experiences, and often during those prayer times you remember people and events from your life. The "Principle and Foundation" of the Exercises begins to teach us that all our choices should be geared and aimed at the reason for which we are created, namely, to praise, reverence, and serve God, and to be happy with God and our loved ones for all eternity. Everything we experience that meshes with that goal should be integrated into our lives; whatever clashes with, or contradicts, our achieving it should be discarded and avoided.

For example, getting "wasted" while worshiping at the altars of Jim Beam and Bud Light a hundred times a year in no way brings us closer to the persons we deeply desire to be. No one in first grade ever announced, "When I grow up, I want to be a drunk and die in a car crash while DUI." However, by pursuing a college education and participating in Mass every Sunday, you are much more likely to attain the meaning for which you were created. No one argues that cheating on your spouse will get you to heaven. More likely, it will land you in divorce court, never a pleasant or inexpensive experience.

The dynamics of the Exercises develop us as free persons. We are freed from all that keeps us from being our deepest, truest selves. We are freed to serve and love others. And we are freed to be with Jesus as we live our lives in relation to him, his teachings, and his kingdom. "Blessed be the God of Israel; he has come to his people and set them free.... This was the oath he swore to our father Abraham, to set us free..., free to worship him without fear" (Lk 1:68 ff.). St. Paul realized, "For Freedom Christ has set us free" (Gal 5:1).

During the Exercises we look for and wait on graces. Grace is the power of the love of God operating in our hearts and minds, and then in our choices. Grace, according to Thomas Aquinas, is the ability to do what you could not do before. You know you have received the grace to stop smoking when you no longer smoke. You know you have received the grace to forgive someone when you reconcile with the person from whom you had been estranged.

I will have more to say on the Spiritual Exercises later. But for now, let's address the main question. Is there a God? Does God really care about us, and about me? Does God really do something? Does living in relationship with God make my life better? Can't I live a meaningful and loving life without God?

Does God Exist?

When I was five years old, we lived in "beeyouteeful" Philadelphia. My mother told me that one day I walked into our kitchen and announced I was going to St. Joe's Prep, the Jesuit high school in Philly. My mother, Brooklyn born and bred, asked, "What's St. Joe's Prep?" I reportedly replied, "That's where all the smart boys go." Even when I was pint sized, I knew I wanted to know what everything was all about. The great Jesuit philosopher-theologian Bernard Lonergan teaches that deep within us is a restless unrestricted drive, a natural impulse, a God-given and inspired dynamism. This is the pure desire to know.[13] No one wants to be ignorant. We all want to know who we are, why we are here, and what we ought to do. The philosopher Immanuel Kant asked three fundamental questions: What can I know? What ought I to do? And for what can I hope? Those three questions lead to the one key question for all human persons: Does God exist?

I always say the real question isn't "Do I believe in God?" The real question is "Does God exist?" If God exists, I should believe in God. Then begins the great adventure about how to respond to the mysterious reality of God. This is the fascinating adventure described in the Bible in the lives of Abraham, Moses, the Prophets, Mary, Joseph, Jesus, the apostles, Mary Magdalene, Peter, Paul. The lives of the saints tell us of many people who took seriously the invitation to open their minds and hearts to God. St. Ignatius once said, "There are very few people who realize what God would make of them if they abandoned themselves into his hands, and let themselves be formed by his grace." St. Francis transformed life in Europe during the Middle Ages.[14] There are dozens of saints of our own time who reached out to the poor and

---

13. See Bernard J. F. Lonergan, S.J., *Method in Theology* (New York: Seabury Press, 1972) and *Insight: A Study of Human Understanding* (London: Longmans, Green and Company; New York: Philosophical Library, 1957). Lonergan is arguably the most brilliant Jesuit who ever lived. These two books are major philosophical and theological works of the twentieth century. Both are intellectually demanding. Hint: tackle *Method* before *Insight*.

14. On St. Francis, see Adrian House, *Francis of Assisi: A Revolutionary Life* (Mahwah, NJ: HiddenSpring, 2001).

marginalized of their society, such as St. Alberto Hurtado, S.J., of Chile, and Dorothy Day, the American who founded The Catholic Worker and is now being considered for canonization. Blessed Mother Teresa of Calcutta, Pope John XXIII, Pope John Paul II, and Pope Francis all have captured the imaginations of young people in our time. Msgr. Oscar Romero and the Jesuits murdered in El Salvador in the 1980s died rather than flee the situation in which they found themselves. John Kennedy,[15] Martin Luther King, Jr., and Nelson Mandela were all imperfect men through whom God changed the world. Kennedy attended Mass regularly. King was a Baptist preacher. And Mandela's relationship with his Methodist roots was real if somewhat muted so as to not misuse religion or contribute to more divisions in his divided land.[16]

---

15. On John F. Kennedy, see James W. Douglass, *JFK and the Unspeakable: Why He Died and Why It Matters* (Maryknoll, NY: Orbis Books, 2008). Douglass argues that John Kennedy wanted to make peace with the Russians and end the Cold War. Douglass cites Kennedy's June 10, 1963, address at American University, among other things, to support his thesis. Until I read Douglass, I had never heard of the American University speech. It is well worth reading. Here's an excerpt. "Let us reexamine our attitude towards the cold war. . . . We must, therefore, persevere in the search for peace in the hope that constructive changes within the Communist bloc might bring within reach solutions which now seem beyond us. We must conduct our affairs in such a way that it becomes in the Communists' interest to agree on a genuine peace. And above all, while defending our own vital interests, nuclear powers must avert those confrontations which bring an adversary to a choice of either a humiliating retreat or a nuclear war. To adopt that kind of course in the nuclear age would be evidence only of the bankruptcy of our policy—or of a collective death-wish for the world." See http://www.american-rhetoric.com.

16. Verashni Pillay, "Mandela and the Confessions of a Closet Christian" (December 13, 2013), http://mg.co.za. "Nelson Mandela was apparently a man of great faith, who kept his Christian beliefs discreet in favor of his great life work of reconciliation. That is the picture emerging from a number of ministers who regularly met to pray with Mandela in prison as well as throughout the latter part of his life. 'He was a deeply religious man; he believed sincerely in the existence of the Almighty,' said Bishop Don Dabula, who first met Mandela in 1962 and met to pray with him whenever he was at his home in Qunu. The former president had the last rites administered by a Methodist minister in his Houghton home on the night of his death. Nearby, in a private room, long-time friend Bishop Malusi Mpumlwana said Mandela's favorite blessing as he died. Mandela's relationship with religion was always significant, if muted. He was raised and schooled as a Methodist, an experience he recalled fondly in his autobiography, *Long Walk to Freedom*. At a religious conference in 1999, he said: 'Without the church, without religious institutions, I would never have been here today. . . . Religion was one of

Does God Make Any Difference?

Many people today face the choice whether to continue in the religious tradition in which they were raised, follow another path, or join the growing numbers of "nones," those who have no religion. Some 30 percent of millennials now say they have no religious affiliation. Many young adults flounder a bit, fearful of believing in a God, or in a religious tradition's version of God. They think, "What if I'm wrong?" and "Does believing in one religion mean I have to be intolerant of other religions?" Many raised in a faith tradition drift away from it in early adulthood or midlife.

A Pew study, "Millennials in Adulthood,"[17] finds that 30 percent of millennials (those born between roughly 1982 and 2000) have no religious affiliation and that this generation is "Detached from Institutions." "Half of Millennials (50 percent) now describe themselves as political independents and about three-in-ten (29 percent) say they are not affiliated with any religion. These are at or near the highest levels of political and religious disaffiliation recorded for any generation in the quarter-century that the Pew Research Center has been polling on these topics."[18]

At 26 percent, the millennials' rate of marriage is much lower than that of previous generations. Most telling for the question of religious faith is the fact that this generation has a very low level of trust. "Just 19 percent of Millennials say most people can be trusted, compared with 31 percent of Gen Xers, 37 percent of Silents and 40 percent of Boomers."[19]

Religious faith is based on a relationship of trust in God and trust in those who claim to follow that God. The revelations of priest sex scandals since 2002 have been devastating to trust in the Catholic Church and Catholic bishops and priests. Even though 96 percent of priests had nothing to do with the abuse, one child abused is one too many. The charge of "cover-up" by bishops I find simplistic. The Catholic Church is the only institution that kept meticulous records of these matters. Still, the damage done to the prestige and honor of the church has been incalculable.

the motivating factors in everything we did.' But Mandela held an aversion to speaking publicly about his own faith for fear of dividing or—even worse—using religion as a political tool, as the apartheid regime did."

17. Pew Research, "Millennials in Adulthood" (March 7, 2014), http://www.pew-socialtrends.org.

18. Ibid.

19. Ibid.

Worse, the scandals have made it difficult for many to trust the church, let alone be proud of being Catholic.[20]

As a result of the scandals and many other crosscurrents coursing through our cultural waters, large numbers of women and men live in an environment where many of their peers do not see any need for God, nor do they feel any great loss at God's absence. "Drugs, Sex and Rock and Roll," texting like it is one's job, following sports teams, and endless work seem to fulfill many persons' wants and needs. Hook-up sex, the never-ending blare of SportsCenter, Pokemon Go, and the latest antics of Miley Cyrus and the Kardashians fill up the ever fewer hours of our free time. There is no noticed need, nor desire, for prayer, liturgy, Bible study, or community service. In such a situation of flux and fury, how does one get started living a "spiritual" life?

The Five P's of the Examen:
Presence, Praise, Process, Penance, Promise

One way to get started paying attention to what is moving in our hearts and minds is the practice of St. Ignatius's Examen, one of the simplest forms of prayer.[21] Many people find the five- to fifteen-minute Examen life changing. The work of prayer, the work of daily loving, can be greatly enhanced and facilitated by practicing the Examen. This spiritual tool has greatly enhanced the awareness and ability of people to follow their spiritual path in greater freedom and deeper love. This short spiritual exercise developed by St. Ignatius of Loyola in his Spiritual Exercises focuses our choosing and directs our loving. The Examen is doable, transformative, and comprehensible. St. Ignatius championed this form of prayer and counseled that it was the one spiritual exercise that should never be left aside.

Michael Sacco, the director of the Center for Student Formation at Boston College, in a presentation to campus ministers from Jesuit universities and colleges across the country, noted that what we ask students to do in Jesuit schools, that is, slow down, be attentive, be reflective, and be

---

20. See Richard G. Malloy, S.J., *Being on Fire: The Top Ten Essentials of Catholic Faith* (Maryknoll, NY: Orbis Books, 2007), 78–86. In these pages, I provide a brief cultural analysis of the priest sex abuse scandals in the Roman Catholic Church. Such analysis does not excuse the horrific crimes of sexual abuse, but it may help us understand the realities of the church's response.

21. Some of this material on the Examen appeared in Richard G. Malloy, S.J., "Mind Your 'P's. Presence, Praise, Process, Penance and Promise: St. Ignatius' Examen Provides Exercise for the Soul," *St. Anthony Messenger* 120, no. 9 (February 2013): 40–44.

conscious about their choices, is quite alien to the culture in which they are immersed. Twenty-four/seven constant texting, tweeting, Instagramming, plus the nonstop flashing images and the hyper realities of video games, all militate against the deep human need to pause, think, pray, and choose wisely and well. The Examen can serve as an antidote to the spiritual detours and dead ends of our age.

In order to make this prayer even more accessible, I offer this description of the traditional five steps of the Examen. Paralleling (1) the prayer to the Spirit for inspiration, (2) Thanksgiving, (3) examination of consciousness, (4) firm resolve to improve, and (5) trust and hope for the future, it consists of the five "P's" of the Examen: Presence, Praise, Process, Penance, and Promise. I suggest you spend one to three minutes on each "P."

1. *Presence:* Stop. Breathe. Be here now. Let the sense of the nearness and closeness of God settle into your consciousness. We spend so much of our thoughts on worries and plans for what comes next. I used to commute most days of the week from Camden, New Jersey, to St. Joe's U. in Philadelphia and could spend forty minutes in the car thinking about what classes and meetings I had that day, who I had to contact, what student I had to prepare to deal with ... and I'd often realize I drove the whole way and had never really "been in" the car.

Just to stop the rush of twenty-first-century living for a minute or two is refreshing, relaxing, and rejuvenating. Being aware of God's presence settles us. We know once again that God loves us, is near and with us. God is for us. God cares. God is interested and concerned with who we are and how we are doing. God gives us all we have, all we are, all we ever will have, and all we ever will be. Realizing and relishing this loving God's presence fills us with peace and a subtle, all-pervasive, deep-seated joy that can be accessed despite any trials and tribulations of the day.

2. *Praise:* This calling to awareness of who God is and how God is for and with ushers forth in praise. I emphasize praise over thanks. You praise someone who does something significant for you. You don't simply thank them. Someone pulls you from a burning building, you say more than thanks; you tell everyone you know what a brave and wonderful person the firefighter is. Someone gives you thousands of dollars to go to college, you don't just say "thank you." You tell all your family and friends how great a grandmother you have. She is paying for your education. Too often college students can take for granted the gift of higher education. You're fifty-two years old and have been unemployed for a year and a half. Someone breaks the pattern and offers you a job. You don't just thank the

person. You praise him or her. And too often we all can take for granted the gifts God gives us: life, health, talents and abilities, family and friends, decent work, and most important, time.

It is so easy to become unaware of all the incredible gifts we have been given. The inevitable stresses and strains of modern life are made much easier by running water, flush toilets, reliable electricity, technology that more and more is just "FM" (freakin' magic), and a society that protects our persons and property better than many other societies have throughout human history. The Wild West of the 1870s was dangerous and deadly. World Wars I and II were terrible times to be alive. Today our planet of seven billion faces great challenges. But we can fly anywhere on the globe in less than a day. We are clothed. We eat. Someone who predicted in 1912 that the world could clothe and feed a population of seven billion would have been laughed off the stage. Lack of food today is more a problem of politics and distribution than production.

If you are healthy, if you can reasonably hope to have help with your pregnancy, if you really don't worry about your child living to be five years of age, if you have a reasonable expectation of living to be seventy-five or eighty, if you have a bank account, if you have a job—you are truly blessed by God.

Just taking time once or twice a day to praise the God who makes our lives possible and pleasant is a practice that maintains sanity and perspective.

3. *Process:* What's going on in your consciousness? What have you been thinking about these past twenty-four or twelve hours since last you made an Examen? Just note and track your thoughts and emotions. What insights, worries, joys, fears, hopes, imaginings are running around in your head? How do you feel? With whom are you "talking in your head" this day?

Are you obsessing about things that really don't matter or over which you have no control? Stop! Freely and consciously, take a minute and ask: What do I want to think about this day? And what am I thinking about today? Instead of running over and over in your head what you should have said to that person in some trivial argument yesterday, or last week or last month, consciously choose to think about what is real and true and meaningful in your life. Rick Curry, S.J., would bake bread in the evening and make his Examen as he kneaded the dough. As Rick folded and pressed the mass of flour, water, and yeast, he shared, "I ask myself, where have I been part of the solution, and where have I been part of the problem?"

Ignatian Spirituality is a method of weighing and making choices. What am I choosing today and why? Am I growing in freedom in what I choose? Do my choices leave me satisfied and joyful or anxious and distraught? It's not a deal of "choose or lose." To not choose is a choice. The Examen is taking time to really pause, ponder, and think about, and ask for the help of God's grace in our choices.

How's your relationship with yourself? Are you doing what you want to be doing in things both small (Exercising enough? Eating right?) and large (How are my spouse and kids? How do I feel about my work? How am I spending my time?).

Most important, ask yourself, "What do I really want? What do I really desire?" If I find myself constantly daydreaming about opening a school in the inner city or starting a small business to employ people in my town, or moving back home to be there to help an elderly parent, maybe I am being led by the Spirit of God to pursue those paths.

Do I find myself infatuated with sexual fantasies about a co-worker, or imagining carrying out angry impulses to do harm to someone? Do I ponder how I could embezzle funds from my place of employment? Am I harboring animosity and anger against my boss, my spouse, my co-workers, or just the guy who cut me off in traffic this morning? Being aware of such dynamics in our inner lives can make us pause, ask God for help, and resist the direction such thoughts take us.

What are my compulsions and addictions? We all have them. Let God help with them. The really dangerous thing is to refuse to recognize our addictive and compulsive tendencies. When we ignore such tendencies, it is then that these dynamics go underground in our consciousness, and we no longer are even aware of how our compulsions and addictions control and manipulate us. We fail to take stock of how constantly annoyed we are, how uninspired we feel, how empty have become our days and routines. It is when we are in such a state that our addictions and compulsions can really control us, even destroy us. Here is where the truly destructive addictions to substances like alcohol and drugs take over our freedom. More and more we are aware of the corrosive and also truly destructive, slow-moving processes of addictions to food, shopping, hoarding, and pornography.[22]

22. See Belinda Luscombe, "Porn: Why Young Men Who Grew Up with Internet Porn Are Becoming Advocates for Turning It Off," *Time*, April 11, 2016, 40–47. For a different view of the pernicious effects of pornography, see Conor Friedersdorf, "Is Porn to Be Feared?" *The Atlantic Monthly*, April 7, 2016.

The Examen opens us to the transformative grace of God. Thomas Aquinas taught that grace is the ability to do what one could not do before. During the Examen we root around in our stream of consciousness and find where lurks the desire to smoke, or drink too much, or act out sexually, or overspend, and we strategize on how to choose what we really want and not what we find ourselves falling into (cf. Rom 7:21–25).

The remedy to addictive and compulsive tendencies is to open our hearts to the freedom with which God wants to grace us. Richard Rohr says freedom isn't doing whatever we want. Real freedom is deeply desiring to do what we should and need to do.[23]

Freedom comes as we begin charting the desolations and consolations of our daily existence. Consolation is what is moving me toward God, toward living happy and healthy and holy and free. We know we are in consolation when we realize what fills us with energy and enthusiasm, joy and justice. Desolation is what worries, frustrates, and diverts us from the goal of transformation in Christ. We know we are in desolation when there is a certain restlessness, listlessness, an "Is this all there is to life?" tone and texture in our soul.

Desolation may be caused by our not living up to the demands of discipleship. Desolation is not always disagreeable and consolation is not always comfortable. Pat O'Sullivan, a famous Jesuit tertian instructor, once said, "The sailors going to the whorehouse may seem happy, but they are not in consolation." And parents doing the hard work of disciplining and loving a recalcitrant teenager may not seem to be at peace, but they are in consolation.

To know true consolation we need to know our deepest, truest desires. The Examen can become the habitual work of discernment, our paying attention to where we are moving and what is moving us in our relationship to God, others, and our deepest, truest selves.

4. *Penance:* Ask God to reveal to you if there is anything that needs tweaking in your life, or if there are major roadblocks that need to be worked on and removed. And then take one aspect of life that is a bit off track and strategize on how to rectify direction in the next twelve or twenty-four hours. Really doing something is the goal here. Do I need to reconcile with someone? Resolve to write a letter in the next twenty-four hours. Am I watching too much TV? Plan a trip to the library to get a

---

23. Richard Rohr, *Everything Belongs: The Gift of Contemplative Prayer,* rev. ed. (New York: Crossroad, 2003), 108.

good book. Have I spent money on goofy latte drinks that cost more than what food costs a family in the Sudan for a day? Choose to give some money to a good charity. Not getting to prayer each day? Resolve to at least make the Examen!

Doing penance frees up the frozen corners of our souls. Actually doing some small thing can set in motion larger, positive dynamics. Something as simple as going to bed on time and getting the rest we need can make us calmer, happier, and saner. Penance is not an exercise in beating up on myself for all my faults and failures. Real repentance is like coaching. Corrections help me play the game better.

5. *Promise: Name and Claim.* Life rushes along at warp speed and we cannot remember what we had for lunch let alone breakfast, or if we even took five minutes to eat. "Don't just do something; stand there" should be the mantra of those who make the Examen. We need to stop and "name and claim" what is happening in our lives. God's promise is that we will have life and have it to the full.

How is life today, now, this moment? We can name what God is doing for us and claim the movement toward God in our lives. I am less annoyed with so and so than I was last week. I really have gotten to writing that novel I've always dreamed about. I did tell my kid she cannot run up the bill on the credit card. I joined my neighborhood watch to safeguard the community. I am getting to daily Mass in Lent. We can trust God's promise that such small, seemingly insignificant choices snowball into the meaning and transformation of our lives.

What do I want and hope for in this day, this week, this month? Ask God to give you what you need. St. Ignatius said we should demand (in Spanish the word is *"demandar"*) the graces we desire from God. The asking for the grace makes us more open to our actually appropriating the power of God's love and justice in our lives.

Where and How

Some people like to sit in a chapel and make the Examen. Some turn off the radio and pray the Examen as they drive home from work. One Jesuit wrote about how he walks seven and a half minutes to a destination. On walking back, he knows he spent a full fifteen minutes on the Examen, an exercise for him both spiritual and physical! Some people pray the Examen in the shower. Some make the Examen before going to sleep. However and wherever you pray the Examen, God will find you and guide you.

What does living the spiritual life do for us and our world? Why bother with prayer and Examen and incorporating ourselves and our lives into a spiritual tradition? Striving to relate to God and then to others in a life of prayer and service will fill us with joy, a joy that resides beneath and within all the trials and tribulations of ours and any age. The graced and great founder of L'Arche, Jean Vanier, reflects from his life in service to, and deep connection with, those seemingly less gifted than some who seem to have full use of their powers:

> The first choice, at the root of all human growth, is the choice to accept ourselves; to accept ourselves as we are, with our gifts and abilities, but also our shortcomings, inner wounds, darkness, faults, mortality; to accept our past and family and environment, but equally our capacity for growth; to accept the universe with its laws, and our place at the heart of this universe. Growth begins when we give up dreaming about ourselves and accept our humanity as it is, limited, poor but also beautiful. Sometimes the refusal to accept ourselves hides real gifts and abilities. The dangerous thing for human beings is to want to be other than they are, to want to be someone else, or even want to be God. We need to be ourselves, with our gifts and abilities, our capacity for communion and co-operation. This is the way to be happy.[24]

The spiritual life is not about the "spiritual" alone. True happiness and joy reside in the efforts to be in loving relationship with one another. Barbara Taylor writes: "The assignment is to get over yourself. The assignment is to love the God you did not make up with all your heart, soul, strength, and mind, and the second is like unto it: to love the neighbor you also did not make up as if that person were your own strange and particular self. Do this, and the doing will teach you everything you need to know. Do this, and you will live."[25]

Living for many people is often hard and painful, excruciatingly painful. Prayer will also see us through trials, sometimes helping us survive terrible times and horrific crimes. From April to July 1994, Rwanda descended into the hell of brutal genocide. The majority Hutu massacred almost 70 percent of the Tutsi of Rwanda. Overall, 800,000 people,[26] some 20 percent of the population of Rwanda, were senselessly murdered in cold blood. An equivalent number of Americans would be more than

24. Jean Vanier, "Our Journey Home," in *Essential Writings* (Maryknoll, NY: Orbis Books, 2008), 122.
25. Barbara Taylor, *An Altar in the World: A Geography of Faith* (New York: HarperOne, 2009), 105.
26. The History Channel, "The Rwandan Genocide," http://www.history.com.

60 million people. Imagine more than 60 million people being killed in less than 100 days in the United States, often by people wielding machetes. Immaculée Ilibagiza survived the horror and was, in her words, "Left to Tell." She relates how she spent three months locked in a bathroom, with six other women, where all she could do was pray.

Rwanda was bitterly divided between Hutu (the majority, about 85 percent of the population) and Tutsi (14 percent before the genocide) tribal groups. Until 1959, the Tutsi were the favored caste, put in that place by Belgian colonial overlords. The Tutsi were cattle herders who occupied positions in society above the farmer Hutus. Violence on a large scale had erupted in 1959 and again in 1973. The hatreds and historically implemented prejudices continued to fester and burn. "Young Hutus were taught from an early age that Tutsi were inferior and not to be trusted, and they didn't belong in Rwanda. Hutus witnessed the segregation of Tutsi every day, first in the schoolyard and then in the workplace, and they were taught to dehumanize us by calling us 'snakes' and 'cockroaches.' No wonder it was so easy for them to kill us."[27] Even churches were not safe havens. People were burned to death as the churches went up in flames.

Locked in a bathroom four feet long and three feet wide, with six others, for weeks, Immaculée took refuge in prayer. She would pray the rosary twelve or thirteen hours a day.[28] But as she heard the news of what was happening outside their cramped cubicle, as she heard killing outside the small bathroom window, and killers laughing gleefully as they murdered, she found her heart filled with anger, and hatred too. She wanted to kill those who were killing. She was as far from forgiveness as one could be. She prayed and prayed but her prayers felt hollow and false.

> One night I heard screaming not far from the house, and then a baby crying. The killers must have slain the mother and left her infant to die in the road. The child wailed all night; by morning its cries were feeble and sporadic, and by nightfall it was silent. I heard the dogs snarling nearby and shivered as I thought about how that baby's life had ended. I prayed for God to receive the child's innocent soul, and then asked him, *How can I forgive people who would do such a thing to an infant?* I heard the answer as clearly as if we'd been sitting in

27. Immaculée Ilibagiza with Steve Erwin, *Left to Tell: Discovering God in the Rwandan Holocaust* (Carlsbad, CA: Hay House, 2009), 86.
28. Ibid., 73, 91.

the same room chatting. *You are all my children . . . and the baby is with me now."* It was such a simple thing, but it was the answer to the prayers I'd been lost in for days.[29]

Somehow in the horror of the atrocities, Immaculée came to a realization that everyone is a child of God—those killed and those doing the killing. God forgives, and that forgiveness opens our eyes to truth, the hard truth that God loves us all, the good and the bad and everyone in between. "The killers were like children. . . . Despite their atrocities, they were children of God, and I could forgive a child, although it would not be easy . . . especially when that child was trying to kill me. . . . That night I prayed with a clear conscience and a clean heart. For the first time since I entered the bathroom, I slept in peace."[30]

Finally, the spiritual life leads us to live trusting God. There's no need to evaluate and measure success in prayer. The practice of prayer is its own "success."

We have a way of bringing into the uncharted land of prayer a false map of what prayer should be like. This expectation is useless. . . . John Chapman writes in his *Spiritual Letters,* ". . . What we want to learn is precisely our own weakness, powerlessness, unworthiness. And one should wish for no prayer, except the prayer God gives us—probably very distracted and unsatisfactory in every way." . . . It's best to become comfortable with the sense of always being a beginner. St. Gregory of Nyssa thinks it characterizes the spiritual life.[31]

We are always beginners. Things take time and we need not rush ahead of the grace of God. Jesuit Pierre Teilhard de Chardin knew this well. His writings were never published in his lifetime, yet, by the grace of God, we are beneficiaries of his profound understandings of the spiritual life.

Above all, trust in the slow work of God.
We are quite naturally impatient in everything
To reach the end without delay.

---

29. Ibid., 93–94.

30. Ibid., 94.

31. Martin Laird, O.S.A., *Into the Silent Land: A Guide to the Practice of Christian Contemplation* (New York: Oxford University Press, 2006), 85–86.

We should like to skip the intermediate stages.
We are impatient of being on the way
To something unknown, something new.

And yet it is the law of all progress
That it is made by passing through
Some stages of instability—
And that it may take a very long time.

And so I think it is with you;
Your ideas mature gradually—let them grow,
Let them shape themselves, without undue haste.

Don't try to force them on,
As though you could be today what time
(that is to say, grace and circumstances
Acting on your own good will)
Will make of you tomorrow.

Only God could say what this new spirit
Gradually forming within you will be.

Give Our Lord the benefit of believing
That his hand is leading you,
And accept the anxiety of feeling yourself
In suspense and incomplete.

—Pierre Teilhard de Chardin, S.J.

CHAPTER 2

What Is Spiritual Direction?

There are very few people who realize what God would make of them if they abandoned themselves into his hands, and let themselves be formed by his grace.

— St. Ignatius of Loyola

If many Christians realized the extraordinary adventure that is offered them, they would throw all their living strength into it.

—Francois Roustang, S.J., *Growth in the Spirit*

After God has gotten us hooked on himself, then he says, "Okay, now we have to go about the serious business of transformation. You're going to have to let me work to make you divine if you're ever going to realize the kind of union with me that you desire."

—Thomas Greene, S.J., *Experiencing God*

Spirituality is most evident in our passions and desires. What we really desire, what we are passionate about, shows what we want and who we are. If I really want to be a teacher, but feel I have to get into finance or accounting because that will let me make more money, I have to grapple with the conflicting desires I experience in myself. If I want to finish writing this book, I can't be out fishing all summer (although fishing is a great time to work through ideas and images for the book). If I want to be at a sane and sensible weight, I can't be eating like a Nebraska football player. We really are going to get what we want. Spiritual direction is all about discovering what we really, deeply, truly desire. If we want a marriage and kids and family life, we cannot desire and fantasize about wild times in Vegas. The truth is that "What Happens in Vegas" doesn't stay in Vegas.

Kevin Kline, Morgan Freeman, Robert DeNiro, and Michael Douglas starred in the movie *Last Vegas* (2013). It's the story of older guys near their seventieth birthdays who meet in Vegas for one last fling. Kevin Kline's character ends up in a room with a naked, nubile young twenty-something who is ready to have him jump her bones (an unrealistic fantasy in itself—what woman has such "Daddy issues" that she wants to hook up with a flabby, gray-bearded grandad?). Kline stops. He movingly tells her, "This would be so wonderful. But you need to know that for forty years, anything wonderful that has happened to me, I have immediately shared with my wife. And I wouldn't be able to share this with her. And that would make it not so wonderful." That guy knows what he really desires and realizes he cannot have his deepest, truest desire if he goes with what he wants in the heat of the moment.

The question of choosing what we want in terms of faith, religion, and spirituality comes down to desires. What do we want? What do we really and truly desire? And what does God desire and want from and for us? Spiritual direction in the Ignatian tradition discerns desires. We pretty much in life do what we want to do. The trick is to get to want to do what we have to do anyway, and not to want to do what we don't deeply and truly desire. True freedom is not doing whatever we want, it is wanting to do what we need to do.[1]

We are composed of body and mind, heart and soul, and each aspect of our being deeply affects the others. If we are physically healthy and fit, the chances are that the spiritual aspects of our being are more in tune with who we really are and what we really want. We are our bodies, and what we do with our bodies is "us." There's an old saying in twelve-step meetings, "Bring the body and the brain will follow." The Catholic faith takes the body very seriously. We are a Eucharistic people, formed by our communal worship of God into the Body of Christ in the world today.

Spiritual direction helps us live our faith in ways that make us happy and healthy and holy and free. The relational nature of spiritual direction empowers us to be more flexible and less rigid, expansive rather than self-enclosed, open to newness rather than closed and determined. Being overly self-determining is seen in fundamentalisms of many kinds, and the excessive "I did it my way" attitude of "me, myself, and I" show that what I do with my life demonstrates little consideration or real care for others. Spiritual direction helps us realize that living in mystery moves us more Godward than certainty. "Prone to black-and-white, either-or thinking,

---

1. Richard Rohr, *Everything Belongs: The Gift of Contemplative Prayer*, rev. and exp. ed. (New York: Crossroad, 2003), 108.

fundamentalism thwarts mature faith, which . . . requires the embrace of paradoxes in the midst of complexity and mystery. . . . In Jesus, Christians have an ideal example of how to strike a healthy balance between being self-determined and Spirit led."[2]

One of the greatest threats to true religious living is the clinging to the Truth with a capital "T" and missing the meaning and spirit of that letter. Love is the living truth that life is complicated and complex while also wonderful and wacky. Good religion helps us float with joy on the sometimes (oftentimes?) stormy seas of life. Real religion, trusting in God and striving to love and serve God by loving and serving others, calls for our navigating calm bays and stormy seas in order to find our deepest, truest selves in our dynamic relationship with the divine reality that resides deep in our hearts and is manifest in the daily realities of our lives. Spiritual direction aims to keep us moving toward that for which we have been created: eternal life in love with God and others. Such life begins as soon as we open our minds, hearts, and spirits to God. Then God can do what God will to make us agents of the kingdom Jesus inaugurated. Spiritual direction helps us chart the course and measure our movement toward our goal, on both personal and social levels of our being.

The late, great Jesuit Tony de Mello taught spiritual truths and principles, often using parable-like stories. One of his stories tells of the eagle raised as a chicken. The eagle spent his days clucking and pecking at the ground in the chicken coop, because all the chickens he saw around him spent their days doing so. One day the caged eagle looked up and saw a beautiful eagle, with a six-foot wing span, soaring high in the sky. The eagle asked, "What kind of bird is that?" An old chicken told him, "That's an eagle, the most beautiful and powerful bird in the sky. Eagles soar where they will, and traverse the world as they will. But we're chickens. We stay here where it's safe." So the eagle spent his life as a chicken, without any awareness of who and what he really could be.

Spiritual direction can help us realize who we really are, and set us free to soar. The relationship between spiritual director and directee is imbued with the grace of the Holy Spirit working in the hearts and minds of both. In this chapter, I want to concentrate on how spiritual direction works over time. In a subsequent chapter, I will share how spiritual direction works during the special time of an Ignatian directed retreat. In both

---

2. Wilkie Au and Noreen Cannon Au, *The Discerning Heart: Exploring the Christian Path* (Mahwah, NJ: Paulist Press, 2006), 10–11.

the short-term direction of a retreat or long-term direction over time the goal is the same: the development of the habitual ability to freely choose the good, the right, and the true. "For freedom Christ has set us free" (Gal 5:1). Spiritual direction is a relational process wherein our freedom to choose to cooperate with God in the living of our personal and social lives becomes strengthened and manifest.

Isabel goes on a SEARCH retreat offered by the campus ministry at her school. She listens attentively to talks from her peers who reveal their joys and sorrows. She finds out that other students share the same struggles she has. As one kid puts it about the retreat, "I found out I'm not weird." Some of her fellow students come from families with deep problems. Others battle addictions or depression. Some students come from loving families and are challenged to reflect on the fact that not all are as fortunate as they are. Isabel learns that going to Mass at the school chapel on Sunday evenings and practicing the daily Examen help her and many of her new friends understand and choose how to live lives that are happy and healthy and holy and free.

Joe, a computer programmer three years out of school, goes on an Ignatian silent retreat. He puts away the cell phone and doesn't go near a computer screen for five days. He prays three times a day for hour-long periods, one in the morning, one in the afternoon, and one in the evening. He goes to Mass each day and spends a half hour talking with a retreat guide about what happens when he prays. Joe comes to some deep realizations about who he is and how he wants to relate to God. He discovers he is fascinated by Jesus. He feels enthusiastic about responding to the needs of God's people in the world today, and is keenly aware of the injustices of our times—everything from racism and sexism to income inequality, immigration issues, and world hunger. Once in a while the fantasy of becoming a Jesuit priest plays in his head. He ponders what this may mean for the future.

Maria, an assistant professor of philosophy, spends Thursday afternoons at the university's medical clinic, translating for Spanish-speaking residents of the city. Service fills her with a sense of meaning and purpose. She had students in her first-year seminar read Jesuit priest Greg Boyle's *Tattoos on the Heart*,[3] about his work with gang members in Los Angeles. She knows she wants to do something with her life that will

3. Greg Boyle, S.J., *Tattoos on the Heart: The Power of Boundless Compassion* (New York: The Free Press, 2011).

help those whom society scorns. She has applied to go as a mentor on a student International Service Trip and anxiously waits to hear where she will be sent.

Steve is a lacrosse coach. He has the whole team spend the Sunday before Thanksgiving filling 150 baskets, each one a complete Thanksgiving feast for a family in need. The team bonds in their shared dedication to the task. Each player realizes a bit more how lucky he is to have food and family this holiday season. And every player senses that this wasn't something they imagined happening when they contemplated attending a Jesuit university. They perceive that they feel lucky to be at a school that calls them to seek the Magis, the ever-greater search for the "more" and the "better" from a stance of gratitude. Their yearly team retreat at the university's retreat house challenges and centers them as young men, and forms them as men who will meet the challenges of adulthood. As their coach, Steve wonders how he can do more to mold these young men into people who will make a world of peace and justice for all.

Ben works with his physics professor studying the marvels of quantum mechanics and helping with a long-term research project. Only a sophomore, Ben is just beginning to grasp some of the deep mysteries of contemporary science and the math that reveals those scientific relationships in a universal language. Another professor suggests he read some of the famous Jesuit Pierre Teilhard de Chardin's writings, which early on in the twentieth century took on the prophetic task of synthesizing science and theology. Teilhard's *The Divine Milieu*[4] rocks Ben's world. He goes on to read Franciscan Sister Ilia Delio's *The Emergent Christ: Exploring the Meaning of Catholic in an Evolutionary Universe*[5] and discovers an intellectual universe mapping the relationships that connect science with the deep wisdom and religious traditions of the human family. He explores *The Language of God: A Scientist Presents Evidence for Belief*[6] by Francis Collins, the biologist who led the team that mapped the human genome. Collins came to faith after having completed his Ph.D. and finding science bumping up against deeper and broader questions and realities of life and life's meanings. While exploring Brown University biolo-

4. Pierre Teilhard de Chardin, *The Divine Milieu* (New York: Harper Perennial Modern Classics, 2001. Orig. English, 1960. French. *Le Milieu Divin*, 1957).

5. Ilia Delio, *The Emergent Christ: Exploring the Meaning of Catholic in an Evolutionary Universe* (Maryknoll, NY: Orbis Books, 2011).

6. Francis Collins, *The Language of God: A Scientist Presents Evidence for Belief* (New York: The Free Press, 2007).

gist Kenneth Miller's book *Finding Darwin's God: A Scientist's Search for Common Ground between God and Evolution*,[7] Ben finds fascinating common ground between evolution and belief in God.

Sean and Mary have been married for six years. They are muddling through what biological anthropologist Helen Fisher calls the "four-year" itch (she claims the "seven-year" is off by three), the time when a marriage will either make it or begin to dissolve.[8] Sean feels that Mary has become too immersed in being a mother to their three-year-old twins and newborn baby. Mary thinks Sean just has to grow up and accept that they are not in their twenties anymore. Life is about responsibility, not having fun all the time. Resentments large and small are building. Sean is drinking a bit more. Sex is a seldom thing. Both wonder if and where God is in all this. They have kept their vows, but they both wonder what those vows mean as they struggle daily to feel something of the excitement and joy of their young love ten years ago. Religious like Jesuits or Sisters of Mercy routinely meet with a spiritual director to help them prayerfully examine, understand, and live their vocations. Who helps married couples live their vocations?

George and Ryan are brothers, both college students, one a senior, the other in his first year. They are shocked on a cool, fall evening: their father has died of suicide. In the weeks following the blur of wake and funeral, they converse with the university chaplain about how they are dealing with their confusion and feelings about their dad's death.

All the people mentioned above could benefit from spiritual direction. Practitioners of Ignatian Spirituality are dedicated to the twin missions of (1) helping people to be aware of, and form, their souls; and (2) guiding people who will make intelligent, passionate, transformative contributions to the common good of our communities and our world.

Sometimes things become clearer if you have a negative example. What happens to a hard-core addict? They literally lose their freedom to the

7. Kenneth Miller, *Finding Darwin's God: A Scientist's Search for Common Ground between God and Evolution* (New York: Harper Perennial, 1999).

8. Helen Fisher, "Is there a Biological Basis for the Seven Year Itch?" http://www.scientificamerican.com. "The four-year divorce peak among modern humans may represent the remains of an ancestral reproductive strategy to stay bonded *at least* long enough to raise a child through infancy and early toddlerhood. Thus, we may have a natural weak point in our unions. By understanding this susceptibility in our human nature, we might become better able to anticipate, and perhaps be able to avoid, the four-year itch."

substance or tendency to which they have become addicted. If Joe has no one to say honestly and lovingly, "Joe, it seems you're drinking a lot more than you have in the past, and it's affecting your life quite negatively," Joe may slip more and more into the hellish addiction of full-blown alcoholism. Joe has no direction about his use of alcohol. Marie is a shopaholic. She has more shoes than she can count. The spare bedroom is so loaded with stuff, no one can see the furniture or the floor. Who will Marie hear saying, "There's a problem here"? Bill and Ann have started a business. They work more than seventy hours a week. Their two teenage kids, thirteen and sixteen, are both beginning to run with the fast crowd in their school. Both are using alcohol and light drugs to stave off the pain of being ignored by their parents. Bill and Ann are working so hard so their kids will have good lives. Who can help Bill and Ann look at their lives and discern how much time should be devoted to their business and how much to their family? Spiritual direction keeps us on track. The more honest we are with our director the more we can maintain our desired course and not get sidetracked.

St. Ignatius in the Principle and Foundation of the Spiritual Exercises teaches we are created to praise, reverence, and serve God, and by doing so come to the fulfillment in love for which we are created.[9] Everything in our lives is given to us in order to help us attain this goal. Spiritual direction is a practice that helps us notice, relish, and choose those realities that help us toward our goal, and recognize, identify, and avoid that which keeps us from being fulfilled in love.

The greatest description of our Christian faith I've ever found is that of St. Athanasius: "God becomes what we are so we might become what God is."[10] Spiritual direction is the process that helps us realize the ways the process of divinization is going on in our mind and hearts and souls. In the conversation between director and directee, often is revealed and brought to consciousness how God is working in one's life.

Spiritual direction is an art that fashions a person into the man or woman they are truly meant to be. The person we are meant to be comes into being through the interaction of God's gifts and graces and our free choices. Discernment is the processes of listening, conversing, choosing, and judging if the choice is ratified by consolation. A spiritual director

---

9. David Fleming, S.J., "The Principle and Foundation," in *Draw Me into Your Friendship: A Literal Translation and a Contemporary Reading of the Spiritual Exercises*, #23 (St. Louis, MO: The Institute of Jesuit Sources, 1996), 26–27.

10. *Catechism of the Catholic Church* (New York: Doubleday, 1995), §460.

coaches, inspires, encourages, and challenges a directee to freely and honestly name and claim what is going on in his or her heart and mind. Life in Christ is one of transformation. We can all use direction as we strive to root our lives in the mystery of Jesus.

Spiritual direction helps us be more attentive and aware of how and why we are choosing what we choose, more conscious of the decisions we make. Our choices are to reflect our love of God by the way we choose to love one another. "The Good News of Christianity comes simply to this, that as a result of Jesus' death and resurrection we can now love God effectively only by loving one another. . . . Probably the greatest difficulty with Christianity is that it is so utterly simple. The real novelty of the Christian gospel is the revelation that I must find God in Christ not 'out there' and not merely 'in here,' in the sense of inside myself; I find Christ upon the faces and in the heart of humanity."[11]

How Spiritual Direction Worked in My Life

As a young man, I entered the Jesuit novitiate in Wernersville, Pennsylvania. Most amazing about the twelve years of Jesuit formation before ordination to the priesthood was the constant message given us: the man God wants you to be is your deepest, truest self. The deepest, truest self is revealed through one's deepest, truest desires. Spiritual direction was one of the gifts the Society of Jesus gave us to discover and discern, fashion and form, choose and create our deepest, truest selves, consciously and authentically. We learned to trust the desire worked in us by God.

When I entered and began Jesuit life in 1976, Henry Haske was approaching his fiftieth birthday. He became my spiritual director for two years, and remained close to me for years after. He mentored and guided me into the depths, meaning, culture, and challenges of Jesuit life. Every two weeks or so, I'd sit down with Henry and tell him what was going on in my life. Much of the conversation was about what was happening when I prayed. Henry had to dispel much of delusion and misinformation about what I expected prayer to be. I remember saying to Henry after a few weeks in the novitiate, "When do the visions start?" I'd read about the saints and their visions. Naively, I assumed these were normal experiences. Henry laughed and cooled my jets. What happens in most people's prayer is much less spectacular or paranormal than mistaken notions of celestial beings appearing in the chapel. From Henry I

---

11. David Stanley, S.J., *A Modern Scriptural Approach to the Exercises* (St. Louis, MO: The Institute of Jesuit Sources, 1967), 228.

learned a great deal about prayer. The first lesson was fidelity. You show up for prayer; you give time to prayer. You struggle at times to stay awake, or fend off distractions. What you get in prayer is more dependence on God, more self-awareness, more and more the ability to live the life you choose in Christ.

Henry was one of the giants of the church in transition. Born in 1927, he was a star football player at Loyola High School in Baltimore. He entered the Society of Jesus in 1945 and was ordained in 1957. In 1959, he was sent with a small group of fellow Jesuits to Osorno, Chile. In those days, Jesuits said a final goodbye to friends and family. The expectation was that they would never return from mission lands. While in Chile, Henry experienced one of the worst earthquakes in history. The long "string bean country" was rocked by several earthquakes in May of 1960. The Valdivia earthquake registered 9.5 on the moment magnitude scale, the most powerful earthquake in history. Henry, a very tough guy, once told me how frightened he was by the experience of the quake.

The shock that hit the Catholic Church with Vatican II (1962–1965) was a comparable eruption of energy. Henry and his generation of Jesuits bridged the Latin church of the 1940s and 1950s and the vernacular church of the 1960s and beyond. Humanly speaking, how difficult was it to give your life to a way of being Catholic and then have that way of life radically reoriented and changed? Cassocks, Latin Mass, and many other aspects of Jesuit and church life changed overnight. Most deeply disorienting and challenging was the whole way Jesuits prayed and related to God. Preached retreats had been standard operating procedure. You went to a retreat house. A Jesuit would talk four or five times a day. You would listen and go off and draw what spiritual guidance you could glean from his reflections.

With Vatican II came a call to religious orders to rediscover their original charisms, in other words, the spiritual gifts and orientations of their founders. Jesuits rediscovered the way of giving the Spiritual Exercises practiced by St. Ignatius and the early Jesuits, one-on-one conversation about one's prayer.

Henry was a pioneer in this rediscovery of the original charism of the Society of Jesus. One-on-one spiritual conversation was the way St. Ignatius and the early Jesuits helped men refashion and mold themselves into the Company of Jesus. A young man needs to be guided as God makes him into someone who can serve God and the church as St. Ignatius did. A man must choose to live and affirm Jesuit charisms and ideals, which can be a challenging process.

The novitiate is a two-year period in which a man lives the Jesuit life and the Society tests his vocation. Pedro Arrupe, the charismatic Superior General of the Jesuit order from 1965 to 1981 who had been in Hiroshima the day the atomic bomb was dropped, had an upbeat and optimistic view of life. Arrupe once said, "To a young man who wishes to be a Jesuit, I would say: Come if serving Christ is at the very center of your life. Come if you have broad and sufficiently strong shoulders. Come if you have an open spirit, a reasonably open mind and a heart larger than the world. Come if you know how to tell a joke and can laugh with others . . . and on occasion you can laugh at yourself."[12] The novitiate is the period in which the man and the Society see if he can become what Arrupe describes: a relatively strong person, centering his heart on Christ, and opening his mind to the sufferings and joys of the peoples of the world.

Henry became my spiritual director for the two years of my novitiate. Along with a couple of dozen other novices, I began to incorporate myself into the Jesuit way of proceeding. Henry began to teach me how to pray. I entered as a young, self-confident (maybe a little too self-confident!), former football, lacrosse, and rugby player. One of the first scripture passages Henry told me to pray over were Paul's words, "my power is best in weakness" (2 Cor 12:9). Henry saw immediately, much more clearly than I, that one of the central spiritual struggles of my life would be learning how to be dependent on God. Childhood family troubles and a troubled adolescence had made me extremely independent and self-sufficient. I didn't need anyone; I could take care of myself. I was here to serve others. I didn't need God to do anything for me. I was here to do something for God. Henry began to chip away at this central dynamic of my being and led me to an awareness of my need to learn how to trust and depend on God, for in that truth lay real freedom. The Jesuit way and the way of the gospel was in the power to transform me into a man who could be "weak" enough to be a Jesuit priest.[13]

About two months into the novitiate, we made an eight-day retreat. This was to gear us up for the thirty-day retreat a few months later. I remember arguing with Henry about the older son in the prodigal son

---

12. Pedro Arrupe, S.J., quoted on a Vocation Card distributed by the Vocation office of The Jesuits, 39 East 83rd St., New York, NY 10028.

13. Michael Buckley, S.J., "Because Beset with Weakness . . . ," in Robert Terwilliger and Urban T. Holmes, eds., *To Be a Priest: Perspectives on Vocation and Ordination* (New York: Seabury Press, 1975), 125–30.

parable. I felt he had a case. Henry began to show me that God's ways were not my ways (cf. Is 55:9).

Henry guided me through the first thirty-day retreat I made. As a Jesuit novice, I discovered that the retreat was both a school of prayer and a time for making an election, a definitive choice. I would pray four or five hours a day, attend Mass, and meet with Henry each day to process what was happening. The first week lasted ten days. After hours of prayer on God's goodness and love, I prayed for several days on how I had responded in the first quarter of my life. Lots of self-awareness of strengths and weaknesses, along with a deep abiding sense of God's presence in my life, took root in me during those days. The full General Confession of all the sins of my life was not easy, but it brought a new sense of hope and healing I had never experienced at that depth.

The second week was easier. I devoted time to contemplating the life of Jesus and his teachings. I remember spending one whole day on the Beatitudes (Mt 5:1–12). The sheer wisdom of those eight truths just dug in and amazed me. The incident of the Rich Young Man (Mk 10:21) also spoke powerfully to my soul. Jesus looked at him, loved him, and invited him to "follow me." I got to know Peter very well, from his fearful admission "Leave me Lord, for I am a sinful man" (Lk 5:8) to his impetuous jumping out of the boat to walk on water (Mt 14:22–33), to his declaration "to whom Lord shall we go? You have the words of eternal life" (Jn 6:68–69), to his shameful denials, to his jumping out of the boat again in John 21 to rush to meet the risen Lord Jesus on the shore. I saw a lot of myself in Peter.

Midway through the retreat, St. Ignatius suggests the retreatant spend some time praying over if and how he or she is to make an election, a choice of a way of life.[14] I really reacted against this idea. I wasn't going to decide then and there to be a Jesuit or a priest for the rest of my life. I just wasn't ready to make that commitment. I told Henry I'd stick out the two years of the novitiate. I told him, "Let's see how things go." Henry just sat there and said, "Keep listening." That was about the fifteenth day of the retreat. I'll never forget the twenty-second day of the retreat. I was down in an area of the retreat house off the dining hall, getting a cup of coffee. It was late afternoon in winter, a rather gray and gloomy day.

---

14. David Fleming, S.J., *Draw Me into Your Friendship: A Literal Translation and a Contemporary Reading of the Spiritual Exercises*, #169–189 (St. Louis, MO: Institute of Jesuit Sources, 1996), 132–45.

All of a sudden a shaft of sunlight burst through the clouds. Somehow I knew in an instant that I was to be a Jesuit for the rest of my life. I hadn't been consciously wrestling with the idea of "making an election"; I'd been praying those days over Jesus' passion and crucifixion. Somehow, on that twenty-second day, the grace hit: You are to be a Jesuit. It's stuck with me for almost forty years now, sometimes better than I've stuck with it.

The fourth week I devoted to praying into the reality and power of the resurrected Jesus. All through the retreat, Henry was a guide and a ballast, slowing and calming me down on days when I was ready "to take on the world for Jesus," and encouraging me when I'd run into times of doubt and discouragement. He always kept pushing me onto the field, while never getting in and playing the game himself.

I did a lot of penance during that first thirty-day retreat, which, though heartfelt and generous, was part of the "muscular Christianity" of my youth. It's not penance that brings God closer, it's the act of removing the false "self" that opens the heart and mind to God. More long lasting were the experiences of three all-night vigils I engaged in during the retreat. Most enduring may have been teaching myself how to play the guitar during those thirty days. That guitar has saved the Society of Jesus a lot of money on psychiatrist bills (one Jesuit buddy joked, "Rick. We'd gladly pay." At least I think he was joking!).

As novices, we were put in situations to test us, to see how we responded to the needs of people, especially the poor. We spent a few months each year in north Philadelphia, in those days a very "inner city" neighborhood. Two days a week I went by public transportation with John Cecero, a fellow novice, out to the home for physically impaired children in Rosemont, Pennsylvania. Located in one of the wealthiest suburbs of Philadelphia, this beautiful home cared for children with severe physical disabilities. Helping these kids swim, play, and get around showed me much about the beauty and love of God shimmering beneath suffering and weakness.

One summer three of us were sent for four weeks to Delaware to work with a priest ministering in migrant worker camps. The conditions in the camps were somewhere between deplorable and minimal; camping would have been a big step up. We three novices were housed in the nice, suburban home of a Catholic family who were on vacation. The priest, a non-Jesuit and a rather conservative guy, said Mass for us the first night we were in the home and then left a two-foot-high tabernacle in the family rec room so we could pray before the Blessed Sacrament. The day we left, we were going to Mass at a parish church and needed to drop off the house keys and the tabernacle to the priest on our way out of town. The priest didn't live at the parish. And the tabernacle had no key. So, we went to 9:00 a.m. Mass, and we had to leave "Jesus" in the car!

The most extensive test of the novitiate is the long experiment. In the second year, for six months a novice is sent to a regular work of the Society, usually a school or a parish. He is to engage in the day-to-day life of a Jesuit community and apostolate. I was lucky and was assigned to Red Cloud Indian School on the Pine Ridge Reservation in South Dakota. Great work, great Jesuits, great times! I learned a lot. How to drive a school bus. How not to freeze to death on 20-degree-below-zero February mornings. How to pray on busy days. Also learned how much I still needed to learn about serving the poor. And that you should show up in the Montessori first grade with valentines on February 14!

My signature experience was falling in love with a young woman who was a volunteer in the school. With some trepidation, I spoke about my feelings for her with the Jesuit superior, a kind old Irishman who had been Jesuit provincial and had seen it all. He calmly told me how normal and common it is for a Jesuit to fall in love. The question now becomes, what do you do? What choices will you make? Those last months on the reservation and in the early summer afterward were agonizing. I felt I would love to leave the Society of Jesus and see where the relationship with her might lead. I also wanted to be a Jesuit, but I wasn't feeling the attraction to the Jesuits all that strongly. But as the days passed and I kept praying, as I kept talking with Henry back at the novitiate, the deeper, consistent, quiet, and demanding desire to be a Jesuit began to win the tug-of-war. To go and be with the young lady would be great. But there was something mysteriously more about the Jesuit thing that wouldn't let go. The Jesuit superior and Henry never told me what to do. They constantly and gently insisted that I closely examine my feelings and thoughts. What did I want? What did I really want? I learned that God's will is present in our desires. She wondered why God's will wasn't present in her desires. I wondered the same thing. If she loved me, and I loved her, why not leave? But deep in my consciousness, I was aware of what I really wanted, even though I didn't really feel like I wanted it at the time. So it is with commitments made and kept. She accepted my decision. Neither she nor I wanted to play games. Over the years she's been in touch. She's married to a guy who is probably twice as good a husband as I would have been. Forty years later, I'm somewhat sure I made a good decision. But at the time it was a risk. I was betting it all on this crazy sense that God wanted me to be a Jesuit. It wasn't until the months of deep consolation after taking vows that I began to trust and believe I'd made a grace-filled choice.

Throughout the novitiate and years of studies, I would see a Jesuit spiritual director once a month or so, sometimes more often if both of us felt to do so would be helpful. John Schwantes and Gene Garcia kept pushing me to follow my desires to work directly with the poor and connect them to the intellectual mission of the Society of Jesus. They also urged me to take prayer seriously. I once told John that I wasn't sure if prayer did anything. Sitting there in the morning trying to stay awake, were my prayers really making any difference? He told me "Find out." I said "Find out? How?" John replied, "Stop praying. See what happens." So I stopped praying. John was right. This Jesuit life, my life, made little sense without prayer. There was something missing without the serious, daily struggle to communicate with God. As I've learned over the years, it takes time to get the false self a bit out of the way so God can communicate with us.

The next stage of Jesuit formation was philosophy studies at St. Louis University. There I had to overcome my initial aversion to the study of philosophy, a seemingly inane and useless way to spend several years of my life. I was very wrong. I literally prayed, "Look, Lord. If you want me to study this stuff, you're going to have to make me like it." That actually happened. I got turned on to the life of the mind, and kicked my already voracious reading habit up a notch. Philosophy challenged me to develop a coherent set of ideas about life, love, God, and the meanings of all three. Spiritual direction during these years dealt with all the normal ups and downs of community life, the struggles to develop habits of prayer and reflection, and the learning to discern the multifaceted ways one is called to be a Jesuit. A street priest needed the same intellectual tool kit as the university professor (no better example of this than well-known Greg Boyle, S.J., out in Los Angeles with Homeboy Industries). Good friendships developed during these years. Dennis Ryan, S.J., and his family in Omaha became one of the most cherished gifts of my life. As I worked through the inevitable family of origin issues everyone confronts in their mid-twenties, the Ryans showed me what a good, normal, loving family is—and can be—in one's life.

Next, from 1981 to 1984, I lived and worked in Chile. The first year in the K–12 San Mateo school in Osorno was challenging and difficult. Spanish came slowly. But a singular grace was the Chilean rector, Fernando Salas, S.J. He was patient and kind with a gringo who was undergoing all the stresses and strains of first-year teaching and the confusions of culture shock. And the kids were great; they were used to somewhat befuddled American Jesuits trying to acclimate. And the Jesuits in general were supportive and helpful.

Once when I went to Fernando, letting him know of my struggles to be a good Jesuit, he shared an image that I've found helpful, and to which I have returned over the years. He said, "We start out as blocks of marble. Within the marble is a beautiful statue. God knocks off the big chunks fairly easily. Then the chiseling starts: chip, chip, chip. And finally the sanding of the marble, which takes a very, very long time. It takes all that for the beautiful statue to emerge." I've often thought of this image. I guess I am still in the "chip, chip, chip" stage.

Later during my time in Chile, I made the major decision to leave the school in Osorno and head up to Santiago to engage in pastoral work in the Zona Oeste. One struggle while I was teaching in Osorno was feeling that nothing was "happening" in Osorno. The issues of the day, La Lucha (the struggle) against the brutal dictatorship of Pinochet, the energies and passions of liberation theology, were all playing out in the capital city, not in the backwaters like Osorno. One Chilean friend told me, "If it's happening in Santiago, there's no use it's happening in Osorno, because Santiago is Chile." I believed that. I told Fernando Montes, S.J., the Chilean provincial, that I wanted out of the school. "This is a great place. But I'm not content here."

There was a need for accompaniment of a Belgian Jesuit, Julio Stragier, in a large parish in the Western Zone of Santiago. I was sent there with another Jesuit scholastic, Ernesto Cavassa. The three of us had a great year, directly accompanying the poor in La Parroquia de la Santa Cruz in Santiago. I went on several demonstrations with "The Movement against Torture Sebastian Acevedo," a loose congregation of protestors mentored by the former Jesuit provincial Jose Aldunante. The young adult members of the *comunidad de base* [base community] of the Capilla San Esteban became my friends and guides to the heart and soul of Chilean life, as they suffered the pains and tribulations of the Pinochet years. In Santiago, I got all I had asked for. Yet, as I spoke with various Jesuits about the currents and flow of graces in my life that year, I had to admit, I had chosen what I wanted. I learned that it's a big old world, and one can do very little by oneself. More and more I wondered if I hadn't been doing more for God's kingdom humbly teaching the kids in Osorno than I was with all the pastoral work in Santiago.

Ignatian Spirituality roots out inordinate attachments. Was I too attached to the image of the "revolutionary Jesuit"? Could I accept where and how God wanted to work through my life? The real challenge was to realize that it was no longer "my" life; now it's Christ's life in me. But it's taken years to grow in the realization of what that all means. As Richard Rohr says, "Your life is not about you."[15]

When I left Chile, I spent the next four years in Cambridge and Roxbury, Massachusetts, while studying theology at the Jesuit Weston School of Theology. The intellectual feast that is Jesuit life was readily spread before us and our lay colleagues as we prepared to become, as the iconoclastic scripture scholar Stanley Marrow, S.J., put it, "let loose on the people of God." My pastoral work at St. Patrick's in Roxbury and the Gesu Parish in Philadelphia during the summers put flesh on the mountains of theological tomes I plowed through during the school year.

As I approached ordination, a strange discomfort began to register in me. I hesitated. Did I really want to be a priest? The whole public nature of ministry really began to make me feel uncomfortable. And I'm no wall flower. What was going on? This took a year or so to untangle. Of course, falling in love with a woman didn't make matters any more clear. To make a long story short, I discovered in conversations with Brian McDermott, S.J., the community's rector, that what was really going on was that I didn't want to have a first Mass. I wanted to be a Jesuit priest, but because of complicated family issues, the last thing I wanted was to have all the attention that a first Mass throws on the newly ordained. The thought of bringing my family together was really paralyzing me. In spiritual direction, Brian suggested I should think about getting some professional counseling to understand better what I was experiencing. My first reaction to his suggestion was, no, I don't need counseling. But with some encouragement, I went. What I learned in the counseling process is that I am counter-dependent, entirely too self-sufficient, and ready and willing to take care of myself with little real help from others. The counseling sort of stalled on that point. Until I could learn to be more vulnerable and in relation with others, I'd be a bit handcuffed in life. This wasn't actually new news. I'd already been challenged by several spiritual directors to address this overly independent stance in life. It certainly was a central struggle in my prayer life. It's tough to have a relationship with God when

---

15. Richard Rohr, "Your Life Is Not About You" (Homily of May 25, 2016), https://cac.org.

you want to be at least "little god" of your life. I was happy to do things for God. I just find it difficult letting God do things for me.

This was a delicate and difficult time. After the first ordination retreat, I called a halt to the proceedings and decided to delay ordination for a year. In the meantime, I grappled more deeply with this counter-dependent dynamic in my life. It was a trait Henry Haske had noticed early on when he suggested I pray on 2 Corinthians 12:9–10: "my power is best in weakness." I had to wrestle with the reality that a man needs to be weak enough to be a priest.[16] Karl Rahner, S.J., the great theologian, teaches that dependence on God and freedom grow in direct, not inverse, proportion. I found I was more free the more I let go and let God be God in my life. But dependence, more on God and less on myself, is a lifelong lesson for me.

A year later, I made a second ordination retreat of eight days back at Wernersville where I'd made the thirty-day retreat some eleven years before. One late summer evening, I sat out on the hills of the retreat property watching a few hawks (maybe they were buzzards?) circling in the sky. It appeared to me that they had it made. They knew exactly what they were and what they were supposed to do. And then the grace broke in on me, dawned in my consciousness. What if I was on the right track? What if I was meant to be a Jesuit priest? What if I'd had it right all along? Soon I was filled with a desire and an energy for Jesuit priestly ministry that was strong and steady. Tom Kane, C.P., who taught liturgy and preaching at Weston, got me through the first Mass. It wasn't too bad. In some ways for me, the first Mass dealt with and healed some family issues that I had been reluctant to attend to in prayer or life over the years.

Rahner teaches that we pray and the Word God speaks is our life; "we experience ourselves as the ones spoken by God."[17] On retreats and in spiritual direction over the years I had had to confront and try and understand my relationship with my father. Family history had made me who and what I was, for better or worse. The better had to be augmented; the worse had to be named, tamed, and healed before I could be sent forth on priestly mission. The first Mass brought it all together. This pivotal

---

16. Michael Buckley, S.J., "Are You Weak Enough to Be a Priest? 'Because Beset by Weakness . . .'" http://www.atlantadiaconateformation.com/weakenough.pdf. This was an address given to Jesuit scholastics (Jesuits in training) in the 1980s.

17. Karl Rahner, S.J., "Is Prayer Dialogue with God?" in *Christian at the Crossroads* (New York: Seabury Press, 1975), 62–69.

moment in my life was a fulcrum that launched me into my life as a priest for the people of God.

The next fifteen years in which I lived and worked as a member of the Jesuit Urban Service Team (JUST) in Camden, New Jersey, were filled with the joys and heartaches of inner-city ministry. My earlier choices to enter the Society of Jesus and seek ordination as a Jesuit priest were greatly confirmed. I learned how to be a priest from the people of Holy Name Parish. During those years, I earned a doctorate, something I hadn't really desired, but the provincial, Jim Deveraux, adamantly insisted I pursue it. I liked school but wasn't wild about the academic life. Yet, as I grew more dependent on God and less insistent on God's conforming to my will rather than my conforming to God's desires, I was beginning to trust God deeply as my life was unfolding. Doctoral studies were fascinating, and I've had a love-hate relationship with academia for years. Still, the doctorate has been an entrance ticket into university work, providing a wonderful opportunity to interact with young adults at a crucial time in their lives.

The horrific revelations of priestly sexual abuse seared the souls of all the ordained and the whole church in the years from 1985 to the present. The avalanche of cases that came forth from the 2002 reporting of the *Boston Globe* and subsequent media attention for the next few years made being a priest a quite turbulent proposition. The turn to the right in matters liturgical and ecclesiastical was not the life, or type of church, I had imagined as a post-"Vatican II"-type priest. As the "John Paul II" priests rose, with steepled fingers, cuff links, and lace-trimmed albs, I wondered, at times, what I was doing with my life. The inevitable difficulties of community life, and other normal realities associated with any life, wore on me. My spiritual director at one point in those years bluntly told me to "shit or get off the pot. It's time to pray for apostolic toughness." She is a wise and tempered sister of the Holy Child of Jesus. She helped me see that most of my "issues" were just life issues, not vocation issues.

Spiritual direction concentrates on the directee's experience of prayer somewhat exclusively when she or he is making a retreat. The range of what spiritual direction deals with expands in the ongoing relationship of spiritual direction over time, and can expand into all that makes us human unto God. After thirty years of engaging in spiritual direction, I grew to appreciate and realize all I had been given to make me the Jesuit I am. One summer, while serving in parishes in Bush Alaska out of the city of Bethel, I was drawn to write out why I was a Jesuit. I share here what I wrote at that time in July 2006. In many ways, this describes what happened to me as I was gifted with the challenges and graces of ongoing spiritual direction over the years.

"Why I Am a Jesuit"

September 3, 2006: The Thirtieth Anniversary of Entrance Day

The primary reason I am a Jesuit is because I am fascinated by God. The only point of life is to try and figure out why we are alive, what we are to do while we are on earth, and what happens when we die. Those three questions all have to do with the mystery of existence, i.e., God. Over thirty years ago I was led to a nursing home to work as an orderly, and that experience of service transformed my life. There, I found joy, assisting the elderly and helping them prepare for death. That job mysteriously was an answer to a prayer I prayed out on the Quad at Lafayette College, "OK, Lord, if you're there, do something." What turned me to prayer was the experience a few days before of falling drunk down the fraternity house stairs and splitting my head open. Sometime it takes a blow to the head to wake up an Irishman.

Ever since, I have been searching for God. This is the God who was part of the thought I had as a little boy at a Lenten daily Mass, as I knelt amidst the entire student body, looked up at the priest and realized, "I'm going to do that someday." On the High School "Encounter" retreat in 1972, I met this God, and then hid from him for several years. This God is the meaning and mystery of my life. This mysterious God saved me from death when I totaled a pick-up truck on the Garden State Parkway, after a wild night in the bars of Margate, NJ, in the summer of 1974. This God has led me, fascinated me, explicitly and directly, ever since calling me to Jesuit life in 1976 when the words of Mk 10:21 powerfully spoke to my soul. This same God refused to be God my way in the thirty-day Spiritual Exercises of 1977 and 2000. This God about whom I've read and read, and thought and thought, to whom I've prayed and prayed, is the reason I'm a Jesuit.

Life in the Society of Jesus is one within which a man is necessarily pursued by God and is freed to pursue God, and to pursue God in a way radically oriented toward service of others, to be "of help to souls." As a Jesuit, I find that I am naturally, constantly, daily impelled to seek

God in all realities, in all personal encounters, in all that is and can be. People in my life support and challenge me as I develop this mysterious relationship with God, a relationship many days muddled and murky, and often cantankerous (eight-day retreats are usually more mud wrestling with God, than halcyon interludes between months of apostolic service). Often, evidence of that primary relationship with God is manifest in interactions with fellow Jesuits, our praying, daily living, sometimes fighting, but always laughing, together. Most deeply, that reality of God and God of all reality is mediated to me by those who love me and those I love.

Those who are not Jesuits of course, are also able to serve others, and to seek and encounter God, and many most likely do so more faithfully, authentically, and integrally than I. For me, the structures and constraints of life in the Society of Jesus focus and free me in the quest for God. If I were not a Jesuit, I'd probably be a truck driver, wandering endlessly, wasting away my life in the pursuit of trivialities and distractions from what really matters, our eternal destiny.

As a Jesuit, I grew and was formed despite my myriad faults and failings, yet also with a flowing forth of abilities and talents I never would have known, had I not taken vows, had I not let go and placed my feet firmly in air, had I not received the grace to keep saying "the Infinite Yes" to God. Preaching and ministering in situations and contexts far, far too numerous to count, has made me a man ready for just about anything: from teaching English and Religion in a High School in Osorno, Chile; to burying a fifteen-year-old killed in the insane violence of the innercity drug wars of Camden, NJ, a young man to whom I had given First Communion just five years earlier; to regularly celebrating Mass with a gym full of mentally challenged children; to teaching Anthropology and Sociology at a Jesuit University; to speaking in contexts as varied as hospitals and retreat houses; to writing of many kinds; to learning from the elders on the Pine Ridge Indian reservation and in Yupi'k Eskimo villages; to the necessary penances of multiple committee and board meetings; to preaching and presiding at Masses in parishes and prisons; to celebrations of Baptisms and weddings; to retreat weekends on hilltops with Jesuit Volunteers; on and on. I am not unique. Most Jesuits lead lives as varied and as interesting as mine. Many Jesuits' lives are even more varied, interesting, and fascinating. When people ask why Jesuits are who and what we are, and do what we do, I don't think we communicate clearly enough that this life is fascinating and fun.

That's a second major reason I am a Jesuit. This life is endlessly intriguing and interesting. There are critics galore in the Society of Jesus, and sometimes the criticism fails to rise above the level of petty complaint, but the one complaint I have never, ever heard is that Jesuit life is boring. The intellectual feast that is Jesuit life means engaging in a never-ending graduate seminar, probing and exploring the endless realms of knowledge, from discussions of theoretical physics' string theory at breakfast to lunch debates about global politics to kitchen talks late at night over ice cream, sharing about the meaning of suffering and death. It really is true that a Jesuit is one with a "flair for prayer, a yearning for learning and an attitude of gratitude."

The mission of deeply entering into the intellectual battles of our postmodern age exacts costs. Paying attention to contemporary church and community conflicts and controversies, which rip at the heart and soul of a Jesuit, can make life painful and confusing, but I imagine less so than many difficult marriages. And, like good marriages, when Jesuit community life is sane and supportive, and when the church community of which a Jesuit is a part is filled with the fervor of Faith and the promotion of Justice which Faith necessarily includes as a constitutive dimension of work for God's Kingdom (or "Reign" if one finds that term preferable), then life is good and wonderful. In such space a Jesuit and his companions and colleagues from other walks and ways of life can grow happy and healthy and holy and free. Our exercise and enjoyment of freedom and love is necessarily measured by the degree to which others have life opportunities like ours. The degree, density, and depth of my solidarity with the poor and marginalized is the measure of the freedom in faith with which God's love has graced me. Freedom's love frees us and our neighbors. It is only in freedom that we can love.

The third and most fundamental reason I am a Jesuit is because I have experienced freedom and love as a Jesuit. I never cease to be amazed at how well and deeply and unreservedly and quickly and openly I am loved precisely as a Jesuit, loved in ways I little deserve or merit, and for reasons I little understand. Wherever I go, from a summer in a parish in Springer, NM, to the students' Hawk Rock café at Saint Joseph's University, to Tee Ball games for Holy Name

Little Leaguers in Camden, NJ, to Jesuit Volunteer Corps' orientations and retreats, to Scranton's parishes and universities, people want to be nice to me, share their food with me, talk with me about their lives and loves, struggles and sins, joys and jubilations. It's not because I'm some kind of special person or priest. It is because they already have met Jesuits, and trust and expect I will be like those fine priests and brothers. At Jesuit parishes, schools and retreat houses, the people we serve never relate to one Jesuit in isolation from other Jesuits. They love us, not just me.

Most deeply, as a Jesuit, I have been made an integral member of many, many families. The love I have experienced at the reunions of the family of a fellow Jesuit, the welcome and support of several families who invite me over, clamor for me to visit, and let me just be me when I am among them, the families who trust me to play with their small children despite the horrific scandals of abuse perpetrated by some priests, are all a direct result of their knowing me as a Jesuit. They call me to be a better and more genuinely authentic son of Ignatius and disciple of Jesus. Great graces too are the many individuals who have loved and listened to me, helping me grow and be a better man of the Gospel and Church, a more authentic human being, a man loving and loved. Love is best expressed in deeds, and one way of expressing love is the practice of prayer.

Finally, I am a Jesuit because of the reality and challenge of prayer. All these realities I mention in this reflection come together in some mysterious and inexplicable way as we pray. Praying the Office, contemplating the scriptures and church teachings, studying spiritual and theological books, and sitting in the silence of Centering Prayer, unite everything in God who is "all in all" (1 Cor 15:28). All these graced/gifted realities of my life are present as the throbbing center at the heart of the daily Eucharist. That pulsating center is charged through, and sustained by, the constant presence of an inexplicable, unfathomable, utterly mysterious God, the God who is love, the God revealed and communicated to us in human history in the preaching, crucifixion, and resurrection of Jesus, the God who lives in our hearts by the gift of the Holy Spirit poured out in our hearts (Rom 5:5). Ultimately, I am a Jesuit because I am made one by the grace of God, the call of Jesus, and the challenge, support and love of others. *Deo Gratias. Oremus.*

To a large degree, spiritual direction over the years, sitting across from dedicated disciples and sharing the movements of my soul, and hearing from the wisdom of their experience of service and prayer, has made me who and what I am. The grace of God, working in and through the processes of spiritual direction, has formed me and given me the abilities to be the Jesuit priest that I am. And the Jesuit I am took years to form.

Spiritual Direction over a Lifetime

Richard Rohr in *Falling Upward* recognizes that in the first half of life, we need to "learn the rules" and form ourselves into good soldiers, those who know how to serve and support the tradition of the community. There is a value to learning how to be a "good soldier," someone who can follow the rules and make the institutions of our lives function. But at some point in midlife we begin to relax and realize the fundamental flexibility of good religious and spiritual traditions. We begin to see things as less black and white; we appreciate the gray areas of everything. We see many more colors as we live more "'both/and' than 'either/or.'"[18] Rohr writes:

> In short, we have not found a way to do the age-appropriate tasks of the two halves of life and both groups are losing out. The juniors are made to think the container is all there is and all they should expect; or worse, that they are mature and free because they believe a few right things or perform some right rituals. The would-be maturing believer is not challenged to any adult faith or ends up in the muddled middle, where "the best lack all conviction, while the worst are full of passionate intensity," as William Butler Yeats put it. I am convinced that much of the pastoral and practical confusion has emerged because we have not clarified the real differences, the needs, and the somewhat conflicting challenges of the two halves of our lives.[19]

Good spiritual directors can help directees in different times and stages of their lives. Sometimes they need to call forth the talents and abilities of someone who is selling herself short. Sometimes the grandiosity or self-pity of a person in midlife crisis needs to be challenged. Sometimes the guy or gal in the fourth quarter of life needs to be consoled as their

---

18. Richard Rohr, O.F.M., *Falling Upward: A Spirituality for the Two Halves of Life* (San Francisco: Jossey-Bass, 2011), xi, 15, and passim.

19. Ibid., 15.

powers and abilities diminish. Our elders need to know that maybe now their prayer is more powerful and more influential than all their years of service. To live out of that truth and vision takes a lot of faith in our golden years.

Ronald Rolheiser names three main stages of spiritual development. We strive to get our lives together in late adolescence and young adulthood. In our adult years, much of our time consists of the long haul of giving ourselves away in service to others (parenting and work receive the lion's share of our life efforts). Finally, Rolheiser teaches that we have to learn to let go and allow our deaths to be gift for others.[20]

In my own life, I've learned the truth of both Rohr's and Rolheiser's observations. Spiritual direction formed me as a Jesuit, and then expanded the meanings and realities of what being a Jesuit means to me. What I used to hold as central to the Jesuit vocation has become broader and deeper. It is more the holding of paradoxes in creative tension to keep them from devolving into destructive polarities than promulgating THE TRUTH of the faith or the ways JUSTICE must be established.

I was once told by a Jesuit contemporary of George Schemel, S.J., a talented spiritual director who founded the Jesuit Center for Spiritual Growth, that toward the end of his life George said, "The older I get, I believe more and more in less and less." What really matters as people get older boils down to some central realities and into some central persons in their lives. As a person grows, roots, and deepens into life, the fires of youth burn lower. A campfire at first has great crackling flames, flashing way up above the wood. But it's when the flames go out and the coals glow that the fire is really hot and can cook food. One wise old man once told me, "At forty, you'll laugh at what you'd have died for at twenty." Spiritual direction, over time, helps us hold certainties more loosely and easily, without the need to defend or prove our views to others, or worse, impose our views on them.

The longer I have been graced with spiritual direction, the more I've come to see that it is all about the prayer. Service must come from prayer, be rooted in prayer, and ultimately be understood and experienced in the light of prayer. Our relationship with God is the only reality of our lives that never disappears. All our possessions will be taken from us. Scranton Bishop Joe Bambera once said, "Everything I have will someday belong

---

20. Ronald Rolheiser, *Sacred Fire: A Vision for a Deeper Human and Christian Maturity* (New York: Image Books, 2014), esp. 284.

to someone else." Our careers and successes will soon be forgotten, and really, they will not even be known by those who come after us. (Think quick. Who won last year's Super Bowl? Oscar? Nobel Prize? But we all remember our first-grade teacher, that coach who kept us out of trouble, that mentor who challenged and taught us our profession.) The good news is that this goes for our failures too! Nobody remembers or cares if you got that promotion or not. Nobody is impressed with our ephemeral successes, nor really cares all that much about our apparent failures. St. Teresa of Avila poetically said it best: *"Nada te turbe, nada te espante, todo se pasa, Dios no se muda. La paciencia todo lo alcanza, quien a Dios tiene nada le falta. Solo Dios gasta."* [Let nothing disturb you, let nothing frighten you. All things are passing. God never changes. Patience obtains all. Whoever has God lacks nothing. God alone suffices.]

Nowhere have I found the lessons of prayer better conveyed than by Fr. Walter Ciszek, S.J., (1904–1984), in *He Leadeth Me*, his fascinating account of his spiritual journey during his five years in solitary confinement in Lubianka [Lubyanka] prison and fifteen years in Siberian labor camps in the Soviet Union. Ciszek, a hard-headed kid from Shenandoah, Pennsylvania, whose cause is now up for canonization as a saint, started his Jesuit life in the same place I did, Wernersville, Pennsylvania. He exemplified muscular Christianity, but his generous heart led him to volunteer for the Russian missions. At the start of World War II, he was serving at a parish in Poland when the Soviet forces overran the country. Accompanying workers, he went deep into Russia. He was soon arrested and charged with being a Vatican spy. The ordeal was just beginning. "There was no one to turn to, no one to talk to, no one from whom I could seek advice, or sympathetic understanding, no one to offer me consolation. . . . And so, as I had done in every other crisis, I turned to God in prayer. I sought his help, his sympathy, his consolation."[21] But all Ciszek received was the God of consolation, which is not necessarily the same as what we conceive of as the consolations of God. "Surely he [Jesus/God] could sympathize with my plight; surely he would comfort and console me. His way of consoling me, however, as had happened so often in the past, was to increase my self-knowledge and my understanding of both his providence and the mystery of salvation."[22] In retrospect, Ciszek realized how

---

21. Walter Ciszek, S.J, with Daniel L. Flaherty, S.J., *He Leadeth Me* (Garden City, NY: Doubleday and Co., 1973), 48.

22. Ibid.

much of "self" had crawled into his prayer. "In how many ways, too, had I allowed this admixture of self, this luxury of feeling sorry for myself, to cloud my vision and prevent me from seeing the current situation with the eyes of God? No man, no matter what his situation, is ever without value, is ever useless in God's eyes. No situation is ever without its worth and purpose in God's providence."[23]

Ciszek spent five long years in solitary confinement in Lubianka prison. There he continued to pray and was schooled by the situation and the Holy Spirit in the difficult but transformative ways of God.

> Being human, I made the same mistakes in prayer every human being makes. I prayed for the conversion of my interrogators, for example, but none ever showed the slightest sign of conversion. I also prayed for more food. . . . I was constantly hungry. . . . Gradually, I learned to purify my prayer and remove from it elements of self-seeking. I learned to pray for my interrogators, not so much that they would see things my way or come to the truth so that my ordeal would end, but because they too were children of God.[24]

Ciszek gradually refined his notions of prayer and, like St. Ignatius in the cave at Manresa, came to understand how God communicates with us. Prayer eventually overcomes the inevitable distractions and "admixture of self" and opens into conversation with a God who loves us and cares for us. "So it is we who must put ourselves in God's presence, we who must turn to him in faith, we who must leap beyond an image to the belief—indeed the realization—that we are in the presence of a loving Father."[25] Lubianka was Ciszek's school of prayer, a graduate school of sorts after years of Jesuit training. He had to learn to believe, hope, and trust in God. Not easy, but necessary, for everyone who is serious about entering into a deeper, more consciously aware relationship with God.

Ciszek's experience of God was extreme and demanding. He eventually buckled under the pressure of his interrogators and signed papers confessing to being a Vatican spy, a trumped-up, ridiculous charge. But it was sign or die.

> Only after several deep breaths could he force himself to say, quietly and icily: "Do you realize, you stupid American, the seriousness of

---

23. Ibid., 49.
24. Ibid., 60.
25. Ibid., 62.

this final procedure? It's a matter of life and death you are fooling around with. . . . Either you sign the document as it is, or we will get rid of you the way we get rid of every spy. There is a bloody war going on outside. If you don't sign those papers, I can sign one right here and you'll be dead before the sun sets."[26]

Ciszek gave in, signed the papers, and returned to his cell filled with shame and guilt. The tough guy from the coal country of Shenandoah, Pennsylvania, had been broken. He felt he had failed—failed himself, his vocation. He complained to God. Why had God failed him in this crucial moment? It was a bitter and agonizing time for the Jesuit priest who had so wholeheartedly and generously given his all to the work of the missions, the work of God's kingdom. How could things have gone so horribly wrong? But Ciszek gradually, over time, under the promptings of God's grace, began to understand things differently. He realized that he had been proud, thinking himself better than others, more capable of handling things on his own. What God taught him was that we must learn to depend on God, not on our own powers and abilities. He had been deeply grateful and aware of God's providential care and concern, "but I had never really abandoned myself to it."[27]

Ciszek learned humility and the peace and eventual joy of abandoning ourselves to God and God's action in our lives. He had pondered the gospel texts about trusting the Holy Spirit, but had thought the Spirit would help him overcome his persecutors. Ciszek thought he could do it for God, rather than open himself to God's working through him. "How foolish and selfish! It was not the church that was on trial at Lubianka. It was not the Soviet Government or the NKVD (Soviet secret police) versus Walter Ciszek. It was God versus Walter Ciszek. God was testing me by this experience."[28] Like St. Peter, Ciszek had to learn to accept that God was God, and he was not God. Through all those interrogations and years of solitary confinement, through that day when he caved and signed the papers under the threat of death, Ciszek learned about the cleansing of self that all true and transformative spiritual practice entails.

The primacy of self that had manifested itself and been reinforcing itself even in my methods of prayer and spiritual exercises under-

---

26. Ibid., 72.
27. Ibid., 74.
28. Ibid., 76.

went a purging, through purgatory, that left me cleansed to the bone. It was a pretty hot furnace . . . very nearly as hot as hell itself. Yet, thanks be to God, I did still endure—and I had learned to the depths of my shaken soul, how totally I depended on God for everything even in my survival and how foolish had been my reliance on self.[29]

As St. Peter learned when he failed and denied Christ, and then went and wept so bitterly, so Walter Ciszek learned that we are dependent on God for whatever we can do. We don't do what we do because we love God; we are able to do what we do because God loves us. "For just as surely as man begins to trust in his own abilities, so surely has he taken the first step on the road to ultimate failure. And the greatest grace God can give such a man is to send him a trial he cannot bear with his own powers—and then sustain him with his grace so he may endure to the end and be saved."[30]

On returning to the United States in 1963, after having left it in 1934, Ciszek took some time to adjust to a country that had been transformed after World War II. But over the years, the lessons he had learned during his long sojourn in Russia stuck with him. In 1964, he writes in his notes on his annual retreats: "Lord, it is not for me to decide or choose what is better for me. I came to the conclusion that abandoning myself to your divine providence and seeking in it thy divine will is the only life for me. Hence the choosing of what is better for me, I leave entirely to you."[31] Ciszek ruefully admits, "But having lived this long, and having tried so often is proof enough for me that I need to select another method of life than I have been using thus far." He critiques himself for having too much of self in all he did, too much "I" in his spiritual life. He writes, "Yet this method of action did not give me . . . peace and contentment. It lacked the perfect surrender of self. . . . A lot of time was spent fighting you [God]."[32] Ciszek finds a new way of allowing the false self to fade away. He leaves everything to God's direction. "This is the way of life I heartily want to accept now . . . no more self-reliance is going to prompt

29. Ibid., 77.

30. Ibid.

31. Walter Ciszek, S.J., *With God in America: The Spiritual Legacy of an Unlikely Jesuit*, com. and ed. John M. DeJak and Marc Lindeijer, S.J. (Chicago: Loyola Press, 2016), 45.

32. Ibid.

me to action again. That is my life, that is my all, that is my happiness ... I'm living your life, not mine. What happens in me now is yours."[33] Ciszek incorporated into his life the final prayer of St. Ignatius's Spiritual Exercises, the Suscipe:

> Take, Lord, and receive all my liberty, my memory, my understanding, my entire will—all that I have and call my own. You have given it all to me. To you Lord, I return it. Everything is yours; do with it what you will. Give me only your love and your grace. That is enough for me.[34]

Spiritual direction will show and teach us that God is enough. Ultimately, God is all we will have. And all we need.

One Jesuit Retreat House's Description of Spiritual Direction

What Is Spiritual Direction? Spiritual direction is about the journey of your soul which seeks to know God, self and others in a deep, loving way. It is about growing in understanding your relationship with God. Your soul thirsts to know God personally. Frequently, it takes another spiritual soul to walk with you so God can mirror through them what your soul needs to know.

A spiritual director is someone you can talk with confidentially about your prayer and spiritual life. Because every aspect of your daily life affects your relationship with God, ordinary concerns such as work, ministry, family, relationships, emotional hurts, joy, anger, sexual concerns, fears, compulsions, addictions, dreams, etc. are properly shared in spiritual direction. A director helps you explore the darkness of self-doubt, confusion, fear and anger so that you are able to be free of what blocks you from God's loving presence. You are helped to truly see yourself through God's eyes as the gift you are.

Spiritual direction helps develop the gift of discernment, which enables you to be more attentive to how God is leading and guiding you. You grow in noticing the ways in which God is touching your life, directly or indirectly.

Some people dislike the term "spiritual direction" because it sounds like one person giving directions, or orders, to another. They prefer "spiritual companionship," or "tending the holy." What you call it doesn't make any real difference. The reality remains: it is conversation about your life in the light of faith.

---

33. Ibid.

34. David Fleming, S.J., *Draw Me into Your Friendship: A Literal Translation and a Contemporary Reading of the Spiritual Exercises*, #234 (St. Louis, MO: Institute of Jesuit Sources, 1996), 177.

What Spiritual Direction Is Not: Spiritual direction is not counseling. It is not therapy. It is not financial advice. It is for anyone who seeks a deeper, real relationship with God.

What Should I Look for in a Spiritual Director? A spiritual director is someone called to and well trained in this ministry. She or he should be grounded in the Scriptures, sustained by a deep prayer life, acquainted with the various ways of spirituality, and carefully trained in the area of discernment. If she or he has experience or has expertise in areas related to your life situation then this may make for a good match. It is imperative that a spiritual director be in ongoing spiritual direction.

How Often Do I Meet With My Spiritual Director? Frequency of direction varies with individual need and circumstance. Some people find that meeting every four weeks is ideal. Others require more or less frequent sessions with their spiritual director.

What Does It Cost? It is customary to offer a stipend to support the spiritual director in this ministry. You and the director should discuss this during your first session.

Manresa Retreat House, Bloomfield IL. "What is Spiritual Direction?" https://www.manresa-sj.org/440_Direction.htm

CHAPTER 3

Engaging in Spiritual Direction: Relationships with Ourselves, Others, and God

Spiritual Direction offers a companion for our spiritual journey, a guide who can more easily spot our movements and unfreedoms. Spiritual Directors actively listen, helping us to find freedom, make balanced decisions and grow closer to God.
—Brendan McManus, S.J., *Redemption Road*

Spiritual Direction is an interpersonal process of growth in which God's call is heard and responded to in faith.
—Bishop Robert F. Morneau,
Spiritual Direction: Principles and Practice

Spiritual Direction: an interpersonal relationship in which one person assists others to reflect on their experience in the light of who they are to become in fidelity to the Gospel.
—Katherine Marie Dyckman, S.N.J.M., and L. Patrick Carroll, S.J.,
Inviting the Mystic, Supporting the Prophet

The question that proved so effective a catalyst in retreats—"What happened to you when you tried to pray?"—also provided an invaluable means of giving focus to spiritual direction outside retreat.
—Madeline Birmingham and William Connolly,
Witnessing the Fire

Keep it relational.
—Pat O'Sullivan, S.J., famed Australian Jesuit Spiritual Director

You have two ears and one mouth. We should use them in the propor-
tion given.
        —Sharon Daloz Parks, former professor of pastoral counseling
                                at Harvard and Weston School of Theology

Spiritual direction, whether during a retreat time or in day-to-day life,
aims to foster the freedom to love and serve ("For freedom, Christ has
set us free" [Gal 5:1]). To be in relation with God depends on the exercise of our freedom. Theologian Karl Rahner once noted that freedom
and dependence on God grow in direct, not inverse, proportion. In other
words, the more we deeply realize and relish reality, and the experience of
God in all things, the more we find ourselves truly free to choose what is
good, what is right, what is loving. The more we can allow another to help
us find our way and make choices out of this freely chosen direction and
meaning of our lives, the more we are transformed in Christ and become
who we deeply and truly desire to be. St. Paul wrote: "I pray that, according to the riches of his glory, he may grant that you may be strengthened
in your inner being with power through his Spirit, and that Christ may
dwell in your hearts through faith, as you are being rooted and grounded
in love." (Eph 3:16–17; NRSV).

Tad Dunne titles his book *Spiritual Mentoring: Guiding People
through Spiritual Exercises to Life Decisions.*[1] For Dunne, following the
philosophy of Jesuit Bernard Lonergan, spiritual direction is the noticing and practicing of paying attention to our experiences, understanding our experiences, and making judgments and decisions on the basis
of such understandings. What Dunne calls "praxis" permeates our lives,
history, images of ourselves, others, and God. Spiritual mentors help us
consciously to root ourselves in our experiences of being human in relation to God.

Frank Houdek, S.J., introduces his description of spiritual direction
with references to Bernard Shaw's St. Joan responding to the interroga-
tor's questioning her about the voices she hears: "You mean you hear
voices?" Joan replies, "Doesn't everyone?" What are, and from where
come, the thoughts, hopes, dreams, fears, and so on, that move through
our interior selves? Our answers reveal what we may think spiritual direction is and can be. Houdek describes the experiences of the disciples on

---

1. Tad Dunne, *Spiritual Mentoring: Guiding People through Spiritual Exercises to
Life Decisions* (San Francisco: HarperSanFrancisco, 1991).

the road to Emmaus. Jesus' enlightening of their experience of the crucifixion helps them change their ways of understanding the event and leads
to a dawning of the meaning of Eucharist. Houdek writes:

> From these two stories we can draw a descriptive definition of
> spiritual direction. Spiritual direction is a conversation, a dia-
> logue between two people. In such a conversation one person aids
> another, often by a process of question and answer, to express his or
> her experience of personal faith and personal mystery. In this way
> one can discover the origin, the character, the quality, the move-
> ment, and the patterns that evolve. One learns to hear more clearly
> and discriminate more acutely the varied voices of personal experi-
> ence. This clarification, this discovery and interpretation, empow-
> ers the individual to make decisions that are congruent with and in
> greater harmony with a personal and unique experience of faith and
> mystery.[2]

William Reiser, S.J., from his perspective as a theologian wondering
about the reality of revelation, provides a slightly more expanded notion
of spiritual direction. God is always revealing who and what God is, he
writes, and we need to learn how to pay attention and respond to what
God is doing in our lives. He quotes William Barry and William Connolly's definition of spiritual direction as "help given by one Christian
to another which enables that person to pay attention to God's personal
communication to him or her, to grow in intimacy with this God, and to
live out the consequences of that relationship." But Reiser goes further
in recognizing that not all spiritual direction occurs in halcyon retreat
house settings.

> Direction provides the occasion for becoming more alert to the
> where, when, how, and why of God's presence in our lives. . . . Spiri-
> tual direction can occur when we read scripture and spiritual writ-
> ers. It can happen in group settings. Married persons often give
> one another spiritual direction (whether the directee wants it or
> not!). . . . the Jesus of the Gospels was not a spiritual director in the

---

2. Frank Houdek, S.J., *Guided by the Spirit: A Jesuit Perspective on Spiritual Direction* (Chicago: Loyola Press, 1996), 5–6.

way we think of the director's role today [but] he clearly conversed with individuals about the Reign of God.[3]

In his moving and challenging set of stories about life with former gang members in Los Angeles, Greg Boyle, S.J., provides many glimpses of "spiritual direction" in real life. He tells the story of Miguel, a twenty-three-year-old who had been abandoned by his family. Miguel had nowhere to go for Christmas, and no one with whom to celebrate the day. So Miguel called some of his buddies who, like him, had no place to be and no one on Christmas. They cooked a turkey and little else, sat around the oven waiting for it to cook, and feasted when it was done. Boyle shares their story: "One would be hard-pressed to imagine something more sacred and ordinary than these six orphans staring at an oven together. It is the entire law and the prophets, all in one moment, right there in this humble, holy kitchen."[4] Sometime after that Christmas, Greg had a chance to speak with Miguel. Greg asked Miguel how he was able to be the way he was, hopeful, happy, willing to reach out to others, after all the pulverizing pain and suffering he had been through in his life. Miguel says:

> "You know, I always suspected that there was something of goodness in me, but I just couldn't find it. Until one day," he quiets a bit "—one day I discovered here, in my heart, I found it . . . goodness. And ever since that day, I have always known who I was."[5]

Spiritual direction is all about realizing and relishing the goodness deep down inside us, the presence of the Holy Spirit indwelling in our hearts (Rom 5:5), the love of God in the relationships of our lives. What Greg Boyle gets at over and over again in conversations is the naming and recognizing the reality of God in gang members' hearts and souls as they struggle to rehabilitate their lives and reintegrate themselves into society. As Greg has called forth God in the homies' lives, so too have they called forth God's presence and love in his own.

The way many come to be rooted and grounded in love, the process of cooperating with the grace of God, is often helped by engaging in ongoing spiritual direction. Usually two (in recent years there have been

---

3. William Reiser, S.J., *Seeking God in All Things: Theology and Spiritual Direction* (Collegeville, MN: Liturgical Press, 2004), 20–23.

4. Greg Boyle, S.J., *Tattoos on the Heart: The Power of Endless Compassion* (New York: Simon and Schuster, 2010), 88.

5. Ibid.

experiments with group spiritual direction[6]) people sit down and first see if they are compatible working together to facilitate the growth of mainly one person of the pair. This is crucial. Not all director-directee relationships work. Both people have to test the waters and see how they feel. If, after a few meetings, both feel comfortable with one another and prayerfully sense that the relationship can work, they can enter into the process of spiritual direction. If one or both recognize hindrances not worth overcoming, either should feel free, and encouraged, to suggest the directee seek another director; no penalty, no foul.

As director and directee enter into ongoing spiritual direction, they will find several areas that will consistently be brought up for conversation and examination. Basically, the directee will be encouraged to look at his or her relationship with God, others, and him/herself. Areas of service (work), play, and relationships with significant people in one's life (spouse, family members, boss, and co-workers, teammates, and so forth) are grist for the mill of direction. Most sessions of formal spiritual direction, in my experience, run about forty-five minutes, an hour tops. There are also the life-transformative moments where we find ourselves "giving" spiritual direction that may be no more than a moment, or spending a day with a person or family in joy or grief (e.g., Greg Boyle and Miguel above).

Spiritual direction is not simply restricted to counseling, psychotherapy, or problem solving. Nor is it just "friends getting together to talk seriously about life."[7] Directors should have a more than glancing acquaintance with psychological theories of transference where a person unconsciously projects ideations of another person onto the director. For example, if the directee is experiencing the director as a father figure or a stern mother, such dynamics should be gently and gingerly addressed. A directee feeling or thinking a spiritual director is a guru who has his or her act all together, and is all-knowing and all-loving, should also see these mistaken ideations deflated for the real relationship of two imperfect disciples to develop in a way that allows for the presence and action of the Holy Spirit in both their lives. Spiritual directors should also directly and constantly challenge and be challenged to realize they are just instruments of God's grace, not the Deity themselves. As noted earlier, spiritual

---

6. George Schemel and Judith Roemer, *Beyond Individuation to Discipleship: A Directory for Those Who Give the Spiritual Exercises of St. Ignatius* (Scranton, PA: Institute for Contemporary Spirituality, 2000).

7. Houdek, *Guided by the Spirit*, 8.

direction is not therapy, and a good director knows when issues need professional help. The director is more a coach or teacher than a therapist, although issues dealt with in more formal, professional therapy often are present and discussed in spiritual direction (e.g., mild depression; death of a loved one; self-esteem; unhelpful, out-of-control emotional reactions to life situations such as excessive anger, fears, grandiosity, addictions, etc.). Many of the realities seldom dealt with in therapy are aspects of our lives that have to do with choice of vocation, discernment about how to live one's vocation, and how to celebrate and enjoy love. Therapy usually exists to help one cope. Spiritual direction not only helps us cope, but leads us to appreciate creation; relish the gifts of life; and feel deep, deep ongoing gratitude for our lives and loves. Therapy may help us be persons who can accept ourselves as worthy of a relationship with God; spiritual direction is all about developing our relationship with God.

Therapy and spiritual direction differ in their sets of underlying values and goals. Although I greatly respect the many ways in which therapy can help people, it seems that therapy is nonjudgmental and free form, allowing people to decide wholly for themselves how they are and ought to be. There's the old joke about a guy who goes to a therapist because he can't control his bladder and often wets his pants in public. When medical doctors can't find anything physically wrong with him, they send the man to a therapist. After a year of therapy, a friend asks him, "How's therapy going?" He responds, "Great!" "So, you no longer wet your pants?" "No, I still wet my pants, but I no longer feel embarrassed about it." Another wry comment on therapy goes, "Therapy works for a light bulb, but only if the light bulb really wants to change." Good therapists like good spiritual directors should be able to laugh at themselves and not take themselves too seriously.[8]

Unlike therapy, the process of spiritual direction has definite aims and goals. It is good at the beginning for director and directee to discuss goals, hopes, and dreams, about what the directee desires to receive as a result of engaging in spiritual direction. For me, spiritual direction aims

---

8. Woody Allen as Alvy Singer in *Annie Hall*: "I was thrown out of N.Y.U. my freshman year for cheating on my metaphysics final, you know. I looked within the soul of the boy sitting next to me. When I was thrown out, my mother, who was an emotionally high-strung woman, locked herself in the bathroom and took an overdose of Mah-Jongg tiles. I was depressed at that time. I was in analysis. I was suicidal as a matter of fact and would have killed myself, but I was in analysis with a strict Freudian, and, if you kill yourself, they make you pay for the sessions you miss."

at helping me live my life as a Jesuit priest. For someone else, it may be to live out their vocation as a married person and parent. Or the goal might be to understand where and how God is calling one to serve. And for all people, spiritual direction hopes to foster a deeper, more disciplined and vibrant life of prayer. Communication with the mystery of God, framed by a religious tradition, is a very different goal from therapy, which aims at adjusting to life. Our hope for our relationship with God is that we become filled with gentle joy, deep trust and faith, ongoing general generosity, and an abundance of true love. But remember the famous words of Dostoyevsky in *The Brothers Karamazov*, words so often called to mind by the great urban saint, Dorothy Day: "Love in action is a harsh and dreadful thing as opposed to love in dreams."[9] Spiritual direction helps us bear the inevitable crosses of life and to remember that there is no resurrection without the cross, which means that there is no cross in life that does not contain within it the seeds of resurrection.

Spiritual direction, ultimately, is about opening our souls to ever deeper, truer transformation in Christ of all we were, are, and ever will be. Remember, "God became what we are so we can become what God is" (CCC §460). That's not some crazy Jesuit spin on theology. That's St. Athanasius in the third century. Thomas Merton, writing in 1963, knew well the point of spiritual direction: "It should be clear that Christian holiness is not a mere matter of ethical perfection. . . . Hence what matters most above all is not this or that observance, this or that set of ethical practices, but our renewal, our 'new creation' in Christ (see Gal 6:15)."[10]

Thomas Merton knew that the essence of the relationship with God is our transformation into persons who can live with God forever. That transformation does not depend on our being perfectly ethical or stunningly virtuous. That transformation in Christ depends on our free choice to allow God to be God in our lives, and in our struggle against all forms of idolatry, the work of resisting all that tries to usurp the place of the divine in our existence. Getting our relationship with God right leads to our being inspired to work to right all relationships in our lives and world.

---

9. Mary Ann McGivern, "Love in Action," *National Catholic Reporter*, October 2, 2015.

10. Thomas Merton, *Life and Holiness* (New York: Herder and Herder, 1963), 70–72.

Justice is the righting of relationships.[11] To enjoy the wonders of a real relationship with God, others, and ourselves, we need to get things and relationships right. Justice is the work of learning and acting in ways that "make things right" (cf. Is 1:18; NAB). To do justice is the primordial challenge and call of the Hebrew Scriptures, and a central tenet of Christian tradition. Justice must begin with ourselves, and then in reaching out to others. In doing so, we are immersed in the mystery of God's action in our lives.

The Spiritual Exercises of St. Ignatius are meant to help us reach and realize true freedom in our lives and true justice in our relationships, and we do so by ordering our lives according to a set of values while resisting being derailed by disordered attachments and dynamics in relation to any person, place, or thing (cf. Spiritual Exercises #21). Spiritual direction, during a retreat or ongoing in daily life, helps us name and tame what is going on in us so we can aim ourselves in the direction in which we and God want us to go, and never blame anyone else for where we place or aim ourselves.[12]

The work of love, the work of prayer, the work of relationship all make up the warp and woof of our connection and communication with God. God is not a thing among other things. God is the mysterious reality that constitutes all reality. "God" is not a noun; "God" is a verb. We experience God differently than we experience things. Both objects and subjects external to us can be confronted, challenged, and categorized by us in contradistinction to them. "I"–"It" relations differ from "I"–"Thou" relations. When someone becomes a "thou" to me, I am no longer just me, but "us." The work of love is to let the "other" in. God is the primordial and constant "other" that makes possible my, and our, being able to relate at all.

The process of spiritual direction must contend with the disconcerting truth of God's being a reality unlike any other. We do not experience God directly. God is always a mediated experience. The great comedian Lily Tomlin once cogently joked, "How come when we talk to God we call it prayer, but when God talks to us, we call it schizophrenia?" It is essential that God be mediated in order to be God. Why must God be a mediated experience? One reason is we are human beings, and any expe-

---

11. See my books *A Faith That Frees* and *Being on Fire* for extensive treatments of this idea of justice as being the righting of relationships.

12. The "Name, Tame, Aim, Never Blame" mantra is from Pat O'Sullivan, S.J., my tertian director in Australia in 2000. I don't know if it's his, or if he got it from someone else.

rience we can have is rooted in the language we speak and our historical and cultural circumstances. So, if God is going to communicate with me, it will have to be in English or Spanish. If the message comes in French or Russian, I will not be able to receive it. As a man born in the twentieth century, I will not be able to comprehend a God who orders me to ignore scientific knowledge, or the truth of historical facts, both welcome and disconcerting. Our understanding of Jesus' historical life has been incredibly enriched in the past century. Our awareness too of the shameful historical moments of the Catholic Church (from the Borgia papacy to the priest sex scandals of our day) contours and challenges a sense of our church being all knowing and perfect. Yet, since historical knowledge has grown in the past few centuries, we are more aware of the reality of grace and dis-grace in the past of our human family.

The second and more intriguing aspect of our relationship with God is that God necessarily seems to maintain a certain separation and distance from us, while still communicating incredible love and concern for us. Why? Why doesn't God just make the reality of the divine unquestionably self-evident? The logic of love shows that God has reasons for not obviously, or self-evidently, that is directly, revealing God's reality. For love to be love, it must be free. If we experienced God directly, we couldn't not do what God wants. We would have to do what God wants. God's direct presence would overwhelm us and determine our choices. The necessary hiddenness of God urges us to freely choose God and God's ways of being revealed to us in Jesus the Christ. When we mistakenly think we could experience God directly, we could be tempted to use God, manipulate and misuse God, in ways that serve our self-centered interests. Such theological misconceptions are the root of various fundamentalisms.[13]

God cannot reveal God's self in a manner that would force our acceptance of, and allegiance to, God's person. When I first began to pray, I assumed prayer would provide a three-beer (or full six-pack) feeling. Immediately, the error of my assuming this became embarrassingly clear. I thought God would be as easy to understand and experience as other realities in my life. God is always much more and much greater than anything, or anyone, else. Truly, the more one "knows" God, the less certain and self-assured one is about God. St. Thomas Aquinas said we could never say anything positive about God. All we could confidently assert is what we do not know about God. In other words, we can never say who or what God is or does. We can only say what God is not.

---

13. Karen Armstrong, *The Battle for God* (New York: Ballantine Books, 2000).

The truth of our relationship with God is that we, as human persons, are made, constructed, and constituted to search for and encounter God. Every human person has a built-in desire to reach out and connect with God. Dr. Gerald G. May writes, "In Thomas Merton's words, 'There is a natural desire for heaven, for the fruition of God in us.' Ultimately, our yearning for God is the most important aspect of our humanity, our most precious treasure; it gives our existence meaning and direction."[14] Karl Rahner, S.J., and others have woven full theological systems based on this bedrock reading of reality, namely, that we are made by God/Love, for God/Love, to return to God/Love. St. Ignatius predicates the whole of the Spiritual Exercises on The Principle and Foundation, the premise that we are created by God to become persons who can live with God forever.[15]

St. Paul's famous speech to the Athenians about their altar to the unknown god reveals a central dynamic of human existence. St. Paul says, "Since [God] himself gives to all mortals life and breath and all things . . . so that they would search for God and perhaps grope for him and find him—though indeed he is not far from each one of us. For 'In him we live and move and have our being'" (Acts 17:25–28; NRSV).

In his seminal work *Addiction and Grace*, Gerald May notes that there is a universal tendency in human persons to substitute attachments to a multitude of realities (persons, work, food, sex, drugs, honors, riches, fame, on and on) for this innate desire for God.[16] The work of liberation theologian Jon Sobrino, S.J., says all of Christian living is the struggle to free ourselves from idols (false gods) and adhere to the challenges and joys of aligning ourselves with the Living God and the mission Jesus inaugurated. In Sobrino's theology, God is always the God of life, desiring life and good for all, especially the poor. God is always in conflict with the idols, the false deities that call for and cause death. "Spirituality is purely and simply a participation in God's own history, history as assumed by God in Christ and the Spirit."[17]

---

14. Gerald G. May, M.D., *Addiction and Grace* (San Francisco: Harper and Row, 1988), 92.

15. See David Fleming, S.J., "The Principle and Foundation," in *Draw Me into Your Friendship: A Literal Translation and a Contemporary Reading of the Spiritual Exercises*, #23 (St. Louis, MO: The Institute of Jesuit Sources, 1996), 26–27.

16. May, *Addiction and Grace*, 92–94.

17. Jon Sobrino, S.J., *Spirituality of Liberation: Toward Political Holiness* (Maryknoll, NY: Orbis Books, 1988), 52.

One crucial aspect of spiritual direction is working together to discover and discern where we are holding on to idols (or where they are holding on to us) and where we are becoming more capable of exercising our freedom as loved sons and daughters of God so that we can give ourselves to the work of the mission of Jesus in our times and places. A spiritual director will want to help a directee prayerfully examine these dynamics in us as individuals, as persons in relation with others, and as persons immersed in societal and cultural systems. These dynamics are always the sea in which we discover and delight in the currents that waft us, hopefully willingly, to the depths of the experience of God in our lives.

Relationship with Oneself

This is inevitably the starting point. Many of us want to change the world, but have a hard time realizing that we must first, as Gandhi said, "be the change we want to see in the world." There comes a time when we discover that we first have to change ourselves, or, even better, allow ourselves to be changed by our cooperation with grace. As we enter into spiritual direction, the conversation begins with how the directee sees himself in relation to the core of his being. As a directee, I want to fill the director in on the main components of my life story. Who and what has made me who I am? What was my family life like? How has life worked out for me? Am I mostly satisfied? Mostly dissatisfied? Am I happy with where I am? What are my strengths and weaknesses? What gets me in touch with myself? How do I work, relax, live? What do I do for fun? What gives me joy? What scares or depresses me? Most importantly, what do I find myself wanting from God at this juncture in my life?

The director gently asks for the directee to reveal him or herself in a safe context. There is no judgment. The director strives to accept the directee as he or she is, not as the director might want the directee to be. This is the discipline called for from the director. He or she is not to run before the grace of God. Rather, allow God to be God in the directee's life. The director may, from a religious tradition, propose to the directee some communally held truths, not in the way of forcing the directee to go in one direction or another, but in order to inform and teach the directee about aspects of the spiritual and religious life of which the directee is unaware.

St. Teresa of Avila said she didn't want holy spiritual directors; she wanted spiritual directors who understood theology. Many people coming to direction today have a tenuous grasp on simple truths of the

Catholic faith. Simple information often helps. One constant misconception is that the church is "against homosexuality." Not true. Check the Catholic Catechism §2357. The church teaches that homosexuality is morally neutral, and views homosexual acts, as all sexual acts outside of marriage, as morally deficient. But the church doesn't just warn against insufficient choices in the area of sexuality. The church calls for chastity, the integration of sexuality into our lives (CCC §2337). These issues surrounding sexuality are increasingly alienating the millennial generation (at some 80 million in the United States, now more than the 75 million baby boomers) who judge the church's opposition to gay marriage as equivalent to country clubs that won't offer membership to Jews or African Americans. Wrestling with one's attitudes and feelings about church teachings is often part of spiritual direction. Discussing women's ordination will often reveal the depth of pain and alienation many women feel by being denied the possibility of serving as priests. But conversation may also make women aware of how much the church has done and does for women, along with letting younger women know about Dorothy Day and the dozens of incredible Catholic women who have greatly and powerfully changed our world. From St. Katherine Drexel, a very rich heiress who used her fortune to start a religious order of sisters to serve Native and African Americans, to Mother Angelica who started EWTN (Eternal Word Television Network), to Sr. Mary Scullion, R.S.M., the great apostle to the homeless of Philadelphia, to the thousands and thousands of women who have served the church in ways great and transformative, the church has been an institution that has given women the opportunities to run everything from hospitals and universities to schools and soup kitchens long before women were allowed to attend male universities or have their own bank accounts. Some who take very strong conservative positions on a plethora of matters theological (often liturgical) may need to learn to see the vast gray areas in what sometimes appear to be black and white.

Despite the ecclesial tensions of our day, the main point is ever present. Most crucial is offering for the directee's reflection the simple, foundational truth that God loves us. I was once directing a Jewish woman, a marvelous gal who had come on the retreat to "honestly, get a few days off from work." She was struck by the idea that God loves us. "I always thought that God wants us to suffer."

More likely with someone who comes for spiritual direction, especially a younger person, the director will find a disciple who intensely desires to serve God and make changes for the better in our church and world. The director can often function as a sounding board to help the person examine and evaluate their hopes and dreams, making sure both are somewhat tethered to reality. More challenging is quietly waiting for the directee to mature and realize they are not necessarily called to reform the church or change the world, all on their own, by the time they are forty. Constant reviewing with directees stories of people they admire and letting them know how those good apostles see themselves and their work is instructive. Most who stand out in their service of the kingdom don't see themselves as all that special. They consider themselves as blessed and lucky rather than as persons incredibly important and to be admired. Sr. Mary Scullion, R.S.M., in Philadelphia, and Greg Boyle, S.J., in Los Angeles, come to mind, both well-known and lauded servants of the poor in those cities. Both laugh at themselves and those who think they are special. I once heard a friend of Greg's relate, "I knew Greg before he was GREG BOYLE." Greg would laugh at that too. I've known board members of Jesuit universities who are incredibly rich and powerful, and who no more throw their weight around than does a janitor.

Tim Russert, the famous *Meet the Press* journalist, a proud graduate of the Canisius Jesuit high school in Buffalo and of John Carroll University in Cleveland, wanted to receive an honorary degree from every Jesuit university. He let it be known he would speak at graduations for no fee. I had a small part in planning his time at the graduation for St. Joe's University in Philadelphia. The plan was Mr. Russert would come, hang out a bit before the graduation ceremony, meet Board of Trustee members, and sign copies of his book *Big Russ & Me*, a powerfully poignant testimony to his dad, a man who worked three jobs to put Tim and his siblings through school. All this was to happen in the building housing the campus ministry offices. The big day arrived and all the bigwigs were waiting. Tim Russert arrived precisely on time and wowed the small throng. He was courteous, polite, relaxed, humorous, and friendly with all. As he sat to sign his books, Thelma, the African American woman who cleaned the building, approached me. She was in her Sunday best, a bright white/yellow pantsuit. "Fr. Rick, could I meet Mr. Russert?" she hesitantly asked. Sensing that Russert was the kind of guy who'd like to meet Thelma, I walked her over to him. "Mr. Russert, this is Thelma. She keeps this place in order." Tim beamed a huge smile at Thelma and said, "So, you clean up after Fr. Rick?" "Yes," Thelma shyly replied. "Well, that's a big job. I'm sure he makes quite a mess. Could I give you one of my books?" He treated Thelma as if she were as "important" as the board members. And in truth she was. Guys like Tim Russert knew that.

For many of us, it takes a while to learn where we stand in life, how we are to serve the Lord and not our own interests, how we are to be Christian in love and service rather than in competition and grades. Spiritual direction can make us realize that we are all just a small part of the Body of Christ, and that no part is better or more important than any other part. Growth in humility characterizes good spiritual direction. Humility isn't humiliation. The word "humility" comes from the Latin *humus*, meaning soil, earth, dirt, ground. Humility means we are grounded, aware of who and what we are, not given to grandiosity and unreal images of expectations of ourselves. In his Spiritual Exercises, St. Ignatius offers an imaginative exercise where one prays over the strategies of Christ as opposed to the strategy of Lucifer, the angel of light. Lucifer attracts to all things that give riches, empty honor, and pride. Jesus counters with acceptance of poverty, insults, and humility. "From these he leads to all other virtues" (Mediation on the Two Standards or Flags, Spiritual Exercises, #136–148). Humility frees us from trying to live up to unreal expectations and keeps us from running ahead of the grace of God.

Especially when we are younger, we are ready to go forth and conquer the world in a flash. We are so eager to change and fix everyone else that we run ahead of the work of allowing God to fix us; we rush ahead of grace. Rather than treat the log in our own eye, we hurry to remove the speck in the eye of another (Mt 7:3–5). It is easy to project our own deficiencies onto the world around us. If only my wife, boss, the kid next door, my neighbor were different, then I could be happy and loving and more generous toward others. If only I had gotten into that college, or gotten that job or that promotion, or earned more money, life would be perfect. One of the great errors we make is thinking and believing that the world outside us completely controls our lives. Actually, we choose the responses we make to the external world.

I learned this lesson from a story I heard about an older, rather mild-mannered Jesuit. He was one of the good guys—even-keeled, never complained about much, got up every day and served the Lord with skilled generosity, good grace, compassion, and kindness. One day he walked into the room where some of the Jesuit community were gathered before dinner. Something very bad had happened in the school that day, and he was livid. What had happened was bad and quite disturbing. It made a lot of sense for him to be royally ticked off about the matter. He came in and ranted and blew off steam for a few minutes. Although no one remembered him being this angry about anything before, no one thought his reaction inappropriate. What he was furious about was worth being furious about. The really interesting thing is that after a few more minutes of enumerating all that was wrong, unjust, and just plain bad about the situation, he stopped. He looked around the room and said, "Damn. I've been angry about this all day. It's not worth my wasting any more of my life being angry about this." And he wasn't angry anymore. Sure, in the days ahead he had to deal with the situation, but he came at it with an interior disposition quite different from that with which he initially came at the matter.

I was struck by this story. You could just decide not to be angry? How? I always experienced anger as something that would hang on for days, even weeks. All I could do was wait it out, and not reach for the shotgun and go hunting for the person who was "making me angry." But, in reality, no one was "making me angry." I was choosing to be angry. In spiritual direction over the years, I learned that nothing outside of us can determine how we will respond. Note: respond. Not react. I was very good at reacting. Learning to respond took . . . well, when I get really good at responding rather than reacting, I'll let you know! But this is a key to real spirituality: consciously choosing how we will respond to the good and bad of life. This is the great gift of grace, that we learn and live out of the truth that "all things work together for those who love God, who are called according to his purpose" (Rom 8:28; NRSV).

As you enter into spiritual direction, you will most likely face the traditional struggles of those who strive to serve God, and other difficulties as well. Aspects of the seven deadly sins—Pride, Lust, Anger, Gluttony, Greed, Sloth, Envy (PLAGGES), one or in combination— seem to be universally experienced. The call to virtue, both theological (Faith, Hope, and Charity) and cardinal (Prudence, Fortitude, Temperance, and Justice), will resonate. Spiritual direction helps us articulate and examine our temptations and strategies for dealing with temptations. And most of what we do to resist the ways of temptation and incorporate the virtues of Christian existence involve our relationships with others.

Relationship with Others

The oft-quoted truth "no man is an island" rings true in every human life. People who try to avoid this truth usually find their lives radically diminished. The false notions of radical self-sufficiency and rugged individualism are deeply ingrained in North American psyches and culture. In contrast, life in Christ is deeply relational. *We* live and move and have our being in God. God is a communal, interrelated reality. As we engage in spiritual direction, we inherently bump into the relationship with others in our lives.

Family-of-origin dynamics, community (family, church, or religious), and work relationships are often the daily circumstances within which we live out our transformation in Christ. Even more, if personal and familial deficiencies keep us off kilter in our relationship with our deepest, truest selves and thus God, societal and cultural deficiencies, that is, social sin, can make it difficult to overcome a sense of separation from God. None of us come to know God in a perfect world, and our imperfect world can make trust and confidence in God hard to entertain, especially if you are on the bottom of the world's distribution scale.

The reality of our spiritual lives is that we live them in a world that often is structured in ways that orient and affect our choices. No matter how well or hard you swim, if the tide is going out, you get swept by the currents in directions you do not personally choose to go. I was born a white male in Philadelphia, Pennsylvania, in the middle of the twentieth century. That is a really good card to be dealt in the history of the world. Yet, I was born three months before Rosa Parks refused to give up her seat on the bus in Montgomery, Alabama. The day I was born, segregation in the United States was legal, lethal, and largely unquestioned.

If I had been born black in Philadelphia, my life would have been very different. And, if I had been born in Latin America, or Africa, my life would be even more different. If I had been born one of the 43 million Americans living in poverty, my life would have been very different.[18] Globally, poverty is more the rule than the exception.[19] Inequality has

---

18. Census Bureau (September 13, 2016), http://www.census.gov. In the U.S. in 2015, 19.7 percent of America's children were living in poverty, down from 21.1 percent in 2014. In 2015, 13.5 percent of Americans, 43.1 million people lived in poverty, down from 14.8 percent, 47.6 million the year before. In 2015, the poverty line was $24,257 for a family of four. Median household income in the U.S. was $56,516 in 2015.

19. "11 Facts About Global Poverty," https://www.dosomething.org. Nearly half the world's population live on less than $2.50 a day. Globally, 80 percent of the people on planet Earth live on less than $10 a day. One billion children worldwide live in poverty. Across our planet, 22,000 children die each day due to poverty. Twenty-five per-

reached extreme levels. CEOs make hundreds of times more than workers. Comedians and athletes are rich. Teachers struggle to earn enough to live middle-class lives. Judge Judy makes millions while Chief Justice John Roberts makes some $200,000 annually.[20] In January 2016, OXFAM reported that 62 people (53 men; 9 women) own the same as half the world. Those 62 are worth $1.76 trillion.[21]

Robert Reich's documentary, *Inequality for All,* and his book *Saving Capitalism for the Many, Not the Few* (2015) are devastating exposés of the deeply entrenched, systemic aspects of our political and economic practices that make life incredibly wonderful for the few, and increasingly anxious for the many, while leaving the vast majority of our brothers and sisters on this planet in distressing to desperate poverty.[22] "The 'free market' serves as a smoke screen for all this."[23]

---

cent of all humans live without electricity. Oxfam estimates it would take $60 billion annually to end extreme poverty. That's less than a quarter of the income of the top 100 billionaires.

20. Michael Sandel, *Justice: What's the Right Thing to Do?* (New York: Farrar, Straus and Giroux, 2009), 8, 162. Harvard professor Michael Sandel teaches undergrads the truths of our contemporary practice of capitalism. CEOs of major U.S. corporations make 344 times what the average worker takes home. In 1980 they only earned 42 times a worker's pay. In 2004–2006, the average CEO in the U.S. made $13.3 million annually. Schoolteachers average $43,000 a year; David Letterman makes $31 million. Chief Justice John Roberts gets $217,000; Judge Judy walks away with $25 million.

21. "An Economy for the 1 Percent," https://www.oxfam.org. The wealth of the poorest half of the world has fallen by a trillion dollars since 2010, a drop of 38 percent. The bottom 50 percent of the earth's population is responsible for 10 percent of global emissions. The average footprint of the richest one percent globally could be as much as 175 times higher that of the poorest 10 percent.

22. Robert Reich, *Saving Capitalism for the Many, Not the Few* (New York: Alfred A. Knopf, 2015), 5, 153. Reich realizes and elucidates the reality that the choice is not between "Government" and "the Market." The truth is that government creates and maintains markets by setting the rules of economic processes. What's really going on is not the oft-trumpeted notion that government is shackling the market with unnecessary and crippling regulations. The truth is that, in the U.S., more and more the government is rigging the game and skewing the distribution of wealth and power to the top one percent, denizens of Wall Street and the shareholders of large corporations. Lower taxes on the rich and favorable rules for corporations have shifted the ways capitalism functions in the U.S. Rather than the somewhat equitable distribution of the 1945 to 1973 era, we now, in the 2010s have the extremes between rich and poor not seen since the era of the robber barons of the 1890–1910 era.

23. Ibid., 156. "Because of it, the system for distributing economic gains appears to be the natural and inevitable result of neutral forces. The meritocratic ideal presumes that people are roughly paid in proportion to their worth. . . . But because the organiza-

Stanford scholar Rene Girard, who is a literary theorist and not a theo-logian, offers an elaborate analysis of the cultural and societal dynamics that get us all off track and cause us "to miss the mark" (the literal mean-ing of *harmatia*, the Greek word for sin in the New Testament). Every group defines itself by being "us" as opposed to "them." As conflicts arise, often the mistreatment of the "other" group is justified by "our" being us: right, good, and in the eyes of "our" God, holy. The abuse and murder of the "other" is then sanctioned and cheered, all in the name of "God." "We" scapegoat "them," because they, we are convinced, are the source of our discontent and problems. Eliminating them will eliminate all that ails "us." One of several stunningly surprising arguments Girard makes on the basis of his reading of universal cultural dynamics is that there is one story that defies this pattern. Only the Christian story reverses the dynamics of cultures constructed on the scapegoat mechanism.[24]

This scapegoating mechanism is clearly evident in the horrific history of Nazi Germany. Since September 11, 2001, we have seen it playing out and becoming ever more deeply entrenched in our never-ending war on terror. We cast all our fears on refugees and other powerless people. We engage in mindless violence of many kinds and on many levels, from drone attacks to closing our borders, and then congratulate ourselves on a job well done. National security (which never seems to be secured) is maintained. "Our" way of life is bolstered and defended. And gospel val-ues are ignored, manipulated, and replaced by the demands of the idols of the globalized, "crony capitalist" system.

The sad permutations and combinations of cultural currents and soci-etal power shifts are addressed cogently and prophetically by the most eloquent global voice of hope, Pope Francis. The first Jesuit pontiff has critiqued and challenged the ways in which business as usual is done, while recognizing the positive contributions business can make: "Busi-ness is a vocation, and a noble vocation, provided that those engaged in it see themselves challenged by a greater meaning in life" (Pope Francis, *The Joy of the Gospel*, #203). Still, as a global community, we must make radical (i.e., to the roots) changes to our social ecology and our planetary

---

tion of the market increasingly reflects political decisions favoring moneyed interests, the system for distributing economic gains through the market does not necessarily cor-respond to what people are 'worth' in any respect other than tautological."

24. See Rene Girard, *The Scapegoat* (Baltimore: Johns Hopkins University Press, 1989); also Gil Baile, *Violence Unveiled: Humanity at the Crossroads* (New York: Cross-road, 1995).

ecosystem. Pope Francis's encyclical *Laudato Si'*, on the need to address the issue of global climate change, goes far beyond the physical care of the planet. As did Pope Benedict, Pope Francis recognizes and argues that the way we treat the physical world in which we live also reveals how we treat one another. And those who suffer most from the degradation of the planet are the poor and marginalized.

> It needs to be said that, generally speaking, there is little in the way of clear awareness of problems which especially affect the excluded. Yet they are the majority of the planet's population, billions of people.... Today, however, we have to realize that a true ecological approach *always* becomes a social approach; it must integrate questions of justice in debates on the environment, so as to hear *both the cry of the earth and the cry of the poor*. (Pope Francis, *Laudato Si'*, #49; italics in original)

"To hear both the cry of the earth and the cry of the poor" should be an aim and norm of our practice of spiritual direction. Living out our spirituality must take into account those most in need. The Good Samaritan is the model for discipleship, and the practice of prayer leads us to serve those bruised and beaten by a war-weary world. But many of the social systems in which we also live and move and have our being militate against such concern for others, especially the poor.

Pope Francis realizes that spiritual direction must help us become aware of and analyze how our relationship with God is impacted and affected by our social and cultural modes of being. The ways we are human, and human-unto-God, suffer when we cannot naturally and easily appreciate the beauty, wonder, and worth of human persons. "Human beings are themselves considered consumer goods to be used and then discarded. We have created a 'disposable' culture which is now spreading" (Pope Francis, *The Joy of the Gospel*, #53).

Recognizing the results of the worship of ideological idols, the pope speaks on behalf of those who have no voice, as did Mons. Oscar Romero in the late 1970s in El Salvador. The poor in El Salvador were murdered by death squads.[25] Much of the killing by the global economy is less bloody, but no less lethal. The indifference toward the Have-nots also

---

25. See Jon Sobrino, S.J., *Companions of Jesus: The Jesuit Martyrs of El Salvador* (Maryknoll, NY: Orbis Books, 1990), and Teresa Whitfield, *Paying the Price: Ignacio Ellacuria and the Murdered Jesuits of El Salvador* (Philadelphia: Temple University Press, 1994).

harms the Haves. We make an idol of money and kneel down and worship it. The pope proclaims, *"No to the new idolatry of money:* . . . A new tyranny is thus born, invisible and often virtual, which unilaterally and relentlessly imposes its own laws and rules" (Pope Francis, *The Joy of the Gospel*, #55–56).

In *Laudato Si'*, the pope begins to teach a way that can help us start to heal what ails us. He analyzes the interconnectedness of all that is and makes us human and all that threatens our common humanity. He tells the world we have to change. "Many things have to change course, but it is we human beings above all who need to change. . . . A great cultural, spiritual, and educational challenge stands before us, and it will demand that we set out on the long path of renewal" (Pope Francis, *Laudato Si'*, #202).

The pope articulates a new vision of human community and justice, firmly rooted in the gospels and Catholic social teaching while improved and updated for the twenty-first century. He invites all of us to embrace a new style of life, a new way of being human that both preserves what is good from the past and responds to the dangers and difficulties of the present and the possibilities and promise of the future. First, we must cease to be enslaved to the erroneous idea of and sacralizing the supposedly independent power of the "market." The market must once again become a servant of the community, not be the community's slave driver (cf. Pope Francis, *Laudato Si'*, #203).

Present-day economic and social forces engulf the vast majority of people in the anxiety and distress we ask to be freed from during every celebration of the Eucharist when we pray the Our Father. The global system itself threatens all with violence and destruction. In the words of Pope Francis,

> The current global situation engenders a feeling of instability and uncertainty, which in turn becomes "a seedbed for collective selfishness." When people become self-centered and self-enclosed, their greed increases. The emptier a person's heart is, the more he or she needs things to buy, own and consume. It becomes almost impossible to accept the limits imposed by reality. In this horizon, a genuine sense of the common good also disappears. (*Laudato Si'*, #204)

As a man of faith and hope and love, the pope encourages and strengthens weary hearts and speaks an imaginative word, describing manners and ways to address our present situation and ameliorate our condition. All is not lost. In Christ, victory is assured. We must cooperate with the social graces extended to us in order to counter the effects of social sin. "Human beings, while capable of the worst, are also capable of rising above themselves, choosing again what is good, and making a new start, despite their mental and social conditioning. We are able to take an honest look at ourselves, to acknowledge our deep dissatisfaction, and to embark on new paths to authentic freedom" (Pope Francis, *Laudato Si'*, #205).

The inherently communal vision of our faith in Christ calls us all to strive to overcome the effects of an excessively individualistic cultural ethos and remake ourselves and our world into a human community more attuned to the will of God and the values of God's reign. "We are always capable of going out of ourselves towards the other. Unless we do this, other creatures will not be recognized for their true worth.... Disinterested concern for others, and the rejection of every form of self-centeredness and self-absorption, are essential if we truly wish to care for our brothers and sisters and for the natural environment" (Pope Francis, *Laudato Si'*, #208).

Our Relationship with God

The ways we relate to other realities in our lives colors and contours how we relate to God. And our relationship with God is ultimately how we will live out our eternal destiny.

I remember the shocking realization I had as a rather young man: either I was going to exist forever, or someday I'd go poof and be no more. I'm reasonably certain I exist now. The question is this: will whatever gives me existence now, whoever keeps me "be-ing," will that force, power, entity, keep giving me existence forever, or will someday the reality that constitutes me as "me" cease doing so? Will I someday be no more? Or will I live forever? I choose to trust, hope, and believe that I will live forever. I've conversed with others who think differently. One told me, "When we die, that's it. Game over. We die and cease to exist." His certitude about this was shaken a bit when I pointed out to him that he too was living on faith in his belief that he'd at some point stop existing. Either way, eternal life or nonexistence, we won't experientially know until we die which of these two beliefs is true.

Spiritual direction banks on the eternal life option. So we believe that eternal life doesn't begin at death; life eternal begins the moment we are conceived, and is radically related to God at the moment of our baptism. Catholics believe in the sacramental nature of existence. All the realities of our existence, both material and immaterial, contain within them the pulsating spiritual realities of the cause of their existence, the ground of "be-ing," the mystery of God. Eucharist especially, but also confirmation, reconciliation, sacraments of vocation, and sacrament of the sick relate us to God at key moments of our lives. Spiritual direction helps us name and claim these ways, moments, and experiences wherein God makes God's self self-evident to us. Birth may be the most universal of these moments. We cannot remember when we were born, but someone certainly does. I've never heard of parents who are not awed at the birth of their child. And also a little daunted. A young woman graduated from nursing school and went to work at Children's Hospital in Philadelphia, on the infant and toddlers intensive care unit. A few years later she gave birth to her own child. In a new-parent moment of panic, she called her mother, who was also a nurse. "Mom, I don't know if I can do this. It's scary being responsible for a baby!" Her mother replied, "Maureen, if you can't take care of a baby, who can?" Parenthood is a prime time to get in touch with the reality of God, whom Jesus reveals to be a good and loving parent.

This work of seeing our lives as given to us by God, and resplendent with the Glory of God, in everything from washing the dishes, to working for a living, to singing in the choir, to making love, to praying, is the work of faith and love. Prayer is when we formally discipline ourselves to stop and let God be God in our lives. It is in times of prayer that we sit and let emerge in our consciousness the ways in which we experience and tell the story of our relationship with God.

God is not a thing among other things. God is the power of life. Our lives depend on God. Spiritual direction orients us to examine, understand, and see how we respond to a God who is the bedrock of our existence, the light of our lives, the love within all the loves of our human history. In spiritual direction, we begin to ask ourselves, "How do I see God?" "What images of God strike me, move me, 'work' for me?" God as loving parent is rather central to the Christian experience. And for those who didn't have a great relationship with their mother or father, I often teach, "God is not my father. God is not your father. God is our Father." God in nature is usually a way of thinking and experiencing God that everyone can click into. God as source of creative energy, God as the bedrock of our lives, God as the champion of the oppressed and afflicted, and as the one who comforts the afflicted and afflicts the comfortable (wasn't it Dorothy Day who said this?), and God who challenges the oppressors, on and on: our image(s) of God are the prime matter of spiritual direction.

A spiritual director will ask about a directee's images of God because that is where the transformation happens. As we pray, our images of God change. The God of our childhood morphs from "the old man with the white beard" or the rainbow we drew at the children's Word of God on Sunday morning, to the God of Jesus. I vividly remember the day in 1971—I was a fifteen-year-old at the time at St. Joe's Prep in Philly—when Vince Taggert, S.J, came into our religion class with the vinyl album *Jesus Christ Superstar*. He had stayed up all night typing out the lyrics and mimeographing them on those old, alcohol-smelling, blue-inked sheets of paper. We sat entranced as we were introduced to a whole new image of Jesus, mediated in powerful song and stirring lyrics. My image of Jesus would never be the same. For young adults at St. Joe's University in Philly, Mel Gibson's 2004 film, *The Passion of the Christ*, made an impact on their consciousness. The students really didn't like a panel of professors' erudite critique of the film (too bloody; reactionary Catholicism with Jesus speaking Latin at the Last Supper; no full depiction of the resurrection, etc.). The critique missed the point. The students' hearts had been touched by the film. They hadn't ever really contemplated the crucifixion. For many of them, it was the first time they realized how Jesus had so suffered and died for them. Their image of God was transformed by Gibson's film.

Movies are often powerful mediators of images that modify our images of God. Martin Sheen and his son, Emilio Estevez, gave us a beautiful meditation on family, father-son relations, and the mysteries of community and God with their 2010 movie *The Way*. It is a fascinating look at the transformation of an eye doctor as he undertakes the pilgrimage of Santiago de Compostela, a journey his son could not complete due to his untimely death. Images of Catholicism can be traced through Hollywood, from Bing Crosby and Ingrid Bergman as Father O'Malley and Sister Benedict elbowing Catholics into the American mainstream in *The Bells of St. Mary's* (1945) to Otto Preminger's celebration of the Church Triumphant and priest as Superman in *The Cardinal* (1963), to Kevin Smith's iconoclastic *Dogma* (1999), wherein the theological questions of salvation, presupposed and answered in the first two films, are again grappled with by Ben Affleck and Matt Damon as fallen angels deeply desiring to get back into God's good graces. And the ever popular *Sound of*

Music may have had a greater effect on Catholic sensibilities than we realize. Maria's leaving the convent in 1965 presaged the exodus of women from religious life. The church in the United States and the world sorely misses those thousands of dedicated, generous, highly educated women who gave so much to so many.

Often God is as much experienced in song and story as God is in our personal life experiences. From popular songs like Simon and Garfunkel's "Bridge Over Troubled Water" and the Beatles's "Yesterday," as well as the scripturally explicit hymns of the St. Louis Jesuits, a whole generation of baby boomer Catholics in the United States have opened their hearts, minds, and souls to the experience of God. The Contemporary Christian Music movement with artists like Matt Redman ("10,000 Reasons") and Chris Tomlin ("Lord, I Need You" and "Here I Am to Worship"), and even more commercial groups like Mumford and Sons ("I Will Wait for You") and Leonard Cohen's "Hallelujah" with various covers, powerfully and deeply connect today's youth to God. Good spiritual directors will ask directees how God is for them: where, when, and in what form God manifests divine presence and power to them. For many, it may be liturgical celebrations like Eucharist or Eucharistic Adoration. For others, it may be time in nature, hiking, or fishing. However God is experienced, that is where spiritual direction begins and the direction in which it moves.

A spiritual director will be interested in a time line of your personal story, your history with God and others. What are the key moments in life that to some degree have made you who you are? How was your childhood and adolescence? Were you the popular kid? The nerdy kid? The athlete? Were you happy? Do you look back on high school with fondness, or chagrin? Did you go to college? What was that like? How are the key relationships in your life, then and now? Who are your friends? What are your hobbies? What books have deeply influenced your life? About who and/or what are you passionate? All this is grist for the mill of spiritual direction, for all this is where God is in your life, and where God has appeared and is going to appear.

One key tool for spiritual direction is usually a more than glancing interest in the Bible. Reading, studying, pondering the gospels, the central Old Testament stories (Abraham, Exodus, Jonah, Job), the New Testament letters, the people of the Scriptures (Moses, King David, Isaiah, Jeremiah, Mary, Peter, Mary Magdalene, Paul), and the key episodes of the gospels (Jesus' birth, temptations, preaching and parables, death and resurrection): all these biblical materials place our life story in dialogue with the salvation history revealed in the communally normative stories of the people of God.

We learn how to relate to God by listening to—actually eavesdropping on—others' stories of how they relate to God. Spiritual reading provides another way to get to know God and how people have come to experience and understand God. There's a vast treasure trove of material out there to dive into, and good directors carefully consider what will be helpful for the directee, depending on the individual's life circumstances. A wonderland of spiritual literature is easily available today, including classic texts like Augustine's *Confessions*, the fourteenth-century anonymous author's *The Cloud of Unknowing*, and the writings of Teresa of Avila and St. John of the Cross (but maybe not for beginners . . .), as well as the works of more contemporary authors such as Trappist monks Thomas Merton, Thomas Keating, and Basil Pennington; Jesuits William O'Malley and James Martin; Franciscan Richard Rohr, and writers Dorothy Day, Ronald Rolheiser, and Dr. Gerald G. May. Jesuit Mark Thibodeaux's *Armchair Mystic* is the best book for one just starting out with prayer. Poet Kathleen Norris's *The Cloister Walk* is a fascinating reflection by a Protestant woman on her experiences in the Catholic worlds of a small convent of Catholic Sisters who extended her hospitality when she was in a difficult situation in New York City and during a longer time among Benedictine Monks in Collegeville, Minnesota. Anything by C. S. Lewis, the most-read Christian author of all time, is worth reading. Bishop Robert Barron's *Catholicism* is a clear and very accessible presentation of an overview of church teachings and history. Former Presbyterian minister, and now mesmerizing Catholic scripture scholar, Scott Hahn's many books are great reads, on everything from his and his wife's conversion story to his take on the sacraments.

One of my personal favorites is *He Leadeth Me,* by Jesuit Walter Ciszek, who lived and worked in communist Russia from 1939 to 1963. Five of those years were spent in solitary confinement in Lubianka prison and another fifteen years of hard labor in the dreaded Siberian Gulag. His spiritual journey through these trials and the lessons he learned from God are profound. Anything by the zany and iconoclastic Anne Lamott is extremely thought provoking and helpful. Immaculée Ilibagiza's *Left to Tell,* about her experience of God and forgiveness in the midst of the Rwanda genocide of 1994, and Mary Karr's bestseller *Lit,* a memoir of her dealing with alcohol abuse and learning to pray, are amazing testimonies to the power of faith and prayer in our lives. The profoundly poetic and powerful sermons of the lyrical writer Frederick Buechner, who spent most of his professional life as a chaplain at a preparatory school, are imaginative and challenging. His moving meditation "The Dwarves of the Stable" tells of his experience as a father whose daughter battles a severe eating disorder, anorexia nervosa. Buechner, an ordained minister, has to deal with the spiritual battle in his own soul as he realizes that his daughter's starving herself is also a reflection of his own inability to accept his own powerlessness and need for God.[26]

There are literally thousands of other great writings. Ask any rabbi, priest, minister, or any other committed religious person: I'm sure everyone has their own top-ten list.

Interaction with church documents can be very helpful if one's taste runs in that direction. I love encyclicals, papal documents, and the Catholic Catechism. Some find the writing tedious. *De gustibus non est disputandum* ("There's no accounting for taste"). But in the actual documents, you find the clear teaching and not someone's version of it. A reading of the Documents of Vatican II, especially the Dogmatic Constitution on the Church, *Lumen Gentium* (Light of Peoples) and the Church in the Modern World, *Gaudium et Spes* (Joy and Hope), go far in deciphering the bitter church battles of the past forty years between "conservatives" and "liberals."[27] Hopefully we are moving beyond those classifications as the millennials move into positions held by baby boomers and their elders.

The documents introduce the directee to the larger community's thinking and articulation of the faith. The good news is we do not have to reinvent the wheel; the challenging news is that the wheels are many, pretty big, and they've been turning for a long time. To become conversant with the tradition takes effort and time. But the reward is a deep appreciation for the extensive and caring ways in which the millions of those people who have gone before us have striven to understand, articulate, and share the gifts of faith we've been given, gifts we are called to pass on to those who come after us.

---

26. Frederick Buechner, "The Dwarves in the Stable," in Darryl Tippen et al., eds., *Shadow and Light: Literature and the Life of Faith*, 3rd ed. (Abilene, TX: Abilene Christian Press, 2013), 97–118.

27. Documents of the Second Vatican Council (Vatican City, 1962–1965), http://www.vatican.va.

All of this, how we relate to ourselves, others, and God, sets a context within which we root our own personal and small communal journeys to and with God.

Engaging in Spiritual Direction

Our willingness to open ourselves and our relationships with ourselves, others, and God, and to allow and trust another person to see us as we really are, is the essence of spiritual direction. Within this relationship the transformative power of the Holy Spirit can become ever more operative and effective in our lives. The sacraments can take on a new vibrancy. And our joy in dedication to the mission of the Lord Jesus can deepen and pervade the innermost parts of our being, even during storms and difficulties on life's surface.

The fascinating dynamic of spiritual direction also plays out in the countercultural way of being for those of us who strive to mold our lives according to the teachings and example of Christ. Here, unlike the world that exists apart from God, power is transformed and utilized in radically different ways. "When power meets power, there is conflict. Where power meets vulnerability, there is oppression. But where vulnerability meets vulnerability, there is intimacy."[28] In spiritual direction, the vulnerabilities of the directee, the director, and God are made available to one another. In that intimacy (at-oneness, "into-me-see"), our hearts and minds and souls can be molded, transformed, and freed up to serve others.

Spiritual direction over a lifetime can help persons reach the end for which they are created. Lack of such direction, lack of careful discernment, and lack of the ability to journey with others can lead to drastic consequences in the long arc of our lives. The example I often note in talking about the dangers of completely "missing the mark" (the literal meaning of the New Testament Greek word *harmartia*, "sin") in one's life is Michael Corleone at the end of *The Godfather II*. Michael has vanquished all his enemies. He has had his brother Fredo murdered as Fredo fished, praying a Hail Mary. We hear the gunshot and then see Michael, smoking a cigarette, sitting in a room all by himself, in his mansion on Lake Tahoe. His wife has left him; he has no close friends. He is all alone with all his possessions, power, and pride. He thinks back to December 8, 1941. Michael, in all generosity and willing self-sacrifice, has signed

---

28. Pat O'Sullivan, S.J., Jesuit Tertian Director, lecture at Sydney Australia, 2000.

up for the Marines. He wanted to serve his country, a cause greater than himself. His older brother Sonny Corleone ridicules Michael. Only a chump would go into the service. Corleones live only for the family. Now at midlife, as he sits alone and isolated, Michael realizes he never really wanted to become the Godfather; he had wanted another life. But his fatal choices turned him into a murderer, and a willing accomplice in unspeakable evils.

What if Michael Corleone had had the opportunity to discern his choice to kill Sollozzo and Captain McClusky? What if he had not chosen to return an "eye for and eye" in retaliation for the attempt on his father's life? How would his life have been different?

We all could use a coach in life, someone who has played the game, knows how to prepare, and can counsel us when we are down three runs in the bottom of the ninth inning. Spiritual direction keeps us talking. The conversation gets what is going on in our souls out there and visible. Spiritual direction allows for another set of eyes to see what's happening in our consciousness. And such conversation helps us to live the spiritual life.

Most people seek spiritual direction because they have begun praying, and desire more from prayer and their relationship with God. If they are able to, they move to something like a five- to eight-day retreat. Let's look at what can happen on such retreats, and then explore what we mean by, and hope for from, the spiritual life.

CHAPTER 4

Eight-Day Retreats: What Can Happen?

The fruit of silence is prayer. The fruit of prayer is faith. The fruit of faith is love. The fruit of love is service. The fruit of service is peace.
— Mother Teresa

How come when we talk to God we call it prayer, but when God talks to us, we call it schizophrenia?
— Lily Tomlin

The greatest revolution of our generation is the discovery that human beings, by changing the inner attitudes of their minds, can change the outer aspects of their lives.
— William James

There was this old Amish woman who went with her family to a mall for the first time in their lives. The Amish family was mesmerized by the hundreds of stores, the lights, the food court. And then, for the first time in her life, the old Amish woman sees two silver doors opening and closing, and people going in and out of the doors. Now, we would know this to be an elevator. She watches as an elderly man approaches the elevator doors and enters. The doors close. A minute later, the doors open and a handsome young man who looks like George Clooney emerges. She sees another elderly man get on, and a minute later a man who looks like Brad Pitt steps out. A third elderly man goes in, and out comes a Matt Damon look-alike. The woman's daughter comes over to her and says, "Mom, this place is great." The old Amish woman agrees and says, "Quick, go get your father!"

Christian life is all about transformation. "God became what we are so we can become what God is," wrote St. Athanasius (cf. CCC §460). God loves us and wants to free us to be the persons we deeply desire to be. God loves us and wants to free us from all that hinders us from being those persons our dogs think we are. God loves us and wants to free us for love, to love and be loved by God and others. Such love transforms us and our world. Retreats are times to focus on and fine-tune these truths. They are times to engage in fierce and fine prayer, to let prayer flame forth into lives of service and love. "Everything is interconnected," the pope insists in the encyclical *Laudato Si'*. Silent, one-on-one directed retreats help us realize and relish the connections constituting our world, our lives, ourselves, our communities, and our relationship with God.

Prayer is the effort we make to open ourselves to the communication of God. God's way of speaking with us is on a level different from other experiences of our human existence. In many ways, when we pray, we are like dogs looking at computer screens. God is ever greater than we are. God is mystery, the somewhat incomprehensible mystery of ongoing creation and committed, demanding love. We are not on God's level. So we actively place ourselves in a position where we can descend into the depths of our being wherein the reality of God can emerge and reveal ourselves to ourselves, and call us to community and mission.

Silence is the traditional manner is which practitioners who conscientiously seek God find the divine revealed. Shutting off all the noise and chatter of life, entering into silence, allows us to begin to pay attention and become deeply aware. What do we hear in silence? What do we notice? As the days of an eight-day retreat roll along we often find that (1) what we thought the retreat was going to be about isn't what the retreat is about; and (2) we find ourselves noticing, remembering, being caught up in, hopes, dreams, desires, and possibilities we hadn't been paying attention to before the retreat. Retreat times are days set aside to allow us to become more deeply and articulately aware of what God is doing in our lives and what we are doing in response. On these retreats, we pull away from everything to experience everything at a deeper level.

St. Ignatius realized God can deal "directly" with the person who takes the time and space to try and open themselves to God. In order to catch what God is saying, we need to learn God's language. And that language is silence. The prophet Elijah learned God is not in the noise of natural forces but in the still, "sheer silence." Elijah is on the run. He hides in a cave where he spends the night. God comes and asks what he's doing there. Elijah professes all he has been doing for God and complains that evil men are now seeking to kill him. He hears God not in the wind, an earthquake, or fire. God comes in "sheer silence. When Elijah heard it, he wrapped his face in his mantle and went out and stood at the entrance of the cave. Then there came a voice to him that said, 'What are you doing here, Elijah?'" (1 Kgs 19:9–13).

Retreats are times to allow God to ask us, "What are you doing here?" When I direct people on five- to eight-day retreats, I suggest that they first relax. Yes, relax. Some people sleep for two days. People today are so busy, so tired out, so exhausted. I tell retreatants to realize that God has gotten them to this place of quiet, silence, pause, and rejuvenation. Trust that. People who go on retreat are courageous and generous people. They have taken time to get away from the strong and heavy wind, from the earthquakes and the fires. They are willing to slow down and allow the silence to seep into their minds and hearts. And I tell them to be patient, to know that they will hear what they will hear. We await the tiny whispering sound of God's transformative presence. And no one knows what will happen when that encounter occurs.

It's not so much about actively doing something as letting something happen, often waiting for something to happen. It's a lot like fishing. You cast, and cast, and cast the lure, and all of a sudden, like lightning, the fish strikes the hook and all hell, or heaven, breaks loose.

Retreats aren't contests to be won. There are no grades. Pray as you are, not some way you imagine you are supposed to be. Karl Rahner, the great Jesuit theologian, taught that we pray to God and the Word God speaks to us is our lives.[1] Paula D'Arcy sagely says, "God comes to you disguised as your life."[2] We place those realities of our lives in relationship with the Word of God, the people and events of our lives, and most importantly, for Ignatian retreats, with our deepest desires. God speaks to us through our desires. When we pray, we often find ourselves wanting something we didn't even know we wanted.

How does an eight-day retreat work? The retreatant speaks with a companion, a guide, or a director once a day for thirty to forty-five minutes. What happens in prayer sessions is the center of the conversation. Ignatius encourages people on retreat to be open and honest with the director. The latter needs to hear what's really going on, what the retreatant desires, how the retreatant and God are getting along. The retreatant begins praying, and we see what happens. The retreat guide may suggest Scripture

---

1. Karl Rahner, S.J., "Is Prayer Dialogue with God?" in *Christian at Crossroads* (New York: Crossroad; Mahwah, NJ: Seabury Press, 1975), 62–69.

2. Richard Rohr, O.F.M., *Falling Upward: A Spirituality for the Two Halves of Life* (San Francisco: Jossey-Bass, 2011), 66.

passages to ponder and pray over, or other ways of praying. When you're on retreat, pray through your life history. Imagine yourself in a situation, for example, in a gospel scene or scene from a favorite movie.

Once I directed a religious sister on an eight-day retreat. She came in the first day and told me how her father had died a few months before, how wonderful the funeral Mass was, and how grateful she was to have her family, members of her order, and many friends there. On this retreat, she thought she needed to figure out whether God wanted her to make a change in ministry. She said she needed to pray more (everybody always says they need to pray more!). So she began to pray. The first couple of days she was tired. Slept a lot. By the third day, she was restless and a bit angry about she didn't know what. I'd given her typical passages to pray on. Psalm 139. The wonders of creation. The annunciation in Luke. Nothing was really striking pay dirt. She began to talk about a relationship with a man, how it had challenged and disturbed her. While being extremely attracted to him, she obviously didn't want the relationship to go further in violation of her vows. She had resolved to have nothing to do with the man. I asked if she could not be friends with the guy. She said that was too dangerous. I asked about her relationship with her father. Often our relationships with members of the opposite sex are colored and contoured by our relationships with our parents, men by their mothers, women by their fathers.

When the sister heard the question about her father, her eyes teared up. She grasped for the Kleenex. Every room where director and directee meet has Kleenex. I gently suggested that she spend the day praying over her father's funeral and her relationship with him. Pay dirt (definition: "ground containing ore in sufficient quantity to be profitably extracted"). As a director, I'm looking for pay dirt. It's in the nitty-gritty grime of our lives and souls that God does divine works of reconciliation, peace, and joy. But the extraction is often oiled by tears.

The sister spent the next four days praying about her father. Turned out he wasn't the figure she'd painted the first day. He'd been alcoholic and abusive. Severely so to her, the eldest daughter, who often had to protect her mother and younger siblings. She cried and cried. After she'd prayed over every passage I could think of to keep her digging into what God wanted to reveal to her through her relationship with her father, I suggested she may want to watch and pray about the movie *On Golden Pond*, a marvelous film starring Jane Fonda and her father Henry. It's a great story of a woman coming to terms with her complex and complicated relationship with her father, portrayed by a real-life father and daughter.

The next day she came in and said kiddingly, "Damn, you want me to keep Kleenex in business for the next three years!" The movie and the retreat broke open for her all kinds of insights, feelings, hurts to be healed, and new hopes in relation to her father. She made connections to choices in her own life that were influenced in ways she hadn't been fully aware of by her relationship and history with her father. She left the retreat with work to do, but having already covered much ground on her journey to God imaged as father; not her father, but the Father revealed in Jesus. Not an easy retreat. But a transformative time in her life.

The important thing for the retreat director is to stay out of the way. The retreat is not about "me." I had to guard against getting into my relationship with my father as I listened to the sister. I'm like a coach; I'm on the sideline observing the game and sending in plays. To put it another way, directors ought to be like glass to a cool, delicious drink of water . . . or beer, or champagne. The focus is on the beverage, not the container or conduit. In the words of Dave Fleming, S.J.:

> A director always provides the balance for us both in times of exhilaration and discouragement. The director is not the one who urges a particular decision—for example to enter religious life, to marry this or that person, or to take a vow of poverty. The director facilitates the movement of God's grace within us so that the light and love of God inflame all possible decisions and resolutions about life situations. *God is not only our Creator but also the director of our retreat, and the human director should never provide a hindrance to such intimate communication.*[3]

The retreat demands some discipline and agreed-to structures. I usually try to ascertain the times of prayer and the length of time a person will pray, as well as to make it a point to ask if these are being adhered to, especially if "nothing's happening." It's good to get some physical exercise, eat sanely, and get lots of good rest. Sometimes the retreatant knows what they need more than the director.

A year before ordination—my eleventh as a Jesuit—I spent the summer learning how to direct retreats at the Jesuit Center in Wernersville, Pennsylvania. For the eight-day retreats, I would direct three or four people and debrief each day with one of the more experienced directors. My

---

3. David Fleming, S.J., *Draw Me into Your Friendship: A Literal Translation and a Contemporary Reading of the Spiritual Exercises,* #15 (St. Louis, MO: The Institute of Jesuit Sources, 1996), 15, my emphasis.

mentors were more interested in what was going on with me as I directed. Confidentiality among directors and directees in my experience is as valued, guarded, and sacred as the seal of confession. I was always glad to direct a religious sister, because these gals had been to the rodeo before, many of them dozens of times. Once I directed a provincial of her order. After a day, she looked at me, and I said, "Yeah, you're right. You know a lot more about this stuff than I do. How would you like this retreat to be 'directed'?" She smiled, and we got along fine.

A director listens for movements in the retreatants. What are the joys, fears, worries, confusions, angers, peace, calm, serenity, enthusiasms, hurts, welling up of old memories or issues, dreams, regrets, and on and on that start surfacing in the consciousness of the retreatant, during hours of prayer and also at times of repose between formal times of prayer? What do they find themselves daydreaming about during the retreat? Night dreams can also play into a retreat.

One time a sister came in who had spent years teaching high school. She was in her late fifties or early sixties. I did the usual preliminary talk, and just assumed she knew what she was doing on retreat, that she would come in the next day and we'd go from wherever she was launching. The next day arrived for our conference and she told me she was saying the rosary three times, had made the stations, and liked the place and the food. I was surprised, and asked if she had ever made a directed retreat before, praying with Scripture, contemplating the gospels in an Ignatian manner. "No," she answered. "My sister friend wanted to come on this retreat. We've never done this kind of thing before. But at the last minute she couldn't come. So I came by myself. Am I not doing this right?"

I assured her it wasn't a matter of doing something right or wrong, it is just a different method. So I took thirty minutes and briefly described Ignatian retreats and spirituality, and gave her explicit instructions on how to pray with a scripture passage. Sit still. Calm yourself. Ask for God's grace. And then read the passage a few times. Then sit and see what comes to mind. One passage I gave her was Isaiah 43:1–7. In that passage, the prophet proclaims God tenderly telling the people, "I have called you by name, you are mine."

The next day she comes in. She was a tough, Brooklyn-born-and-bred gal. As she walks by me to her chair, she whacks me on the shoulder and says, "Rick, I messed it all up. I don't know if I have the hang of this." I laughed a bit and asked what had happened when she prayed (and you have to imagine all this said in a thick, Brooklyn accent!).

I did what ya told me. Sit. Breathe. Be quiet. Read the passage a few times. And then I'm sitting there, and I'm sitting there and I'm thinking about that "called by name." Me being called by name. Called by name. And all of a sudden, I'm back in Brooklyn. I'm little, like three or four. Maybe two. Wadda I know? And I'm in the basement of my house, and it's all dark and musty smellin', and all of a sudden I hear my fadda, he's callin' me, callin' me by my name. And he calls again, louder. And I run up the stairs and I jump into his arms, and he's spinnin' me around and around, and I'm laughing and laughing. It was like I was back there. His big, strong arms. Smellin' of cigars and after shave. He was a great guy. I hadn't thought about that in years, YEARS! And, I couldn't believe it, like forty-five minutes went by like that [snaps fingers]. All I was doing was remembering when I was a little girl and my father would do nice things for me. I'm sorry, see. I screwed it all up. I was supposed to be praying and I wasted the whole prayer time!

Stunned, I sat there and said, "No! You got it exactly right. That's the kind of thing that can happen when you pray this way."

She began to learn how God communicates with us through our memories, our awareness of our graced (and sometimes dis-graced) life stories. Her remembering, really reliving, her wonderful relationship with her father was a marvelous consolation. She began to dig into scripture passages and milk them for all they were worth.

As the retreat progressed, she ruefully realized that she'd gotten into a bit of a rut in religious life. She (as do all the sisters!) worked very hard for years and years teaching young teens. She cared about and for them. Often she had to show them some tough love; after all, she was teaching in northern New Jersey. But life hadn't quite turned out the way she had hoped. And she became aware of her anger. She was in many ways, in some very deep ways, an angry woman, angry at her religious order, angry with life.

About day five she came in and shared that she'd had a dream. There was a huge, ugly pit bull sitting in front of the convent where she lived. The dog was digging a big hole in the front lawn of the convent. As the hole got bigger, a large beautiful collie was revealed, buried in the ground, barking loudly and trying to get out. But the pit bull, though digging the collie out, didn't like it and wouldn't let it come to the surface.

Now, I had just a smattering of training in dream work. The one rule of thumb I learned is that as the director of the retreat, you don't interpret a dream for a retreatant. Wait for them to draw their own conclusions about the meaning, if any, of the dream. So I suggested she keep that dream in her awareness and ask herself what it meant.

Now, you don't have to be Carl Jung to figure it out. The next day she came in and shyly said, "Dat damn dream. I think it's something like dis. I'm like both those dogs, see. I've gotten too mean and too tough. I'm too angry about everything. And there's this beautiful collie dog deep down inside me that's wantin' to get out. Does that make any sense to you?"

To me, it sure sounded like it made a lot of sense. On that retreat she recognized where she'd gotten off track, where she'd missed the mark. In the collie and the pit bull, she had been graced/given a wonderful image to work with. She really wanted to let that collie part of her come to the surface, and she wanted to tame the pit bull. She resolved to try to find a spiritual director and keep opening herself to this kind of Ignatian prayer.

On eight-day retreats, people often find ways to name and claim ways of praying that work for them. They slow down, take long walks, get eight whole hours of sleep (something we in the United States are less and less likely to do in the twenty-first century!). Retreatants learn to wait and listen for that "sheer silence" Elijah heard at the mouth of the cave.

Beginners are particularly delightful. For the past several years, I've been privileged to be a part of the team that provides the MAGIS retreats for teachers and administrators from Jesuit universities and colleges around the country. Given the pluralism of our times, Jesuit schools often see new faculty who are not Catholic, or even religious. Some who get a position at a Jesuit school aren't all that interested in the Catholic nature and Jesuit tradition of the institution. But most, in my experience, are super-intelligent, hard-working "type A's" who have gotten their Ph.D., are in line for or have received tenure, are in their mid-thirties to early forties, and are asking, "Is this all there is?" They are teachers and administrators, with families and children, and they are beginning to ask the big religious questions that have been on the back burner since adolescence. They are ready to light a fire under that pot and see what bubbles up. All the Jesuit schools offer programs and workshops to help these not-so-young adults find out more about Ignatian approaches to God. From service sites and immersion trips to book reads and courses, many are discovering and enjoying the riches of living in the academic world with this added-on sense of Jesuit mission and identity.

On one MAGIS retreat, I was paired with a young psychology professor. She had grown up in a family where religion just wasn't present. She harbored no animosity toward religion; it just wasn't something her completely secular family dealt with in any way. After nine years at an East Coast Jesuit university, she had tenure, a loving husband, a nine-year-old daughter, and a dog. Life was great. When she heard about the Ignatian Colleagues Program, a year-and-a-half to two-year program of formation for teachers and administrators at Jesuit schools, she was intrigued. She got into it. As part of the program she had done a lot of reading about St. Ignatius, Jesuit history and tradition, and the ideals and meaning of Jesuit education. She had gone on an immersion trip to Nicaragua. And now, as part of her Ignatian Colleagues Program, she was making her first silent retreat. And trying prayer for the first time in her life. That's right. She had never "prayed" at all. She was going to give this prayer thing "a try."

She was a dream retreatant. She would follow my suggestions. She'd spent a lifetime doing "assignments," and it took a day or two to help her realize she could "color outside the lines" a bit if she wanted. She liked praying with scripture and had some fascinating questions about the Bible, but resisted getting into huge head trips about this or that meaning of the passage. She just began seriously and deeply to entertain the notion that there is a personal God who loves us and wants good for us, and specifically wants good for her. She was particularly moved by the story of the Annunciation and fascinated, as a mother, with the whole reality of Mary giving birth to Jesus.

About the fourth day, she shyly asked me about Mary, and we chatted a bit. I went through the old routine about how Catholics don't worship Mary. Mary isn't a goddess but a poor Jewish girl, almost a young woman, whose "Yes" response God needed in order to become incarnate among us. She paused and quietly asked me more pointedly, "But how do you Catholics actually pray to Mary? What's that all about?" Oh. I gave her the ten-minute version. Hail Mary. The rosary. I even threw in something about Pope Francis's interest in Mary the Un-tier or Un-doer of Knots. At the time, I'd vaguely heard something about this thing with the pope and Mary the Un-doer of Knots. I looked up a lot more after this young psychology professor's retreat. She asked, "Can I do that? Can I pray to Mary? Can I pray a rosary?" I said, "Sure. Here." I had a rosary. "Give it a whirl. See what happens." She continued, "There's this statue of Mary that I like in the little chapel on the lakeside of the house." (I hadn't seen the statue but found out it was a statue of the Black Madonna, the one with Mary holding little Jesus in her lap.) "I want to pray that my brother gets a job. He's been out of work for three years." I said, "Sure. People have been praying to Mary for centuries asking for favors."

She came back the next day and reported, "I prayed the Mary thing, the rosary. And I tried praying for my brother, that he gets a job. And you're not going to believe this: he called yesterday afternoon about three. He hardly ever calls me. He says he got a job. He had had an interview in the morning. That's when I was praying in front of the Mary statue. And he got the job. You're not going to believe this," she said again. "His interview was at eleven o'clock! Right when I was praying the rosary. I didn't even know he had an interview. And it was yesterday, a Saturday! Who has a job interview on a Saturday? But it's one of those computer places. They have crazy hours. Do you think I should tell him I was praying for him?"

I was amazed. I had to confess to her that prayer doesn't always work this way. She shared this experience of praying to Mary, and the surprisingly quick result, with the larger group on the retreat at a reflection session on the last evening of the retreat. The room exploded in clapping and laughter. One person jokingly called out, "Can you pray over my lottery ticket?"

I particularly enjoy the privilege of directing beginners on retreat. I get to teach more. What does it mean to "pray for a grace"? How exactly should a retreatant structure the day and prayer times, and so on? But it is fascinating to witness and listen as someone clicks into how to experience God in their lives. A previous generation had to be freed a bit from ossified ways of experiencing God that were no longer working for them (wordy litanies, forty-hour devotions, Eucharist as obligation, not celebration). Today, many are making retreats with little in the way of formal religious practice. Many college students coming to the sacrament of reconciliation, confession, on a SEARCH retreat, are making their second confession, the first since their First Confession. A lot of people come to silent retreats clear out of the blue.

Listen to the experience of a woman without a religious background who tried the Ignatian silent retreat. Hers is one of the most intriguing testimonials to the reality and power of experiencing this silent retreat. Her article appeared in the *New York Times*. As far as I can tell, she went on the retreat without any plan to write about it for a larger audience, but I'm glad she did.

Susan Gregory Thomas, "a 43-year-old mother of three wrung out from three years of panic attacks triggered by the specter of financial ruin, needed a solid period of quiet to recombobulate. Cheaply." In late November, she traveled from New York City to the quiet lands of Wernersville, a few miles west of Reading, Pennsylvania. She had never made a retreat before but "yearned for a snippet of the no-frills spiritual solitude. The Jesuits, I'd read, were the guys to go to concerning such matters." She didn't want high-end, new age, spa experiences, and the price was right at the Jesuit Retreat Center in Wernersville. Having spent two years as a Jesuit novice at Wernersville, I laughed out loud at Susan's apt description of the place.

> The facility itself, an English Renaissance-style building constructed in the late 1920s, was gigantic and dark—attributes intensified by the resident Jesuits' ubiquitously posted wish to keep the light bills low. . . . There was also an ineffable sphinxiness about the place. For example, I got there an hour and a half late the first night, and there was no one to tell me where to go or what I should be doing. The only signpost was a list of names and room numbers tacked to a corkboard, so I found mine and rollerbagged down the building's spooky, caliginous hallways until I tracked down my assigned spot. I creaked open the lockless door and found a jumbo crucifix resting on the bed pillow. *If Stanley Kubrick had found this place, he'd never have shot a movie anywhere else.* [My emphasis. I had to laugh out loud at her description!]

The next day, Susan met with her retreat director, Sr. Barbara, "an upbeat grandmotherly woman with a plumose crown of lovely white hair." Susan poured out her heart.

> I told her about my stress-related illnesses, which had hospitalized me twice earlier that year; about my sparkly-minded children; about watching my Lear-like father die in front of me; about my divorce, subsequent remarriage and unexpected conception of my son; about my dip into poverty; my husband's unemployment; my darkest fears; of aloneness. Sister Barbara listened closely and then said, "What I hear you saying, Susan, is that you feel forsaken."

Sr. Barbara provided the central gift of spiritual direction. She listened to Susan and tried to help name, from her own spiritual experience of directing people, what was going on for Susan. Barbara's suggestion struck a chord. Susan continues:

Not dealing with abandonment issues: forsaken. Sister Barbara did not then press me to process my relationship with, say, my mother or to consider that I should "own" my feelings. Rather, she opened her Bible and turned to Matthew 3:17. This is the verse in which Jesus is baptized by John the Baptist, and God opens the heavens and says, "This is my son, the beloved; my favor rests on him." Sister Barbara read the passage and closed the book. How would it be, she asked, to personalize this passage—to pray with the words, "You are my beloved daughter, Susie; my favor rests on you"? How would it feel to know that God loves you as you love your own children? And then I wept and, finally, cleared my throat. It would feel pretty good. Sister Barbara advised me to go outside, walk, and pray with this. "See you tomorrow at 1:15, and we'll see what God says," she said.

Susan then went and did what Sr. Barbara suggested. Susan learns to sit with a passage, letting it roll around in her head and heart, stretching into her soul. And she sleeps. With exquisite detail, Susan describes her experience of the silent retreat.

I followed her suggestion. I brought a pack of cigarettes, Thomas Merton's "Book of Hours," and a paper cup of coffee with hazelnut nondairy creamer, and I walked. The grounds of the Jesuit Center in Wernersville number some 250 acres of Wyethesque country, replete with undulating hills; groves of shy trees; a pond that's home to monster koi; a cemetery. Benches positioned perfectly for quiet contemplation appeared providentially every so often.

I sat on one of these at the top of a hill, closed my eyes and sat. I don't know how long I was there, not meditating "on the breath" or deliberately clearing my mind, but simply internally rolling over the words of my custom-tailored Matthew 3:17. Slowly, though, I grew to feel still and happy.

Later that night, I peeked into the center's adytum, a dark and lovely stone chapel whose altar glowed with candlelight. I approached a pew and knelt. I thought about my closest family and friends and how Matthew 3:17 might be custom-fit for them, too. Again, time evaporated. That night, I slept 12 hours straight. I hadn't slept half that much in more than a decade.

One sage director once said, "A lot of spiritual problems can be greatly helped by a bowl of hot soup and a good night's sleep." Rested, Susan was able to hear what she found in Matthew 3:17, the text describing

Jesus' experience at his baptism by John. The heavens open and Jesus hears, "You are my beloved." The first thing Ignatian directors listen for is directees' experiencing God's love, God's concern for them right here and now, God's acceptance of them as they are, God's desire for them to open their hearts and receive God's graces. Susan heard that while pondering Matthew 3:17. She knew God's love. She realized that God loves her the way she loves her own children. She had wept with Sr. Barbara, but soon felt pretty good. And rested.

A silent retreat is usually not all lights and rainbows. Susan describes feeling antsy on the retreat, worrying about her kids, wondering about all the work waiting for her back in Brooklyn. But she sticks with it. So often we were counseled as young Jesuits to "stay in the retreat." You never know when something will strike, like a trout hitting a fly on the end of your casted line. Sr. Barbara toward the end of the retreat asks Susan about her relationship with Jesus.

> She exhorted me to talk, pray to Jesus directly, with the Scripture from Exodus in mind. "Just see what comes to you." That afternoon, I ventured into the chapel again and stayed a long time. It would be awkward to report on what I experienced there; possibly, implausible. Suffice it to say, I left with the strong feeling that I did, indeed, have everything I needed—if only I would stay quiet long enough to remember.
>
> I left the Jesuit Center on a clear, icy night, turning on my cellphone just in time to receive a call from my husband hollering that he and a fellow he'd hired needed to be picked up at 30th Street Station in Philadelphia, followed by a call from my daughters' father saying that financial aid applications needed to be completed by the next day, latest. Seven voice mails and 108 e-mails left. O.K. For now, at least, I had more than enough to do all the work, and more.[4]

Susan describes the dailyness and the strange sense of closeness that grows in the silence. Having been struck on arrival by the crucifixes "everywhere," she found a comfort develop with the place and the process. "[B]y the end of my five days, I'd come to see my room as my sanctum sanctorum. I would regard crucifixes as heralds of human suffering and spiritual light. And I'd come to feel a strange closeness with my silent

---

4. Susan Gregory Thomas, "In Pennsylvania, a Quick Shot of Peace, on a Budget," *New York Times*, December 29, 2011.

companions. All this was chaperoned by my spiritual director, Sister Barbara Singer." Susan put herself into the hands of this stranger and was led to Jesus. At one point in the retreat, Sr. Barbara "asked the startling: Did I believe in Jesus? Sure, I did; in fact, as a punky, truant teenager, I had believed that Jesus was the greatest anti-establishment radical of all time. Sister Barbara laughed and clapped her hands: 'Great—so you can relate!'"[5] The silent retreats in the Ignatian tradition are usually about getting in touch with the reality of Jesus in our lives. Some may concentrate more on the Father, or the Spirit, but Ignatian Spirituality is deeply cristocentric opening unto a more Trinitarian sense of the divine. Whenever people are struggling on retreat and nothing is happening, or, on the other end of the spectrum, are all into excessively "spiritual" things (e.g., obscure saints, romanticized liberation theology, plans desired by God for them to reorder their parish/school/retreat center/business, on and on), it is always good to steer them toward an experience of Jesus.

Some retreats are more peaceful and calm, but often beneath the surface much is happening. I often tell retreatants to wait six months to see if the graces received solidify and take root in their lives. One administrator at a large Jesuit university who had a very demanding job went through the retreat without any huge movements or swings. He just had a quiet and growing sense of gratitude for his life, for his wife and family, and for the work he did, as well as a dawning realization that he'd like to develop and grow in his relationship with God. Several months later, I happened to be at the university where he works, and was fortunate to enjoy dinner with him and his wife. His wife definitely wanted him to find some way to work less. Seems the need to balance life and work is universal, and we all need to carve out time for God and relationships that really matter. We've all heard the old line, no one ever received a cancer diagnosis and said, "Gee, Doc, I wish I had worked more weekends."

The real way to kick a short, silent retreat into high gear is to come in and lay out the issue with your director on day one. One guy came in and spoke for about fifteen minutes the first day about how good life was and how grateful he was for so much of his life. And then he paused, took a deep breath, and laid it out. He and his wife were having sex about four times a year. He wanted more. She always seemed to want things to be perfect in order to feel ready to engage in intimacy. They had a great time

5. Ibid.

on a short vacation without the kids a few months before, but in the ordinary times of their lives, sex wasn't happening. He spent a lot of time on the retreat hearing that he wasn't weird, or a sex fiend, for wanting more sex. And he prayed over his and his wife's relationship with their parents and how that might be affecting things. Overall, he came to an awareness that some marital counseling could be a good thing for his wife and him. And toward the end of the retreat, he really made some connections with how all this played into his relationship with God.

I shared with this man a true story of a couple I've known for years. The guy was tall, very good looking, very successful (made really way high-end "money money"). His wife was extremely attractive. They had three small boys. One day she announced, no more sex. She was done with all that. He was shocked and crushed. Confused and angry. Feeling rejected and abandoned. He insisted they get counseling. She wouldn't go. After trying for months for some kind of resolution of the situation, he gave up. They divorced. He loved his boys and wasn't going to pay someone to mow the lawn and clean the gutters of his house, so he got a house a few streets over. He began drinking a little too much and chasing women. But, living where he did, he stayed in close proximity to his former wife and his sons.

Long story short, she finally got some counseling. Turns out she had been sexually abused as a young girl by cousins. Sex for her was never pleasurable. She had never spoken with anyone about her suffering. When she realized what had happened to her and how she could move beyond it, she reached out to her former husband. The process took seven years, but they eventually reconciled and now their marriage is stronger than ever. When they got some counseling together before resurrecting their marriage, the counselor told them how lucky they were to have stayed close enough to leave open the possibility of reconciliation. Too many couples give up too early and move on too quickly. On the other hand, a decision to divorce may be the only solution. One woman I know used to say, "My kids aren't from a broken home. I had to divorce him to fix our home." Never easy discernments.

Spiritual direction would be a help to many as they live the demanding vocation of married life. I don't know whoever got people to think that celibate priesthood is a more difficult or demanding call. Listening to married couples makes me realize how relatively easy my life is in many ways compared to those who struggle to maintain a loving relationship with a spouse and deal with children, especially teenagers!

Another group who could greatly enjoy spiritual direction and retreats are the elderly. (One "old" Jesuit once told me, "Don't call us elders. Bullshit! I'm a veteran of the long campaign!") I once had the privilege of directing a sister of St. Joseph on her annual eight-day retreat at a Jesuit retreat house. When she began the retreat, she was very hurt, sad, and upset. After sixty-three years of teaching small children, she was being sent to the Motherhouse to "stuff envelopes and wait to die." She was feeling sorry for herself, angry at her superiors, and really very distant from God. "I've loved Jesus all my life and he has left me high and dry!" She began praying. She came back the next day and told me she'd been out walking. The area was near water, and there were many boats in the waters near the retreat house. She had spent a lot of time gazing at an old beat-up rowboat. "I felt just like that boat," she remarked. "All used up and thrown aside." That image was sticking with her. I suggested she contemplate the great catch of fish in Luke 5 and Peter walking on water. Not much happened for a day or two. She couldn't imagine herself in those gospel scenes. She was a bit stuck in her sadness and depression over the forced retirement she was facing.

I was struck by the sister's image of the worn-out rowboat. I asked her if she could imagine setting out on the waters with God. The next day she returned surprisingly super-energized and enthusiastic. She had gone out and sat near the rowboat, and imagined Jesus passing by and suggesting she set out to sea. Then Jesus asked her, "What kind of boat do you want?" She spent the day imagining the two of them going and buying a boat. As I'm listening, I'm amazed at all that's happened to her in twenty-four hours. She's smiling and happy. This little eighty-three-year-old sister is beaming with joy, after having been so dejected and upset. "Jesus said I could have any boat I wanted. We walked around everywhere looking at boats. Can you believe it? He said I could have any one I wanted! And he got me one. The one I wanted!" Many beautiful sailboats graced the nearby marinas, and I thought she'd probably picked one of those. When I asked, "What kind of boat did you get?" she smiled with such great joy and happiness, and spoke with such heartfelt conviction, "I got a yacht!"

Such great consolation is often a gift of these retreats. The sister spent the last couple of days realizing all the new possibilities of her relatively lighter work schedule at the Motherhouse. "Just think. I won't have to be grading papers every night! I may even have time to read a novel!" On that retreat, God had touched her and helped her see her life anew.

The last night of the retreat, I had to run out to the mall and get some toothpaste or something. I was walking by one of those cart kiosks they have in the wide hallways of malls. The kiosk was filled with little knick-knacks of bronze, things made of some bronze alloy: books, hats, butterflies, figurines of children, leprechauns. They could serve as paperweights or decorations. They all were heavy and solid, with green felt cloth on the bottom. And there it was: a little bronze yacht. It was about the size of a golf ball and cost ten bucks. I bought it. The next day, our final session, the sister came in all grateful for the retreat and more willing and ready to move to the Motherhouse and her new assignment. As she thanked me for the retreat and was readying to leave, I said I'd found something for her that I thought God would want her to have. And I gave her the little bronze yacht. Her eyes filled with tears. You'd have thought I'd given her some great gift, not just a little, cheap knickknack.

Several years later, I met the provincial of her order. Her eyes lit up when she heard my name. "Are you the Rick Malloy who directed Sister Mary [not her real name] on retreat a few years ago?" Surprised, I said I was. "She still has that little bronze yacht you gave her. Thanks so much for that retreat. It did so much for her." I said it wasn't really me. And the wise Sister Provincial smiled and said, "Yes. We both know God is really the director on retreats."

God is the director of these retreats. Spiritual directors are just coaches. We get to listen and watch and see what God is doing in people's lives. I often suggest to people that they look for a symbol of the retreat, something that will quickly remind them of this time and what they experienced.

There was a laywoman who made an eight-day retreat. She was facing many challenges and difficulties in her life. It was summer, and she spent a lot of time watching a spider build a huge web. Each day, she'd notice more and more how the web grew and caught insects. Her life felt just like that web: Everything was clawing at her and she couldn't break free. Until the last day of the retreat. She felt a newfound sense of freedom. She realized that she could try a number of strategies to confront some of her life challenges and had choices she could make to free her from some oppressive realities. She left our last session smiling and hopeful. Later on, she came by and shyly knocked on my door. "I had to tell you. The spider web is gone!" The night before there had been a spectacular thunderstorm. The web had dissolved. For her, that web was the symbol of the retreat.

These retreats form us into persons who can be servants of Christ's mission. God's will is clear: that the kingdom come. A reign of peace and prosperity, joy and justice, hope and healing, faith and freedom, life and love, as we pray in the preface for the feast of Christ the King. Pius XI inaugurated the Feast of Christ the King as a way of calling the church to stand against the idolatries of fascism and Nazism. These retreats exist within the community's call to form a world of peace and justice for all.

As a spiritual director, I have great trust and faith that something will happen on the retreat. No one can predict what will happen, which makes it all so fascinating. But I've never seen or heard of a silent retreat where nothing happened. To give ourselves over to serious silence and concentrated prayer reorients, changes, modifies, and reinforces what we desire and what God desires for us. Something's happening, God's doing something when you find yourself wanting something different from what you wanted before. Or wanting more deeply and ardently something you've already chosen. Or being able to make a choice you hadn't expected to entertain. Or something completely surprising.

One of the most startling experiences of "retreat" I've had was with a student on spring break. This guy had already made a few retreats with campus ministry during his undergrad years and really liked the silent retreat weekends. So he came to me and asked if he could do something during a spring vacation before his graduation. I suggested we try a few days of the Exercises in daily life. He would pray one hour a day and come and chat with me every other day. To tell the truth, I've found that students can rarely stick with the Exercises in their daily routines. Too much busyness and the hectic nature of student life crowd out a desire for daily prayer. But this young man stuck with it for the eight days we'd agreed upon. The last day, he comes in and says how grateful he was for this last chance here at school to engage in prayer and spiritual direction. He added that he'd realized more deeply all he'd received while an undergrad. And then he said, "And one thing really surprised me these past few days. I never told you, but my sophomore year me and my roommate, a good friend, we had a real falling out." In short, the grace of this "spring break retreat in daily life" was that this guy reached out and reconciled with his old friend. They hadn't spoken for two years, but a few months later they graduated in a very different space. Grace of the retreat.

The most often repeated phrase in the Bible is "Be not afraid." On retreats we hear loud and clear that *God loves us*. Five- and eight-day retreats give us the space, silence, and chance to revel in that truth of our relationship with God. That primordial relationship relates us to everything else. Remember what Pope Francis says over and over again in his encyclical *Laudato Si'*: "Everything is interconnected."

What do we hope for from engaging in Spiritual Exercises? I hope we can become like those wonderful people in South Carolina who forgave the killer of their loved ones. In Charleston, South Carolina, in June 2015, a deeply disturbed racist, twenty-one-year-old Dylann Roof, sat in a prayer meeting in Emanuel African Methodist Episcopal Church for over an hour before brutally murdering nine African American people, among them the church's pastor and State Senator Clementa C. Pinckney. Roof, a seemingly stone-cold killer, was hoping to ignite a race war. I sat amazed watching CNN a day after the massacre as Roof was shown listening to family member after family member of those persons he had murdered. Each one of those African Americans, through their tears and agony, found it in their hearts to offer Roof forgiveness. That's grace. That's the power of the gospel, calling for reconciliation with our sworn enemies, hopefully challenging and changing hearts and minds sickened by the sin and disease of racism.

On these retreats we pray. What is prayer? Prayer opens us up to grace, the ability to do what we could not do before; retreats are times to discover what it is we can do that we couldn't imagine doing before. Prayer is simply paying attention to God, something that is not so simple in our times. There are many ways to pray, but all transformative prayer gets us into relation with God. Prayer is getting to know your deepest, truest self and how that true you relates to the mystery of God. Prayer is work. As Tom Hanks barks at the female baseball players in *A League of Their Own*, "Baseball is hard. If it wasn't, everyone would be playing." Prayer is much more like walking on water like Peter, or even better, it is like floating on your back and allowing the current to take you where it will. On these retreats, we place ourselves before God and await God's response.

Ignatius was a genius in many ways, but most of all when he taught directees to use their imagination in prayer. Imagination is the pictures in our heads that become words in our minds, feelings in our hearts, meaning in our lives, and actions in our world. Imagination is both personal and social. Transformation of ourselves, our relationships, and our world begins and is carried out in our personal and communal imagination. Retreats put us in touch with the deep currents running in our imaginations. And on these retreats, much more than we can imagine and hope can occur, changing us and our world.

CHAPTER 5

Spiritual Direction and Retreats as Meaning-Making Adventures

Our problem now is that we seriously doubt that there is any vital reality to the spiritual world, so we hear no life-changing voices—true even for many who go to church, temple, or mosque. For postmodern people, the universe is not inherently enchanted, as it was for the ancients. We have to do all the enchanting ourselves. This leaves us alone, confused, doubtful. There is no meaning already in place for our discovery and enjoyment. We have to create all meaning by ourselves, and most do not seem to succeed very well. This is the burden of living in our heady and lonely time, when we think it is all up to us.
—Richard Rohr, *Falling Upward*

Mimesis sutures the real to the really made up—and no society exists otherwise.
—Michael Taussig, *Mimesis and Alterity*

On day three, I decided that a power outage would make a great spiritual practice. Never mind giving up meat or booze for Lent. For a taste of real self-denial, just turn off the power for a while and see if phrases like "the power of God" and "the light of Christ" sound any different to you.
—Pastor Barbara Taylor, *An Altar in the World*

There are no hard and fast rules on retreats or in the spiritual life. Directing people in a multicultural, interreligious world means being aware that most people today have not been recipients of intact cultures. Years ago, when I was studying cultural anthropology, I had an extended discussion with a Jesuit philosopher who specializes in the philosophy of religion. My world was a little rocked as I realized more and more the cultural diversity and relativity of the various thousands of tribes and peoples throughout history, and that their ideas of God, the spiritual, namely, the what and who transcending empirical reality, so drastically differ one from another. I believe in the Roman Catholic tradition, but if I'd been born in Iran or Iraq, I'd most likely be a Muslim. Wondering what all these various readings of reality and deeply held beliefs meant for the truth value of the various and serious religious claims, I asked him, "It just seems that it's all made up. Is there any way to adjudicate between all these ways of being and believing?" His reply was enlightening. "Sure it's all made up. But what isn't?" Profound. His words "But what isn't?" helped me appreciate that all readings of reality, even those that assume science is universal, trans-cultural, and trans-historical, are based on accepted first assumptions. Science itself assumes truth is replicable, that the simplest explanation is the best (Occam's Razor), and that all truth claims can be falsified (the principle of falsification). But much of what really matters in life cannot be known scientifically. You, as one person, cannot live and experiment by having fifty twenty-five-year marriages, and then pick the one you want.

We live in a time when we are more aware than were the ancients of competing and conflicting ways of understanding God and ultimate matters. We must sit in silence and see what happens. We need to let the upheaval of our times quiet down. We need to discipline our minds and hearts to turn away from the endlessly flickering and chattering screens. We need to learn to listen to the "sound of sheer silence," as did Elijah (1 Kgs 19:12). Matthew Fox observes:

> Perhaps the poorest-kept secret of our times is that Western civilization finds itself in a mighty upheaval. . . . We live . . . in one of those periods "that visit mankind between millennia, between the death and birth of the gods, when there is nothing to steer by but sex, stoicism and the stars." A culture is the world (or the worlds) one lives in and the collapse of that world, with a basic shifting of the powers that support it, constitutes a cultural crisis.[1]

---

1. Matthew Fox, *On Becoming a Musical Mystical Bear* (Paramus, NJ: Paulist Press, 1972), xxvii. Fox quotes the character Freddy Thorne in John Updike's novel *Couples* (1968).

Fox made that observation back in the 1970s, long before cable television's thousands of channels; long before the Internet; long before the iPhone; long before the dawn of the cyber age's pseudo-realities. The monks of the twelfth and thirteenth centuries saw their power wane as commerce and people moved to the cities. By the end of the twentieth century, the global migrations of billions of people from rural to urban settings were well under way.[2] In the twenty-first century, the vast majority of people will live physically in urban environments. The crucial shift in our times, though, is the shift of consciousness to the environs of cyberspace, the lands and worlds of the vast new communicative technologies wherein "we live and move and have our being" (Acts 17:28). If it's not on Facebook, does it really happen? If it doesn't get tweeted, does it really exist? And who knows what Instagram means?

In reviewing Elizabeth Drescher's book on the growing numbers of "Nones," those who profess no religious affiliation, now some 25 percent of Americans, Thomas McGovern writes:

> Nones are not interested in being "re-captured," going back through a narrow gate. When asked if they are looking for a new religion that would be right for them, 88 percent said, Thanks, but no thanks. Yet, "Becoming None does not erase or overwrite whatever came before it, whether that includes elements of cultural identity, spiritual practices, moral values, or re-configured personal relationships. . . . Nones shape spiritualities that alternately draw a boundary and bridge their religious past and present."[3]

For many years, young adults would tell me, "You know, Fr. Rick, I went to twelve years of Catholic school. I had Catholicism shoved down my throat." I'd gently respond, "Well, it didn't get shoved very far!" Many young adults had tenuous and sporadic relationships with their families' religious traditions. Many families are less the weekly Mass or church

---

2. "Today, 54 per cent of the world's population lives in urban areas, a proportion that is expected to increase to 66 per cent by 2050. Projections show that urbanization combined with the overall growth of the world's population could add another 2.5 billion people to urban populations by 2050, with close to 90 percent of the increase concentrated in Asia and Africa, according to a new United Nations report launched today." See http://www.un.org.

3. Thomas V. McGovern, "Nones Beyond the Numbers," review of Elizabeth Drescher's *Choosing Our Religion: The Spiritual Lives of America's Nones*, in *America*, September 12, 2016, 37.

goers of the 1950s.[4] Among Catholics, the shocking and sickening revelations of priest sex abuse of minors in 2002 caused many parents to be
much less likely to force their children and teens to take boring CCD
classes or undergo irrelevant confirmation programs.

One inspiring and enlightening young man I've had the privilege of
accompanying a bit on his journey is Michael Goonan, a deeply thoughtful and intelligent searcher. He didn't fully accept the traditions of his
elders, nor did he totally reject the search for a spirituality that fits him
and his friends. A year after he graduated from the University of Scranton with a master's degree, he sent me this reflection (lightly edited for
this book) on his spiritual journey. In it, Goonan captures a lot of young
adults' experience with spiritual direction.

The Benefits of Spiritual Direction

Those who knew me during my days in Scranton would be unlikely
to identify me as a pious person. While I was baptized and confirmed in the Catholic Church, I have always "questioned all the
answers," as Crosby, Stills, and Nash would say. I have, however,
always tried to be open-minded to the spiritual aspects of human
existence. And I must say, throughout my six years at Scranton as a
Bachelor's student in Philosophy and Master's student in Secondary
Education, the Jesuits on campus—particularly University Chaplain Fr. Rick Malloy—have been extraordinarily good to me.

I ended up in the Cura Personalis dormitory by accident freshman
year when my roommate, whom I had met at orientation, signed up
for it. At the time I was, generously speaking, an agnostic. I did not
find, however, that my RA or dorm mates were annoying or preachy
toward me in any way. Everybody involved seemed to embody the
"culture of encounter" that Pope Francis now speaks to the importance of so frequently. In the spirit of reciprocity, I decided to take
part in the Examen from time to time with my RA. It was the most
beneficial form of prayer I had ever learned, and while I still didn't
know what I believed in, it was enough to leave the door open a
crack for me to keep considering the merits of faith.

Over the next few years, I participated in several retreats at Chapman Lake, but often half-heartedly and as an excuse to be in nature.

---

4. See Robert D. Putnam, *American Grace: How Religion Unites and Divides Us*
(New York: Simon & Schuster, 2010).

I more deeply explored other forms of philosophy and spirituality such as Buddhism, Taoism, and Hinduism. I always remained
"spiritual but not religious," but practicing mindfulness meditation
opened me up to the church in a way that I had previously been
closed [to]. During my senior year, a period of much fruitful explo-
ration marked by many bumps in the road, I had a dream. I was
walking down the commons and saw some kind of Catholic ritual
being performed, and a priest mentioned that it was available every
week from university ministries. Lots of people were very happily
taking part (not in the somber, serious way that I had come to expect
from Catholics) and I was basically mocking the whole thing: calling people sheep, saying it's meaningless, etc. I then walked down to
the library and went to the bathroom, and while I was in there I was
suddenly levitated about eight feet off the ground and spun around
at all different angles. I then came crashing down to the floor, totally
humbled, and woke up.

After this dream, I had the strong sense that I had long been
missing something about the faith I had been raised with. Fr. Rick
met with me and recommended that I take part in that year's silent
retreat. I had been intrigued by the idea of silent retreats from my
explorations of Buddhism, so I decided to give it a try. It was only
a three-day retreat, but it really opened my eyes in a profound way.
I had an amazing spiritual director who respected who and where I
was, and who recommended spiritual reading that has turned out
to be very relevant and nourishing: Anthony De Mello and Jesuit
Pierre Teilhard de Chardin.

For a variety of reasons I drifted away from the spiritual life in
many ways over the next couple of years while I was completing my
Master's program. I again took part in the three-day silent retreat
during my second year as a Master's student. Again, it was extremely
nourishing. So much so that I ended up signing up for the five-day
silent retreat, which was quite regrettably cancelled due to a snow
storm. This led me, however, to seek out Fr. Rick for spiritual direction once more. I wanted to truly give Christian practice a chance,
particularly focusing on the Spiritual Exercises. It was senior week,
and I was busy with family in town preparing for my Master's graduation. Still, it felt very important to pray and reflect at this time,
particularly in a way that honored the Jesuit tradition. I participated
in a "retreat in the real world," where I would take an hour a day

for prayer and reflection, and then meet with Fr. Rick to discuss what happened during that hour. I don't think I'll ever be able to fully express how grateful I am for those experiences praying over scripture, meditating on the life of Christ, and just allowing God the space to work in my life. During this time I was introduced to the work of Fr. Greg Boyle, an amazing person who has been working with gang members in Los Angeles since the 1980s. I was also introduced to Richard Rohr, an incredible contemplative ecumenical Franciscan, and Matthew Fox, a former Dominican priest and profound thinker in the realm of spirituality and ecology rooted in "deep ecumenism."

What do all these inspirational figures have in common? They have no doubt had wonderful spiritual directors. They have experienced the benefits of opening up to mystery in silence. They have prayed and meditated over scripture in a way that goes far beyond simply reading an instructional manual. I have been humbled to discover that the Catholic Church, with all its faults, really has throughout history been fertile soil for extremely profound spiritual and mystical insights, and the Jesuits in particular have found a unique way to channel that into real, tangible service in the world.

I just moved to the Czech Republic about a week ago. I'll be teaching second grade here at an international school this year. I spent much of the last year or so living and working in the Netherlands, New Zealand, and Australia as well. I'll probably never stop being a "seeker." That's who I'm called to be. But silence, meditation, and prayer—and dare I say, God's presence—have been indispensable "rocks" on the journey. I am very grateful that the Jesuits run the English speaking church here, and look forward to deepening the seeds of faith that were sown during my days seeking in Scranton. "Catholic" means "universal," and the truest wisdom is universal. No matter who you are or what you believe or don't believe—I heartily recommend taking part in the university's silent retreats and personal spiritual direction. Listen for how God is working in your life.

"Now, listening is not as easy as you might think it is. Why? Because we're always listening from fixed concepts, fixed positions, fixed prejudices. Listening does not mean swallowing, though. That's gullibility. 'Oh, he says it, so I take it.' When Jesus taught the good news, I think he was attacked not only because what he taught was good but also because

it was new. We hate anything new. I hated anything new. Give me the old stuff. We don't like the new. It's too disturbing. Too liberating. So, the ability to listen: Buddha formulated it beautifully. He said, 'Monks and scholars must accept my words not out of respect, but must analyze them, the way a goldsmith analyzes gold: by cutting, scraping, rubbing, melting.' You must not accept my words out of respect, but should analyze them by cutting—the way the goldsmith analyzes gold, see? Cutting, scraping, rubbing, melting."
—Anthony de Mello, S.J., *Rediscovering Life*

Directing Millennials

Having lived for over a decade in first-year dorms on college campuses, I realize how extensively and deeply different my experience of young adulthood was from that of today's young adults. The revolutions of omnipresent cell phones, helicopter parents, and change at warp speed make my world of the 1970s and 1980s seem like a horse-and-buggy era.

Many campus ministers and others who work with young adults ponder why twenty-somethings often seem estranged from church and religious practices. Why does Charlie Sheen's way of life appeal more to the average undergraduate male than Jesus'? Why do the ways of the Kardashians touch the souls of some young women more than the lives of Dorothy Day or Mother Teresa? In a world where "New Jersey's finest," Snooki and The Situation, rule, how can we get the millennial generation interested in God and the practices of faith?

In February 2010, the Pew Research Center reported that members of the millennial generation (born after 1982) are much less likely to participate in or be affiliated with any particular faith than were members of Generation X (born between 1965 and 1982) or the baby boomers (born between 1946 and 1964) at their age. Fully one-quarter of today's young adults do not profess allegiance to any faith tradition. Compared with their elders, current twenty-somethings find religion to be a much less needed or important part of their lives. While 56 percent of the Greatest Generation (born before 1928) attends religious services weekly or more often, only 18 percent of millennials do so. Forty-four percent of the Silent Generation (1928–1945) and 36 percent of boomers attend church weekly.[5]

---

5. Pew Research Center, "Millennials: Confident. Connected. Open to Change," http://www.pewsocialtrends.org, February 2010), chap. 9, 85 ff.

Judging by these findings, it seems many of the young are ignoring God and church. Sexual scandals involving the clergy and a plethora of other reasons are given for the alienation of young adults from the church. But maybe young adults want to find a way to connect to God. The problem may be that they are just afraid and confused.

"Look Jesus in the Eye"

Amy Hoegen, an experienced pastoral minister, was leading a prayer exercise with students at the University of Scranton. She encouraged the group to pray, imagining Jesus right in front of them. "Look Jesus in the eye," she counseled.

After the prayer time, Amy invited the members of the group to share their experiences. One student described what happened but studiously ignored the "looking Jesus in the eye" part. Amy asked, "What was it like to look at Jesus face to face?"

"Oh, I couldn't do it."

"Why not?" Amy gently asked.

Pause. Shuffle of feet. A glance at the floor. "Oh, I'm not worthy."

What gave all of us on the campus ministry team pause was the next detail. Amy went on: "And I'm looking around the group, and all the heads were nodding. They all felt that way."

A few weeks later, Rob, a stellar freshman from St. Joe's Prep in Philadelphia who went on several retreats this year and is involved in many service projects, is hanging around the office late one night.

"Yo, Father Rick, how come before we get Communion we say that thing about not being worthy? That really sucks. Man, so many kids today don't feel worthy of anything. Why reinforce it right when we're receiving Communion?" (Such questions always seem to emerge late at night!)

Is the problem that young adults feel unworthy of approaching God? Are the young afraid of getting too close to Jesus? If those are the issues, then pastoral approaches and responses need subtle to radical revision. We need to be asking why the young adults feel so unworthy and what we can do to assure them that they are loved by God and worthy of God's attention. We need to communicate that they can be in relationship with Jesus and the saints, no matter how good or bad they think themselves to be.

Spiritual directors of young adults need to realize that the issues of those born 1982–2000 (millennials) are very different from those of us born 1946–1964 (baby boomers) and even 1964–1982 (Gen Xers).

Reading the currents of contemporary culture and societal permutations are prerequisites for accompanying people on their spiritual journeys.

Cathy Seymour, who has been a campus minister at the University of Scranton for more than thirty years, connects the feelings of unworthiness before God with feelings of lack of worth in relationships in general. "What our students most want is to be closer to Jesus," she says, "but they do not feel worthy. Just like what they most want is real, lasting relationships with another person, but instead they 'hook up,' thinking they are not worthy, or 'who would want me with all my flaws?' They either feel they can't be perfect, so 'Why try?' or 'What if I make a mistake and choose the wrong person?' The 'how do you know' question always comes up on the senior retreat. Unfortunately, drinking helps them forget their faults and overlook others' as well, and hooking up precludes being real and the work they perceive it would take to become better, more desirable and committed to another."

Guidance for the Over-Parented

The paradox is that this is the generation whose parents took the 1970s mantra "I'm OK, You're OK" to the max. They made sure every kid got a trophy, and that every report card affirmed their child. Today's college students react in horror to descriptions of the corporal punishments my generation received. But most of us were not abused. In the 1960s it was called parenting. Lori Gottlieb, a therapist, reports that the over-parenting today's young adults received (from what she calls "helicopter parents") gave them an inflated sense of self and self-worth.[6]

I suspect many twenty-year-olds are aware that they cannot live up to the false assurances of competency and character proffered by their well-intentioned parents. When these young people slow down, quiet their thoughts, stop texting, and open themselves to God, they realize their intrinsically flawed humanity.

This is the classic dynamic of the First Week of the Spiritual Exercises of St. Ignatius. When we meet the living and true God, our obvious distance from God's holiness becomes readily apparent. The difference is that in the Exercises the confrontation with our sinfulness follows an experience of God's love and grace. But in the lived reality of the twenty-

---

6. Lori Gottlieb, "How to Land Your Kid in Therapy: Why the Obsession with Our Kids' Happiness May Be Dooming Them to Unhappy Adulthoods. A Therapist and Mother Reports," *The Atlantic*, July/August 2011.

first century, Catholic young adults who are tangentially connected to God and church too often realize their sin and sinfulness without having had that foundational experience of God's transformative love.

The trick is to get these young adults to understand the truth in "I'm not OK; you're not OK; but that's OK." The good news is that we are not perfect. We are not even all above average. Yet the consolation is that we do not have to be perfect. Only Charlie Sheen has "tiger blood" and "Adonis DNA," and look where it gets him—into rehab. The truth is that God loves us precisely as "unworthy" sinners. God comes to save us from our sinfulness. God transforms us into persons who can believe, hope, and love.

What can we do to foster among the young the twin dynamics of overcoming fear of God and dealing with a sense of one's unworthiness and sin? In spiritual direction we can do much to help millennials make meaning.

First, challenge young adults more directly and deeply. Their coaches yell at them, while we teachers "ask" them to do the assigned readings. If professors could be as tough as coaches, we would see less grade inflation and more real engagement with the life of the mind. Meeting challenges will foster in young adults a sense of self-worth. Making things too easy leaves them, on some subtle level, knowing "they are missing the mark," which is the literal meaning of *hamartia*, the Greek word for sin in the New Testament. Thomas Merton wrote in *Love and Living*:

> The function of a university is, then, first of all to help students discover themselves: to recognize themselves, and to identify who it is that chooses. . . . To put it in even more outrageous terms, the function of a university is to help men and women save their souls and, in so doing, to save their society: from what? From the hell of meaninglessness, of obsession, of complex artifice, of systematic lying, of criminal evasions and neglects, of self-destructive futilities. . . .[7]

How drastically Catholic universities would change if we took seriously, and made our students take seriously, the task of saving one's own soul and in doing so saving our society. Priests and other campus ministers need to challenge students to meet the demands of discipleship.

Second, preach a God who loves us and who not only calls us but also demands that we love one another. Many college students today know infi-

---

7. Thomas Merton, *Love and Learning* (New York: Harcourt, 1965–1979), 4.

nitely more about how to work a cell phone than they do about simple, bedrock theological concepts. Too many think of God as the all-powerful punisher, condemning them for what they are doing "wrong." They have too little sense of a God who rejoices in who they are and in the good they do. Ours is a God who gives us the graces, that is, the power to truly love one another.

Real love always includes the hard work of naming our sinfulness, asking for and receiving forgiveness. Amy Hoegen and Brian Pelcin, both married campus ministers, were teaching a class for the Jesuit Jack Begley's marriage course. Amy noted how deeply struck the class was by the section she and Brian presented on forgiveness and redemption. The idea that we can be forgiven and redeemed was not only attractive to the students; it came as news. Most in the class did not seem to know that God's forgiveness is part of the deal.

Third, teach transformation. Many students think their sexual hooking up and wild partying have stamped them for life. They need to learn what the anonymous author of the spiritual classic *The Cloud of Unknowing* realized: "It is not what you are, nor what you have been, that God sees with his all-merciful eyes, but what you desire to be" (chap. 75). Our young need to know that God can change and transform us, no matter what we have done in the past. St. Athanasius said, "For the Son of God became man so that we might become God." God does not transform "perfect" people. God loves, saves, and transforms sinners.[8]

Religion as Recipe Book, Not Rule Book

Real religion, the practices of spirituality that routinely and concretely connect us to God and others, can foster a sense of the grace of God transforming us daily. Young adults need to be led to experience religion more as a recipe book than a rule book. Authentic religion frees and empowers. Young adults (and most thinking, responsible adults of any age) will ignore religious institutions and ministers who make religion an oppressive force. Unchristian dynamics make too many fear God instead of run toward God. And real religion, the deep and transformative binding of things together, does not always happen inside a church building.

---

8. Much of this material on ministry with youth appears in my article, "You Are Worthy: Helping Young Adults See Themselves as God Sees Them," in *America* (February 2012), http://www.americamagazine.org.

There was a student I met during the years I lived and worked at Holy Name Parish in Camden, New Jersey, and taught at St. Joe's University in Philadelphia. After graduation, this fellow's 2.0 grade point average from the business school was not making his phone ring with job offers. He was feeling really bad about himself: no job, nothing to do, and drinking too much, as he had during his college days. He called up Dan Joyce, S.J., who was also working at Holy Name. Father Joyce got him working in Sr. Helen Cole's Camden summer camp. This graduate, it turned out, was a genius at working with kids. All the Camden kids wanted to hang with him. All the campers wanted to ride with him. Everyone loved him, and he found his true self in that inner-city setting.

This young man finally found his worth. That he missed all the opportunities for service while he was at St. Joe's amazes me. But it is in meeting the challenges beyond our comfort zones and growing that we feel our intrinsic worthiness. The multitude of service venues on Jesuit campuses force college students to look themselves in the mirror and see who they actually are. The lesson is that "in serving one another we are set free," as Sean Connery's King Arthur tells Richard Gere's Lancelot in the film *First Knight*.

Students need to meet the challenge of experiencing Jesus in service to others and in prayer. In doing so, they will discover their true worth. The Christ of God has come among us and remains present in the Eucharist to transform us in the reconfiguration of ourselves and our world. Go ahead. Look Jesus in the eye. In that divine gaze, we will see not condemnation but the reflection of our deepest, truest self.

Young people, people in mid-life "confusion" if not crisis, and people in their golden years all now live in a world where the signposts guiding us where to go to find and create our deepest, truest selves have all been knocked down. Our choosing a religious tradition, and usually some current or particular manifestation of that tradition, will always be a risky choice these days, for we know there are other paths, and it is difficult to honestly argue or assume that our way is true, perfect, better, or more "right" or "correct," in comparison to other ways. We have to do the hard work of prayer and the spiritual life to come to a comfort with, and a trust in, the way we've chosen, a way that is no longer bolstered by fundamentalist assertions that my religion is "right" and all others are "wrong."

We are like the first disciples of Jesus who needed to be courageous and open to something new God was doing in the world. I've written elsewhere that the question is not, "What Would Jesus Do?" The question is, "What would Peter and Mary Magdalene and Paul do?" In our times we are much more like those three than we are like our Irish grandparents (great-grandparents?) in Philadelphia or Brooklyn, where Monsignor Murphy had all the answers and forcefully said you needed no questions. The church taught it, you believed it, and that ended it. Some Catholics today still try and live that way. Despite much good the Catholic TV network EWTN does, it leans, in my humble opinion, too much toward an unquestioning and triumphalist faith. Some people freely choose to put on blinders and not question anything. But for most young adults I know, doubt is part of the deal. We live with an awareness that our religious readings and choices are ones of multiple options. For me, doubt is inherently an accompaniment of faith, or if not full doubt, at least wonder. The opposite of faith is not doubt. The opposite of faith is certainty.

We need to read the religious and spiritual realities of our times. We need, through spiritual direction in many venues and arenas, to call all to the great adventure of faith, and living the implications of faith in all the gospel's splendor and challenge. Back in 1973, Pedro Arrupe turned the Society of Jesus in a new direction, aimed at new horizons, and called on our institutions, especially our schools, to engage in new ways of thinking about ourselves and our work.[9] The mantra "Men and Women for and with others" was born.

For years, mostly young people, many from Jesuit schools across the United States and Canada, have joined together for the Ignatian Family Teach-In for Justice. The Teach-In grew out of Fr. Roy Bourgeois' calling people to protest at the gates of Fort Benning, Georgia, in memory of the six Jesuits killed in El Salvador in November of 1989. After many years of journeying to Georgia, the Teach-In moved to Washington, DC. In November 2016, I was in the huge hotel in Arlington, Virginia, as, once again, over two thousand teens and young adults came to hear speakers like Jesuit Greg Boyle, Sr. Norma Pimentel, Sojourner's Lisa Sharon Harper, and a host of others giving workshops on multiple issues of justice. The prayer service on the first night remembers Jesuits who have died when standing up for justice since the 1970s. Over fifty Jesuits have been martyred. This year the candlelight prayer service adds the names of the religious sisters who have been slain.

---

9. Pedro Arrupe, S.J., "Men for Others" (Valencia, Spain, 1973), http://onlineministries.creighton.edu.

It's amazing: two thousand kids sitting in a humungous ballroom, lit by the glow of small hand-held candles as the names are read, one candle for each martyr. If you had told Jesuits in 1989 that by the 2010s we had to get two thousand college and high school–age students from all over to come to Washington, DC, for a weekend learning about faith and justice, engaging in day and night workshops, and staying to lobby Congress on Monday (and get them to pay their way!), we would have said, "You're nuts. No way we could make that happen!" But it has happened and it does happen. Men and women for and with others isn't just a slogan, it's a gospel-inspired movement. What will come of these annual meetings? What will God do in the future with the minds and hearts touched by the Ignatian Family Teach-In? Only God knows. It will be wonderful to watch where it all goes.[10]

---

10. Ignatian Family Teach-In for Justice, https://ignatiansolidarity.net/iftj.

CHAPTER 6

Lessons to Learn in Spiritual Direction

I think the most important question facing humanity is, "Is the universe a friendly place?" This is the first and most basic question all people must answer for themselves.

—Attributed to Albert Einstein

What is to give light must endure burning.
—Viktor Frankl, *Man's Search for Meaning*

There is only one absolutely necessary starting point! The experience of powerlessness is where we all must begin.
—Richard Rohr, *Breathing under Water*

There is a price to pay. Honesty with the real must be maintained through thick and thin. Honesty with the real may lead us where we did not expect to be led. We must be faithful to that reality, regardless of where it may lead.
—Jon Sobrino, S.J., *Spirituality of Liberation*

What are the lessons a person can expect to address and learn in spiritual direction? Here, in no particular order, are some of the central lessons that many spiritual writers highlight in one way or another. Thomas Merton, Richard Rohr, Ronald Rolheiser, Anne Lamott, and others inform my imagination about these lessons. Those who have graced me with their service as spiritual directors in various ways have tried to impart these lessons to me, or better said, have tried to direct me toward where I could learn these lessons myself. To be honest, I know a lot more about the need to learn these lessons than I do about how to actually appropriate these truths and live by them. Many of us are perpetual beginners! So it goes—and that's OK.

The Power of Silence

"Silent" and "listen" are spelled with the same letters. In our times of constant noise and chatter, endless tweets and blaring headlines, 24/7/365 news, the ability to turn it all off and listen is a skill and ability much more admired than practiced. So many of us sincerely try to discipline ourselves and engage in silent prayer and meditation. I have tried to consistently give myself over to Centering Prayer, but often realize I'm too busy to find twenty minutes to sit, do nothing, and enter into the silence. Even when I do find the place and time to sit for twenty minutes, I spend much of the time fending off distractions and the miasma of thoughts that run around in my head.

Silence is a welcome space wherein we settle down, relax, and just be. Silence allows us to get beneath the endless symposium going on in our heads. To allow the quiet to well up and calm the turbulent tumbling never-ending stream of consciousness gives us pause and allows us to consider and choose from a different level of our being. Spending time in silence allows us to listen better to what's going on deep inside us. When we know on a deeper level what's going on inside us, we are able to better choose how to respond, rather than react.

I remember one time when the noise took over my life for almost an entire day (unfortunately not a onetime occurrence!). I'd gotten snookered into taking a wedding for a Jesuit who all of a sudden couldn't fulfill his commitment to the couple. I met with the bride and groom—nice young adults, friendly, and very much desiring a Catholic Church wedding. The one thing the bride was kind of set on was the couple's writing their own vows. I explained the power of using the traditional vow choices, how all the couples there would have said those same words, how the wedding is not the couple's wedding ("my" wedding) but a celebration of the entire community, and how the vows were a strong symbol of that reality. She seemed to accept that explanation.

So the evening of the wedding rehearsal comes. It's being held in Philadelphia, and everyone is late on this hot, muggy, summer Friday. Traffic is a mess, and rain showers screw up everything in the city. We get started late at a big church downtown, where they have a lot of weddings, and I've got to get us through the rehearsal quickly, because there's another rehearsal on the heels of ours.

When we come to the part where we rehearse the vows, the bride announces they have the words memorized. I usually feed the words to the couple at a voice level only they can hear. But no need to practice that now. They have memorized the vows. I don't think much about what she's just said and wheel along, scooting us out of there in time for the next crowd that's waiting in the back of the church.

Later that evening, it hits me. They are going to use a vow formula they've written themselves. What am I going to do? Is the sacrament valid if they don't say one of the approved vow forms? Will I have to stop them? Or let it go and do the vows later in the sacristy after Mass? Why the hell did I ever agree to take this wedding? Why are brides so obsessed with having the wedding "their" way? On and on my thoughts raced from 9:00 p.m. to around 3:00 a.m. Sleep was a long time coming. The next morning, all I could think about was this damn mess with the vows. By noon, I was at the church for the 2:00 p.m. wedding. Over and over, I kept running the scenario of a vows fiasco in my head. Once, I was a spectator at a non-Catholic wedding where the bride and groom had written their own vows. Among other things, they vowed to never get "pissy" with one another. What would this couple say with "their vows"? What would I do? Was it a sacrament if they didn't pronounce the approved vows? Would I have to take them aside after the ceremony and make them "do it right"?

The moment in the ceremony arrived for the vows. And they pronounced the simple, Catholic vows, word for word! Perfectly memorized and said with loving, heartfelt conviction, eyes tearing, and evidencing deep commitment. Nothing problematic at all!

I had wasted almost a day of my life ruminating, wondering, imagining, agonizing over something that not only wasn't ever going to happen; it was something that wasn't even close to happening. I had been utterly consumed with unrealistic fears. My stomach was in knots, and I had lost sleep over something that was only a figment of my untrusting imagination. Why?

Most likely because I allowed the worry and fear about a wedding couple not saying the vow formula correctly crowd out any of my awareness of, or trust in, God. What if I had sat down into the silence for twenty minutes and just breathed that Friday evening? I might have gotten to sleep before 3:00 a.m. I might have realized there was no way to know what the couple would do or say. I might have relaxed and become aware that God is God and I'm not God. Silence may have saved me from my own often present insanity. Fr. Martin Laird, O.S.A., notes:

This insight is behind Mark Twain's famous line. "I'm an old man now and have had a great many problems. Most of them never happened." A lot goes on in our heads that is quite worthless. . . . Contemplation is a way out of the great self-centered psychodrama. When interior silence is discovered, compassion flows. If we deepen our inner silence, our compassion for others is deepened. We cannot pass through the doorways of silence without becoming part of God's embrace of all humanity in its suffering and joy. Silence is living, dynamic and liberating.[1]

Silence teaches us that God is with us. Silence allows us to become aware of ways to respond to people and situations, rather than react.

Once I lost a book, Richard Rohr's *Falling Upward*. I knew I'd had it on a Thursday. Then I went away to another university on Friday and returned Monday. On Tuesday, I began looking for the book. I really mark up books, so the idea of getting another copy was out of the question; I needed to find that book with all my margin notes. I knew exactly the last time I had it: Thursday's meeting at the university. I went to the office, but it wasn't there. So I started reviewing the Thursday, trying to remember everywhere I'd gone. I looked and looked for the book, and grew more and more frustrated. Rohr's book had to be somewhere in my office or room. No book. I continued searching for several days, looking everywhere and often in the same places. Finally, I just sat and tried to allow myself to sink into silence. Again, I played the whole Thursday of ten days or so ago. All of a sudden, I remembered I had gone out to dinner with one of the deans that day, to a Thai restaurant near the university. But I hadn't taken the book to the restaurant. I'm sure I would have put the book somewhere. Yet the more I thought about the restaurant, the more I wondered. Finally, I went to the restaurant, figuring it was a long shot, but what the heck did I have to lose? I explained to the nice Thai woman that I might have left a small, brown book in the restaurant over a week ago. Had they seen any such book? She said "No," but looked under the counter anyway. She stood up and said, "Sorry, no book." Then suddenly, a Thai gentleman who had been listening to our conversation said, "Wait." He walked over to a coat rack and began rummaging through hats, scarfs, and gloves on the top of the rack. Moments later he takes

---

1. Martin Laird, O.S.A., *Into the Silent Land: A Guide to the Practice of Christian Contemplation* (New York: Oxford University Press, 2006), 115–16.

out two books and a folder. I had left all three there. And the folder was important! I wouldn't have wanted to lose that. It was the calming down in silence that allowed me to imagine and relive the Thursday, with all the possibilities of where the book could possibly be. And I hadn't even realized I'd lost the other book and the folder!

Shirley Turkle is an expert who studies how communication technology is changing the way we relate to others and ourselves as computer and TV screens and cell phones colonize our times and lives.[2] She points out that especially young people today never have time to be alone. The omnipresent cell phone is a literal addiction. Kids cannot not respond to a cell phone's ping. Many even sleep with the phone and must wake up at the slightest tweet or Facebook post. The danger here is that without time to be alone, young people cannot learn who they are.

We all need time in quiet and silence to reflect. It amazes me how shocked people are at the idea that one can enter into a silent retreat. The almost universal response to the invitation to make a silent retreat is, "Me? A silent retreat? I could never do that!" When did we become so unaccustomed to spending time alone, in solitude, with only ourselves for company? And in our solitude, in the quiet silence, we will discover who we are: persons in relation.

Keep It Relational

The essence of our faith is the truth that God is relational. Our God is three persons in relation. In the silence of our hearts we discover who we are, who others are, and who God is. And all of these discoveries are in the relations that constitute us as persons and communities. The relationships are carried and communicated in our stories. God is the relationships of the Trinity.

> We can say that the history of humankind should be the external projection of the intimate story of God: God lives in himself a mysterious, inexpressible, and most profound covenant whereby the Father is everything for the Son, the Son is everything for the Father, and this, in the Spirit, is the glory, the fullness of God. God wishes to spread forth the project that is himself; hence God constitutes in the Son a people that can be his as the Son belongs to the Father, a people to whom he can say, "You are mine and I am yours." The covenant is the very Trinity projected into history.[3]

---

2. Shirley Turkle, "Ted Talk: Connected but Alone," https://www.ted.com.

3. Carlo Maria Martini, *A Prophetic Voice in the City: Meditations on the Prophet Jeremiah* (Collegeville, MN: Liturgical Press, 1997), 36.

Comparisons Are Odious

So much of who we think we are or should be is condemned by the mischief of comparison. Henry Haske, S.J., used to say, "Comparisons are odious." Comparisons smell. They are offensive. Prayer and spiritual practice are not competitions. They are not zero-sum games. If someone is a "better pray-er" than I (whatever "better" could mean in this context), so what? Someone is always better than I am at anything. And I'm probably better than others at a few things. So what? In God's eyes, we are all loved as we are, for what and how we are. The freedom of the daughters and sons of God (Gal 5:1) graces us with the awareness that we are all given gifts, abilities, and missions, and that all ought to be placed at the service of God's kingdom. If someone is a better teacher, or preacher, or more "successful" academic or pastor, or whatever, than I, so what?

We all have bad days. Sometimes we have good days. A Jesuit friend of mine asked how long it took me to get my doctorate. I said seven years. He said, "It took me three!" Some grace overtook me, and instead of trying to justify why it took me longer, I just replied, "OK. You win." He paused, smiled, and realized how dumb his initial comparison was. He laughed and said, "Good answer." There is no one on earth who cares how long it took either me or him to get a degree. And if you measure your self-worth by money earned, or academic honors gained, just remember: B.S. is bullshit! M.S. means "more of the same." Ph.D. is "piled higher and deeper." There was a famous baseball player who said, "You're only as good as yesterday's box score." We can take justifiable pride laced with gratitude at our successes and achievements, but we should always realize that whatever we are able to do is because God and others make it possible. We can never take full credit for our success, and only rarely is failure all due solely to our shortcomings alone. We don't do what we do because we love God; we are able to do what we do because God loves us.

Better to always strive to praise and celebrate others' achievements and successes. And to live with the humble realization that whatever you do, there are at least 7 billion people who will never hear or care about it. My buddy Brother Dennis Ryan, S.J., once told me, "Look. You don't have to live your life as if the world is anxiously awaiting your autobiography." You don't need to know why Dennis was telling me that, but he was a wise man.

Address and Battle Addictions

One of the most serious obstacles to living a life centered in God, a life filled with joy, serenity, and love, is our all-too-human tendency to become addicted to persons, processes, and things that give us temporary satisfaction, but soon leave us empty and wanting more of what never seems to satisfy. Dr. Gerald G. May, in his classic work *Addiction and Grace*, defines addiction as "any compulsive, habitual behavior that limits human freedom." According to Dr. May, addictions force and compel us to waste our lives and give our hearts to things that are not our true desires or wants. "Addiction is a *state* of "compulsion, obsession, or preoccupation that enslaves a person's will and desire."[4] God gives grace, the power to do what we could not do before, and helps us be free from all that limits our ability to choose what makes us happy and healthy and holy and free.

Everyone experiences addiction to large or small degrees. Certainly, hard drugs like heroin, alcohol, and tobacco have robbed people of their ability to avoid these substances. But there are myriad other ways in which we lose the ability to "take it or leave it." From mild addictions like an inability to turn off a re-run of M*A*S*H to a compulsive need to always be right, to more life-disturbing addictions to anger, overworking, sex or gambling, to life-threatening addictions like eating disorders, alcoholism, prescription pills, and hard drugs, virtually everyone finds it difficult to always live and choose what is objectively right and good. St. Paul describes this universal human experience of wanting to do what is good, but finding ourselves, almost against our will, choosing what is to our own detriment. "I do not understand my own actions. For I do not do what I want, but I do the very thing I hate. . . . For I do not do the good I want, but the evil I do not want is what I do" (cf. Rom 7:14–25; NRSV).

For St. Paul, flesh (Greek *sarx*) and spirit (Greek *pneuma*) are two realms, or as we might say today, "zones," in which we place or find ourselves. When I'm in a good zone, I'm up early, I've gotten coffee and prayed, and I'm at the computer writing my quota for the day. When I'm not in the zone, I've hit the snooze button seven times (because I got caught by Netflix, binge watching just one more episode of *House of Cards* after already having watched two . . . or three). And I'm tired, running late, and there's no more time to set aside for writing before the work day begins. More seriously, when addicts feel good, their desire "to pick up and use" isn't too strong; they're in the zone of *pneuma* or Spirit. When the craving for the drug high is too strong to resist, they find themselves falling into the zone of *sarx*, or the flesh.

---

4. Both quotes are from Gerald G. May, *Addiction and Grace* (San Francisco: Harper and Row, 1988), 24.

In his Spiritual Exercises, St. Ignatius presupposes we will move between experiences of consolation and desolation. By consolation, he means when interiorly, in our thoughts, moods, and feelings, we feel excited, enthused, on fire, up, ready to do whatever for God and God's people. Desolation is the opposite. We feel, "Ugh! What's the use?" What used to give us joy and peace is now weighing us down. We avoid praying, and when we try to pray we're constantly distracted. The soup kitchen we so enjoyed working in last week holds no attraction. We are filled with thoughts of old resentments and angers. St. Ignatius considers the tugging and pulling, the going back and forth, of desolation and consolation—the normal condition of people who are serious about their life with God. I suspect that addictions are ways we fall into of avoiding the challenge of dealing with consolation and desolation. We find the numbing of addiction easier than the work of dealing with how God is active in our lives.

Addictions are ways we develop to avoid the depth of our spiritual experiences. They keep us on a treadmill, like a hamster in a cage, constantly running on that wheel, getting nowhere. The more we are captured and enslaved by our addictions, the more difficult it is to become aware of the grace and power of God in our lives. Extremely serious addictions seem to be confronted and dealt with by the genius of the Twelve Step programs, a way of life rooted in the wisdom tradition of the Spiritual Exercises of St. Ignatius.[5]

Many are familiar with the famous Serenity Prayer, popular with Twelve Step programs, but few are aware of the full version of the prayer. The words are usually credited to theologian Reinhold Niebuhr.

> God grant me the serenity
> To accept the things I cannot change,
> Courage to change the things I can,
> And the Wisdom to know the difference.

---

5. Robert Fitzgerald, S.J., describes that meeting of Fr. Ed Dowling and Bill Wilson, http://www.barefootsworld.net. Jim Manney writes on Loyola Press's Ignatian Spirituality website: "Fr. Edward Dowling, SJ, a friend of Bill Wilson, the founder of Alcoholics Anonymous, was convinced that the *Spiritual Exercises* influenced the Twelve Steps of AA (which guide many other twelve-step programs). Bill Wilson said he had never heard of Ignatius or the *Exercises*. He said he sat down at his kitchen table one day and wrote out the Twelve Steps in about twenty minutes. To this Fr. Dowling said, 'If it were twenty weeks, you could suspect improvisation. Twenty minutes sounds reasonable under the theory of divine help.'" See http://www.ignatianspirituality.com.

Living one day at a time,
Enjoying one moment at a time,
Accepting hardships as the pathway to peace,
Taking as He did this sinful world
As it is, not as I would have it.

Trusting that He will makes all things right
If I surrender to His Will
So that I may be reasonably happy in this life
And supremely happy with Him
Forever and ever in the next. Amen.

The good news in all this is that addictions are often avenues to the reality of God in our lives. After his extensive experience battling his own addictions, and helping people as a psychiatrist, Dr. May concludes, "I believe that humankind's ongoing struggle with addiction is preparing the ground of perfect love."[6] May analyzes addiction as our contemporary form of idolatry. Our addictions come between us and God. We sacrifice our energy, attention, power, and ability to love to these idols that promise us security and peace but never deliver those realities. And God, perfect love, places in our minds, heart, and souls the desires to be free of our idols/addictions. May writes:

Our freedom is not complete. Working against it is the powerful force of addiction. Psychologically, addiction *uses up* desire. It is like a psychic malignancy, sucking our life energy into specific obsessions and compulsions, leaving less and less energy available for people and other pursuits. Spiritually, addiction is a deep-seated form of idolatry. The objects of our addictions become our false gods. These are what we worship, what we attend to, where we give our time and energy, *instead of love*. Addiction, then, displaces and supplants God's love as the source and object of our deepest, truest desire. It is . . . a "counterfeit of religious presence."[7]

In freeing us from addictions, God rescues us from our blindness, slavery, and the misery caused by addictive tendencies and dynamics. God places us, or helps us place ourselves, in the zones and realms of freedom, serenity, hope, and love. The power of faith gives us the sense that there is

---

6. May, *Addiction and Grace*, 12.
7. Ibid., 13.

a way out of our self-created cages and self-constructed prisons. May has found in looking at his own struggles with addictions, in looking at the freedom of Jesus and the Saints, in looking at the truly free and holy people he has met, that "true freedom from attachment is characterized by great unbounded love, endless creative energy, and deep pervasive joy. . . . Compassion takes the place of attachment. Where there was the agony of clinging to and grasping one's own attachments, freedom brings a feeling of unity with the pain of the world."[8]

My own battles with addictions are fewer than many others', but like those of many others. I smoked cigarettes from when I was twelve to when I was thirty-five. Luckily, I wasn't a heavy smoker, usually five or six cigarettes a day. After ordination, while working in Camden, New Jersey, we got very involved in the battle against drug dealing that was the scourge of our North Camden community, literally enslaving some of our young men, often the best and the brightest. I also was smoking a half to three quarters of a pack a day. As I reflected more and more on the contradiction between our laboring to eradicate the drug dealing and drug use in our culture, I began to feel the need to try to quit smoking.

George Will writes for the *Washington Post*. He is a conservative, and I often disagree with his analysis of political and social matters. But he is very intelligent, and his writings on baseball are excellent. His rare reflections on being the father of a son with Down syndrome are heart-warming and challenging to many people in our culture who see such persons as less than human. Will once wrote an article showing that more people were killed by cigarettes each year than in auto accidents and that it was a scandal that the government subsidized big tobacco companies. When I had to agree with George Will, I sensed there was something going on to which I had to pay attention.

I had never tried to quit, always thinking I wasn't smoking that much. Finally, I decided to try. And I chanced upon an extremely helpful way to go about quitting: I told the entire Holy Name grade school that I was going to quit smoking. On Pentecost 1990, I had my last cigarette. Giving up smoking wasn't easy, but it wasn't as hard as it would have been to disappoint all those little kids. The second graders badgered me for a year: "Have you started smoking again?" In many ways, I see my quitting smoking as a great grace, something I was given the power to do that I

---

8. Ibid., 144–45.

had not been able to do before. Freedom from addictions necessitates our asking for the graces we need to be free and happy.

The hardest attachments to hold lovingly and loosely are those we have to people for whom we care deeply. Friendships that resemble more the taking of hostages than free and easy relationships; romantic entanglements from drunken hook-ups to swept-off-one's-feet infatuations, to dangerous liaisons like adultery—all such attachments are more addictive than loving, more destructive than edifying, building up.[9] And even wonderful, loving relationships will call us to realize we can't hold on to them tightly, but we must hold them loosely and freely.

Addictions are often our futile efforts to control life. But life cannot be "controlled." One inescapable truth of life is that we will seem to lose to death some of those we love. The rock band Coldplay's Chris Martin wrote a song, "Fix You," to comfort his then-wife Gwyneth Paltrow when her father died. It's a beautiful ballad expressing the longing and love we have for those who suffer. "Lights will guide you home / And ignite your bones / And I will try to fix you." Compassion streams through this song like sunbeams piercing the clouds of a dissipating storm. The light of love, the reality of God, guides us home and ignites our bones as we are stunned by the grief and pain of death. But those who love us will be with us through it all. They will hold us and will try and "fix" us.

Let the False Self, the Ego, Dissolve and Die

After his baptism, Jesus went off into the desert where he was tempted by the devil. What were the temptations? All three begin with the devil's scoffing, "If." "*If* you are the Son of God ..." Jesus is tempted to satisfy superficial hungers, to grasp for power and glory, and finally, to test God by throwing himself off the parapet of the Temple. "*If*" he is the Son of God, God will protect and save him. Jesus fends off all three temptations with quotes from the Hebrew Scriptures: "One does not live by bread alone"; "You shall worship and serve God alone"; "You shall not put the Lord your God to the test" (Lk 4:1–12). It's as if someone fended off the temptations to riches by saying, "Blessed are the poor"; the temptation to step hard on others on the way to the top by saying, "You shall love your neighbor as yourself"; the temptation to place our trust in things rather than God by saying, "Our Father, who art in heaven ..." Jesus had to learn to discern the

---

9. See Richard G. Malloy, S.J., "Just Sex: Giving Young Adults What They Truly Want" (January 2008), http://bustedhalo.com.

difference between a possible false self and the true self that he discovered in his relationship with the God whom he experienced in prayer as Father, or better translated, "Abba/Papa/Daddy."

We, too, must labor in prayer and spiritual direction to discard the false self, which is rooted in ego and built up by the familial and cultural expectations that lead us away from our true self, our deepest, truest self known by the God-inspired desires emerging from our hearts.

Richard Rohr provides a powerful meditation on Thomas Merton's sense of the true and false self.[10] Rohr finds in *New Seeds of Contemplation* Merton's description of the false self: "Everyone of us is shadowed by an illusory person: a false self. This is the man [or woman] that I want myself to be but who cannot exist, because God does not know anything about him [or her]." Merton goes on: "My false and private self is the one who wants to exist outside the reach of God's will and God's love—outside of reality and outside of life. And such a self cannot help but be an illusion." He argues that all sin starts from the false assumption that the false self is real and is the bedrock reality of our lives. This false self, built on and enmeshed in my egocentric desires, burns up my life in pursuit of power, pleasure, and possessions. Merton consoles and challenges: "You have been given something so much better: 'For all belongs to you, you belong to Christ, and Christ belongs to God' (1 Corinthians 3:22–23). Your true self is already home free! To know that is to be 'saved.'"[11]

Rohr elucidates the meaning of the unreality of the false self. It's all about who we think we are and ought to be independent of, and separate from, God.

> The false self is so fragile. It's inherently insecure because it's almost entirely a creation of the mind, a social construct. It doesn't exist except in the world of perception—which is where we live most of our lives—instead of in God's Eternal Now. When you die, what dies is your false self because it never really existed to begin with. It simply lives in your thoughts and projections. It's what you want

10. Richard Rohr, "The Illusion of the Autonomous Self" (August 3, 2016) and "In God's Eyes" (August 4, 2016), https://cac.org.

11. Thomas Merton, *New Seeds of Contemplation* (Boulder, CO: Shambhala Publishers, 2003), 36–37, quoted by Rohr in "The Illusion of the Autonomous Self" and "In God's Eyes" (see previous note).

yourself to be and what you want others to think you are. It's very tied up with status symbols and reputation.[12]

The true self is who and what we really are in our relationship with God, in our rootedness in our humanity unto divinity. Our true self connects to everyone and everything. Thomas Merton experienced this in the famous moment at Fourth and Walnut Streets in downtown Louisville, Kentucky. He writes:

> I was suddenly overwhelmed with the realization that I loved all these people, that they were mine and I theirs, that we could not be alien to one another even though we were total strangers. It was like waking from a dream of separateness. . . . If only they could all see themselves as they really are. If only we could see each other that way all the time. There would be no more war, no more hatred, no more cruelty, no more greed.[13]

Rohr comments that this peculiar gift, the contemplative mind, relinquishes unreal thoughts about itself and is grace/gifted to see and enjoy with "a much broader, deeper and more compassionate set of eyes." To consciously live out of the true self and avoid dwelling in the illusions and often painful un-freedoms of our false self is one of the signature benefits of the practices of contemplative prayer and spiritual direction.

In a humorous song with an infectious beat ("We Are the People Our Parents Warned Us About"), Jimmy Buffett sings, "I was supposed to be a Jesuit priest or a Naval Academy grad / That was the way my parents perceived me / Those were the plans that they had / Though I couldn't fit the part too dumb or too smart / Ain't it funny how it all turns out / I guess we are the people our parents warned us about." Buffett and his pals know they are made to make music, even if they do not live up to the expectations of others. The magnificent meditation on this theme is the late, great Robin Williams's *Dead Poets Society*, a profound portrayal of a gifted teacher trying to open up the hearts and minds of young men. The truth the film teaches is that the living out of the true self makes for life and love; being forced to kneel at the altar of the false self leads literally to death. One gifted student desperately wants to try acting, but his

---

12. Rohr, "The Illusion of the Autonomous Self" and "In God's Eyes."

13. Thomas Merton, *Conjectures of a Guilty Bystander* (New York: Image Books, 1968), 156–58, also quoted in Rohr (see note 12 above).

father will not allow him to follow his dreams of becoming an actor. The consequences are devastating.

God wants us to follow our dreams. God's will is absolutely clear: that the kingdom come. Our part in fostering the kingdom is communicated to us in our deepest, truest desires. We often have a hard time receiving the messages of our hearts; the ego gets in the way. The ego is like the shell around the seed. The shell must disintegrate so that the seed can grow, transform, and bloom. If a caterpillar never trusts its desire to enter the cocoon, the butterfly will never emerge. So it is with the spiritual life. We need to allow the disintegration of our false self so that our true self can emerge and fly.

Tony De Mello's wonderful story exemplifying this theme bears repeating: There was a farmer who found an eagle's egg. He placed it with the hen's eggs and pretty soon a little eaglet emerged and began to hang out with all the little chicks. Like the chicks, the eaglet learned to cluck and peck for food on the ground. This went on for a few years, and he grew into an amazing-looking eagle, clucking and plucking along with the chickens. One day, all in the barnyard looked up and saw a magnificent eagle soaring high above the plains, heading for the mountains. The eagle who thought he was a chicken asked, "What's that?" The chickens replied, "That's an eagle, the most magnificent bird of all. Eagles soar all around the world. But we are just chickens. We're stuck here in the barnyard." And the sad end of the tale is that the eagle spent his life as a chicken, for that is what he had been taught he was.

Let the false self dissolve, and strive to discover and choose to be your deepest, truest self. Know you are not a chicken. You are an eagle. So, soar!

Get in Contact with Reality

God is reality. The more we get in contact with reality, the more we get in touch with God, and then we and our realities, both personal and social, become transformed. This is why the Superior General of the Society of Jesus, Peter Hans Kolvenbach, S.J., urged Jesuit schools to get students in touch with the "gritty reality of our world."[14] Too many live in the unreal

---

14. Peter Hans Kolvenbach, "The Service of Faith and the Promotion of Justice in American Higher Education" (October 2000), http://onlineministries.creighton.edu. "We must therefore raise our Jesuit educational standard to 'educate the whole person of solidarity for the real world.' Solidarity is learned through 'contact' rather than through

worlds of screens, images, and protected/constructed environments. Our gyms are full; our parks are empty. We spend millions of dollars in bars consuming alcohol to ease the stress of our lives, while our churches and meditation centers are vacant. We watch endless hours of sports on TV in the comfort of our La-Z-Boys, no longer enjoying real ballparks because they can't provide endless instant replays. Leaving our comfort zones by coming into contact with people different from ourselves by, for example, serving at a soup kitchen or visiting a nursing home, can help us realize the constrictions of our comfortable world. God exists in the encounter with the other. Only associating with those just like ourselves results in myopic awareness of our world and a blindness about ourselves and the social structures in which we exist.

Pain Is Inevitable, Suffering Is Optional

Sr. Linda Stilling, S.S.N.D., who taught me much in my early years as a priest at Holy Name Church in Camden, once said: "You stay with people in their pain until you begin to feel the joy of resurrection."

There is no one who escapes the pain of the world. Our parents are not perfect, and we spend years coming to terms with our feelings about our mothers and fathers. We soon learn in life we don't always get what we want. Some children die way too young, and some people are seemingly doomed to live lives seriously circumscribed by illness and disability. Some deep loss and tragic heartache mark most lives. The radical possibility for those who live in Christ is an awareness that our pain, our losses, the inevitable effects of the human condition, can be experienced as Godward movements.

We suffer when we assume we are to live pain-free lives. But we can respond to our pain with hope and trust in a God for whom all things work for our good (cf. Rom 8:28). Pain is real, but the lesson to be learned

---

'concepts,' as the Holy Father said recently at an Italian university conference. When the heart is touched by direct experience, the mind may be challenged to change. Personal involvement with innocent suffering, with the injustice others suffer, is the catalyst for solidarity which then gives rise to intellectual inquiry and moral reflection. Students, in the course of their formation, must *let the gritty reality of this world into their lives, so they can learn to feel it, think about it critically, respond to its suffering and engage it constructively.* They should learn to perceive, think, judge, choose and act for the rights of others, especially the disadvantaged and the oppressed. Campus ministry does much to foment such intelligent, responsible and active compassion, compassion that deserves the name solidarity."

is in how to respond to pain. The grace of acceptance gives us the power to endure pain without suffering. The wisdom of Anthony de Mello, S.J., tells us:

> Because what is suffering? Suffering is, "I don't want this! I want to get rid of it! I want to run away from it! How long is this going to last?" But as soon as you can accept something (by accept, I say approve of it, or enjoy it, or even be resigned to it), you can just be with it, not run away from it. If you can rid yourself of it, fine, but as long as it's there, you're peaceful with it. That's when you get the experience of pain without suffering. Now if you can do this, it brings you great depth as a spiritual person.[15]

God Really Exists and Operates In Our Lives

This is the crucial challenge for those of us who live in a secular age and culture. Not just believing, but believing in a way that radically informs and contours our choices and commitments in life, is the real demonstration of the reality of faith in God. Charles Taylor in his seminal *A Secular Age* cogently asks, "Why was it virtually impossible not to believe in God in, say, 1500 in our Western society, while in 2000 many of us find this not only easy, but even inescapable?"[16]

Many of us in twenty-first-century America are stone-cold materialists. We find it really difficult to wholeheartedly and whole mindedly accept that nonmaterial realities are "really real" (although science reveals that most atoms are composed of empty space! And quantum weirdness is a real challenge to simple materialism). Still, too many of us think that if something cannot be in some way touched, physically experienced, physically felt, it cannot be actual and real. And those who do accept the reality of the nonmaterial can really spin off into "Woohoo land." When someone is convinced that Elvis comes and sings to them every night, or the squirrel outside is the presence of their long lost uncle, or that Jesus is telling them to play these lottery numbers and do I have fifty bucks to lend them to put on those digits, we can retreat into our certainty of the reality and intelligibility of the material universe and leave the nonmaterial to the wackos. And the bloodthirsty actions of religious groups like

---

15. Anthony de Mello, S.J., quoted in J. Francis Stroud, S.J., *Praying Naked: The Spirituality of Anthony de Mello, S.J.* (New York: Doubleday, 2005), 141.

16. Charles Taylor, *A Secular Age* (Cambridge, MA: Harvard University Press, 2007), 25.

ISIS, or of those who murder abortion providers "in the name of Jesus," repulse many thinking persons.

But, what if there are true and trustworthy nonmaterial realities to which we can have access? What if the transcendental God, angels, and saints—those who have died and gone before us—what if these are real? What if we can cogently and sanely appreciate and interact with such realities? Spiritual direction can be a key process by which we can separate the wheat of real religious and spiritual experience (the two are not mutually exclusive!) from the chaff of wacky assertions about figments of overheated imaginations.

While many people in today's world no longer firmly assert or hold that religious realities exist or matter, it is difficult to argue that religion and God will disappear anytime soon. Karen Armstrong notes:

> Even though so many people are antagonistic to faith, the world is currently experiencing a religious revival. Contrary to the confident secularist predictions of the mid-twentieth century, religion is not going to disappear. . . . There is a long religious tradition that stressed the importance of recognizing the limits of our knowledge, of silence, of reticence, and awe. . . . It is not easy to talk about what we call "God," and the religious quest often begins with the deliberate dissolution of ordinary thought patterns.[17]

Although, as Armstrong notes, there are still robust faith traditions, Taylor analyzes and articulates the present state of affairs for many of us in the secularized sectors of our global community. He points out that there has been a great decline in belief and practice among societies that a short time ago saw great percentages of the population practicing their faith. In 2015, Pew Research reported the "Nones," those with no religious affiliation, have increased from 16 percent to 23 percent of the population in the United States.[18] They have left or not joined church communities for a plethora of reasons. Many "Nones," 49 percent, report lack of belief and/or a sense that science trumps and negates their trust in the truth or meaning claims of religions. Eighteen percent report they are simply unsure about their religious beliefs or lack thereof.[19]

---

17. Karen Armstrong, *The Case for God* (New York: Anchor Books, 2009), xvii.

18. Michael Lipka, "A Closer Look at America's Rapidly Growing Religious 'Nones,'" Pew Research Center (May 13, 2015), http://www.pewresearch.org.

19. Michael Lipka, "Why America's 'Nones' Left Religion Behind," Pew Research Center (August 24, 2016), http://www.pewresearch.org.

Taylor recognizes that the enchanted world of 1500 has given way to where we are today. "We no longer live in societies in which the widespread sense can be maintained that faith in God is central to the ordered life we (partially) enjoy.... In a pluralist world ... [o]verall fragmentation has increased."[20] This results in religion's retreat from the public square. People like Karen Armstrong who are aware of religion's presence and power need to also recognize that in much of the first world, religion is considered little more than a fairy tale. For much of the rest of the world, religion is central to communities' sense of reality and self. The conflicts have been playing out for the past two decades, if not the past two centuries. From 9/11 back to the demise of the Ottoman Empire, the secular West and "the rest" have been on a religious trajectory of conflict rather than communion. The challenge for the twenty-first century is to reduce the conflict and foster the constitution of communion across and between such divides.

To rebuild our sense of God as active and real in our lives and in the lives of our communities, cultures, and societies, we need to both update our notions and images of God, and understand theologically who and what a reality revealed in the light of faith actually is, and how such reality operates. "For surely I know the plans I have for you, says the Lord, plans for your welfare and not for harm, to give you a future with hope" (Jer 29:11; NRSV).

Sr. Ilia Delio, O.S.F., a shockingly provocative theologian, argues in *The Emergent Christ* that Christianity is based on disturbing and amazing beliefs: "One is that God became a human person" and, two, "that a dead man is raised to new life."[21] The whole teaching on resurrection is startling. Jesus' resurrection is not the revivification of a corpse. It's a "new mode of physicality, an event for which there is no precedent and of which there remains as yet no subsequent example."[22] Christian faith teaches that our ultimate destination is life with God forever in heaven. "Heaven is not the place of non-materiality. It begins in this earthly life.... Heaven is the reality of God's indwelling presence.... [E]arth is not the training ground for heaven. It is rather the very place where heaven unfolds.... Heaven, therefore, is not another world, but this world clearly seen."[23] Matthew Fox preaches the same insight. "Thus the sense of 'eternal life' is

---

20. Taylor, *A Secular Age*, 531.
21. Ilia Delio, O.S.F., *The Emergent Christ: Exploring the Meaning of Catholic in an Evolutionary Universe* (Maryknoll, NY: Orbis Books, 2011), 72.
22. Ibid., 73.
23. Ibid., 75.

intimate converse with God, a relationship already begun. 'Eternal life' is what we all have now (John 17:2)."[24] Anglican bishop and scholar N. T. Wright makes a similar point: "There is no sense that this 'age to come' is 'eternal' in the sense of being outside space, time, and matter. Far from it. The ancient Jews were creational monotheists. For them God's great future purpose was not to rescue people out of this world, but to rescue the world itself, people included, from its present state of corruption and decay."[25]

According to Jesuit David Stanley, the resurrection means that the kingdom of God has arrived on this earth. New Testament authors intimate that heaven means we join Jesus in his reign over the "course of world history. Heaven . . . is not a kind of perennial 'Old Folks Home.' It is not simply a place of retirement and celestial repose for senior citizens of the kingdom of God. . . . Heaven consists in the active participation in the glorified Christ's direction of history."[26] Richard Rohr teaches that we access heaven here and now, or we don't at all. "Jesus said, 'I am life.' He came to promise us that this mystery called life and love is eternal, but that we have to enter into it *now*. It's heaven all the way to heaven."[27]

What does it mean to live consciously every day aware and impacted by this heavenly destiny that is ours? It means to take seriously that God exists and loves us, and that our relationship with God effects and affects all we are and do, all we can be and desire to become. God's love and real relationship to us means that eternal life doesn't begin the day we die. Eternal life begins the moment we are baptized. Confirmation and Eucharist reaffirm and impart grace, the power of God's love, to help us live as those destined to be resurrected, saved, brought to the culmination of our existence in heaven. St. Ignatius starts out the Spiritual Exercises with this primordial truth: "God who loves us, creates us, and wants to share life with us forever. Our love response takes shape in our praise and honor and service of the God of our life."[28]

---

24. Matthew Fox, *On Becoming a Musical Mystical Bear* (Paramus, NJ: Paulist Press, 1972), 56.

25. N. T. Wright, *How God Became King: The Forgotten Story of the Gospels* (New York: HarperOne, 2012), 44–45.

26. David Stanley, S.J., *A Modern Scriptural Approach to the Exercises* (St. Louis, MO: Institute of Jesuit Sources, 1967), 282–84.

27. Richard Rohr, *Everything Belongs: The Gift of Contemplative Prayer,* rev. ed. (New York: Crossroad, 2003), 165.

28. David Fleming, S.J., "Principle and Foundation," in *Draw Me into Your Friendship: A Literal Translation and a Contemporary Reading of the Spiritual Exercises,* #23

To be a believer, to be a person of faith, is to be a person living consciously and actively aware of, and trying to consistently choose out of, the lived sense that one is on a journey to exist for all eternity with God. From this faith understanding flows forth service of others and work for justice, love as the center of our lives, and worship of God as replenishing of grace and impulse for growing in our relationship with the depth of all reality, that is, the love that is God.

"Love is relational," writes Ilia Delio. "Love the potentiality of what can be because relatedness is energy and energy is always renewing itself; hence love is always new. . . . Because this energy is full of potentialities, the Spirit of new life is always creating the future. Hence the fullness of Christ is always on the horizon; the complete unification of all that exists into a unified whole is always before us."[29]

The life of faith takes God, and the transformation of all in Christ through the action of the Holy Spirit in our lives, as truth and promise.

Learn to Float and Live with Ambiguity

Jesuit Thomas Green's books on prayer are some of the clearest and most perceptive on how prayer actually develops in us. He emphasizes how prayer more transforms us than shows us off as great "pray-ers." He provides an image of prayer that calls us to be relaxed and trust in God. He says we need to learn how to float: "It is puzzling to see what a difficult art floating really is—difficult not because it demands much skill but because it demands much letting go. The secret of floating is in learning *not* to do all the things we instinctively want to do. We want to keep ourselves rigid, ready to save ourselves. . . ."[30] Green says we need to choose. Do we want to float or swim? The aim and point of the spiritual life, the life of prayer, is to grow to totally trust God and float. No matter how hard we swim, the tide will take us where it will. Go with the flow.

Richard Rohr ruminates on the relationship between the two halves of life. In the first half, we become good soldiers, following the rules, learning what we have to do to make institutions and organizations function and serve well. But, in the second half of life, we have to discharge our loyal soldier. Now that we know the rules, we need to discern where God may be calling us to bend them. Pope Francis is forcing some in the

---

(St. Louis, MO: Institute of Jesuit Sources, 1996), 26–27.

29. Delio, *The Emergent Christ*, 86–87.

30. Thomas H. Green, S.J., *When the Well Runs Dry: Prayer Beyond the Beginnings* (Notre Dame, IN: Ave Maria Press, 1979), 142 ff. (italics in original).

Catholic Church to realize that God is heard and pleased not so much in the black-and-white ways of rule observation, but more in the gray and murky relationships of truly loving one another. Rohr writes: "Paradoxically, your loyal soldier gives you so much security and validation that you may confuse his voice with the very voice of God. *If this inner critical voice has kept you safe for many years as your inner voice of authority, you may end up not being able to hear the real voice of God.* Please read that sentence again for maximum effect!"[31]

Both Green and Rohr are teaching what good spiritual direction helps us realize and live. God is God. We are not God. No matter how things seem to us, whether we think things should be this way or that, ultimately, we can relax and know that God is God and we don't have to be God. Smile, the universe is user friendly![32] Einstein asked the question, "Is the Universe a Friendly place?" Spiritual direction helps us answer, Yes!

Forgive

There's a great movie, *Dad* (1989). It's the story of a hard-charging, Wall Street type, John Tremont (Ted Danson), whose career took over and kept him far from his family. When his father, Jake Tremont (Jack Lemmon), is ailing, John returns home. He rediscovers the challenge and joy of being a good son, helping his parents in their time of need. At one point, John tries to reconnect with his own son Billy (Ethan Hawke), a child he's neglected. Billy is not really enthused about this long-lost father suddenly being all interested in really talking with him. Billy belligerently says to John, "What advice do you have for me?" And John replies, "Learn to forgive. That's real important."

Ernest Kurtz and Katherine Ketcham tell a story. Former inmates of a Nazi concentration camp meet up. One asks the other, Have you forgiven the Nazis yet? The reply: "I'll never forgive those bastards. I will always hate them." The first gently suggests, "Then they will always have you in prison."[33]

The inability or refusal to forgive is one of the great obstacles to the spiritual life. The old Native American legend of the two wolves applies

---

31. Richard Rohr, *Falling Upward: A Spirituality for the Two Halves of Life* (San Francisco: Jossey-Bass, 2011), 46 (italics in original).

32. See Richard G. Malloy, S.J., *Being on Fire: Top Ten Essentials of Catholic Faith* (Maryknoll, NY: Orbis Books, 2014), 165 ff.

33. Ernest Kurtz and Katherine Ketcham, *The Spirituality of Imperfection: Storytelling and the Journey to Wholeness* (New York: Bantam Books, 1992), 213.

to all of us. An old chief tells a young brave there are two wolves at war within us all, one striving to be loving, the other struggling to keep us at war with ourselves and others. Which one wins, asks the young brave? The one you feed, replies the old chief.[34] As we feed our desires to be loving and peaceful and true, we starve the part of us that wants to give in to anger, resentment, and hate.

Be Kind

The week before I was ordained, I met up with another Jesuit who would be ordained with me. We got to talking, and I asked him if he was ready to hear confessions. He said, "I got the best advice from Hugh Kennedy." Now Hugh was an elderly Jesuit, a legend in the Maryland Province, who had done all kinds of jobs and service over the years. In my time, he seemed to me to be rather quiet and severe. He was the last Jesuit I knew to regularly wear the black Jesuit cassock that most left aside after Vatican II. What would Hugh have to say about confession? "Hugh told me, in confession, just be kind to people." Great advice.

Writer George Saunders gave a remarkable commencement speech in 2013. His message was simple: be kind. He tells a story of a little girl in his school who was teased, and rues that he had not defended her more vigorously. "What I regret most in my life are *failures of kindness*." Saunders reminds the crowd that the people "we remember most fondly" are those who are kindest to us. "It's a little facile, maybe, and certainly hard to implement, but I'd say, as a goal in life, you could do worse than: *Try to be kinder*." It's a little scary that this address received so much attention. Our times and culture are in desperate need of kindness. Saunders says our sickness is selfishness and the antidote is sacrifice of self-centeredness for love. Success isn't worth it if it costs our ability to love and be kind. "Do all the other things, the ambitious things —travel, get rich, get famous, innovate, lead, fall in love, make and lose fortunes, swim naked in wild jungle rivers (after first having it tested for monkey poop)—but as you do, to the extent that you can, *err in the direction of kindness*."[35]

---

34. See under Cherokee Legends "Two Wolves," http://www.firstpeople.us.

35. Quotes are from Joel Lovell, "George Saunders's Advice to Graduates" (July 31, 2013), https://6thfloor.blogs.nytimes.com.

CHAPTER 7

Prayer over the Long Haul: Holding Fire in Our Hands

If you can sit and do nothing, then you can do virtually anything.
—Michael Elliston

That prayer is a combat has been said hundreds of times. . . . "Believe me, I think there is nothing which requires more effort than to pray to God. . . . Prayer requires combat to the last breath," says a desert Father.
—Jacques Ellul, *Prayer and Modern Man*

In far more pungent language, Daniel Berrigan once said, "It all comes down to this: whose flesh are you touching and why? Whose flesh are you recoiling from and why? Whose flesh are you burning and why?"
—Barbara Taylor, *An Altar in the World*

In both our more reflective moments and in our more desperate moments, we feel our need for prayer. We cannot sustain ourselves all on our own. We need prayer. But too often we think of this in pious rather than realistic terms. Rarely do we grasp how much prayer is really a question of life and death for us. We need to pray not because God needs us to pray but because if we do not pray, we will never find any steadiness in our lives. Simply put, without prayer we will always be either too full of ourselves or too empty of energy, inflated or depressed. Prayer . . . is meant to do two things for us . . . prayer is meant to connect us to divine energy, even as it makes us aware that this energy is not our own, that it comes from elsewhere, and that we many never identify with it.

—Ronald Rolheiser, *Sacred Fire*

L ittle Johnny was being completely impossible, driving his mother crazy as he kept getting into trouble. Finally, she grabbed him by the arm, led him up the stairs, and put him in his room, telling him he was on a "time out" and that he needed to pray and ask God to help him be a good little boy. Later, Johnny wandered into the kitchen. His mom wasn't as perturbed as earlier. Johnny asked if he was still on "time out." "Did you ask God to help you be a good little boy?" "No," replied Johnny. "I asked God to help you put up with me."

I always say that I stand in awe of parents. The difficult tasks associated daily and over the years with disciplining and raising children seem beyond heroic to me. Johnny's mother probably, and most parents likely, find themselves praying to God for help. We all find ourselves praying when times get difficult, tough, and painful. We wonder if God is there, if God is listening, if God is doing anything.

Many were shocked to hear that Mother Teresa had long and deep doubts about faith, God's existence and power, the efficacy of her prayer. Irreverent and bombastically anti-religious comedian Bill Maher ridiculed her on his TV show, as he held up the September 3, 2007, *Time* magazine cover showing Mother Teresa and the headline "The Secret Life of Mother Teresa: Newly Published Letters Reveal Beloved Icon's 50-Year Crisis of Faith."[1] Maher, a militant atheist and producer of the screed *Religulous*, a mockumentary focusing on the extremes of religious expression, gleefully exclaimed, "See! She agrees with me!" It was fascinating to hear the response of two of his guests that night. Actor Tim Robbins produced the movie *Dead Man Walking*, about the courageous prison ministry of Sr. Helen Prejean, C.S.J. (Sean Penn was nominated for Best Actor and Susan Sarandon won the Best Actress Oscar). Michel Martin is a well-known NPR host and very respected journalist. Both Robbins and Martin vigorously defended now St. Mother Teresa of Calcutta. An observer of the encounter writes:

> He [Bill Maher] thinks having doubts about your religion is the "opposite of faith." But Tim Robbins argued that even *Jesus* had his doubts. And at this point, it was clear to me that not only was Michel Martin the one driving this debate, but she was the surprise star of the show. Maher let out "Wow" after "Wow" as the NPR host made her case for doubts being part of one's faith; she recounted

---

1. Charlie Doherty, "TV Review HBO's *Real Time with Bill Maher*," Episode 515 (August 31, 2007), http://blogcritics.org.

that the Methodist Church founders had their own crisis of faith just like Mother Teresa.[2]

I had a cousin, the daughter of my mother's half-sister, a great gal who taught math at university level. She was nearly forty and had never been married. One day she comes home and announces she's marrying a widower with six kids. Wow, we all thought. Is this a good idea? How's this going to work out? Well, it worked out great. They had a fine marriage. His kids loved her, and Thanksgiving, Christmas, and graduation celebrations at their house on Long Island were filled with laughter, food, and joy. And they had their own bouncing baby boy, Kevin. A great kid, loved by his parents and brothers and sisters and everyone. He grew to be tall and athletic. He had a little bout with epilepsy when he was eleven or twelve, but that seemed to disappear in his early teens. He had a great personality and a wonderful sense of humor. He was a great baseball player. He got a driver's license. In his senior year of high school, Kevin came down to check out St. Joe's U. where I was teaching. He wanted to look the place over. Hoping he'd attend St. Joe's, I wanted him to experience all the school and the city had to offer. We went to 54th and City Line, to "dine" at Larry's "Home of the Belly Filler," a popular Philly cheesesteak place. Kevin, at the time 17 years old, 6'2", 180 lbs., polished off the signature sandwich of the City of Brotherly Shove in about three minutes. I asked how he liked it. Wiping his mouth with about four paper napkins, he wryly joked, "Well, I was really expecting a little more grease."

Kevin ended up at St. John's in Queens where his mother taught. In his sophomore year he was planning on spending the spring semester in Italy. He was excited and ready for the great adventure of being out of the country for the first time. A few nights after Christmas, he crashed at the house of a buddy of his. He went to sleep and never woke up. He had died from a grand mal epileptic seizure. I had never heard of anyone dying from epilepsy. But it happens more than I knew.

Walking into the funeral home for his wake, I had a really hard time looking at him. He looked great, like he was sleeping, as if you could gently shake him and tell him to quit screwing around and get up. But he was dead. And I really began to wrestle with God in the mud pits of faith. This made no sense. Even though I'd seen a lot of death, Kevin's made me question more than other deaths. During my first two years as a priest in Camden, I presided at many funerals of young men who had

---

2. Charlie Doherty, "TV Review."

been ensnared by the drug epidemic during its crack cocaine phase. Some close family had friends who had died. One was a Jesuit brother who had a heart attack at thirty-four. At his wake his sister said to me, "This makes no sense." And I learned a definition of death: that which makes no sense. Kevin's death made no sense to me. He was too young. You don't die of epilepsy. He had his whole life ahead of him.

Like most people who have been around death, I found myself thinking long and hard about God and God's promises when confronted with the hard and painful death of Kevin, with the death of a loved one. Does life and death make any sense? Why do things so seem to contradict God and his promises?

Over several months of mud wrestling with God, it gradually dawned on me that I was looking at Kevin's death in a skewed fashion. I was assuming he would have a great life. But what if he would have suffered greatly? From ALS or cancer? What if he'd messed his life up with drugs? In prayer, it seeped into my consciousness that maybe God knows better for Kevin than I do. Maybe God did something and is doing something with Kevin's life that I cannot understand now.

I've come to the conclusion over the years that prayer is a risk. When we pray, seriously or just "trying it out," sometimes things can happen. Perspectives can shift. Choices can be reevaluated. We can find ourselves being turned upside down and all around by God, or gently, quietly moved to a different place and space within ourselves. Prayer is amazing and mysterious and often hard work. Prayer changes what we desire. Prayer changes how we see things. Graces, gifts from God, the power to do what we could not do before, come in prayer.

Mark Thibodeaux, S.J., in his marvelous introduction to prayer, *Armchair Mystic*, provides a beautiful image of what happens when we pray. Prayer is like rowing out to the middle of a lake. We sit in silence and wait for the graces that lie at the bottom of the lake to float to the surface, freed by our prayer. We have to row over and grab the graces. We need to put them in our boat and carry them back to land. We cannot let them float away.[3]

Ronald Rolheiser shares a Buddhist parable.[4] The Buddha is sitting under a tree. A physically very "in shape" soldier notices how fat the Bud-

---

3. Mark Thibodeaux, S.J., *Armchair Mystic: Easing into Contemplative Prayer* (Cincinnati, OH: St. Anthony Messenger Press, 2001), 96 ff.

4. Ronald Rolheiser, *Sacred Fire: A Vision for a Deeper Human and Christian Maturity* (New York: Image Books, 2014), 217.

dha is. The soldier says, "You look like a pig." The Buddha replies, "You look like God." The surprised soldier says, "Why do you say I look like God?" The Buddha sagely notes that we see what is inside us and project it outward. The Buddha sits all day under a tree and thinks of God, and so sees God in everyone and everything. He says to the soldier, "You must be thinking about things other than God."

Richard Rohr notes that most of us don't see things as they are; we see things as we are.[5] Prayer is the work we do that helps us to see as God sees, to feel as God feels, to want what God wants. Prayer is something we receive, not achieve. A wonderful image of prayer is that of the small plane being refueled while in flight. It has to slow down and connect to the larger tanker plane in order to receive the energy needed to keep flying. If it doesn't connect, it will lose power and crash. But if the plane flies too close to the tanker, it will collide with it and perish in a ball of flame.[6]

God's distance is a gift, and paradoxically, both God's nearness and distance are experienced in prayer over the long haul. If we simply knew who and what God is, and what God wants, we would lose the freedom to choose to respond. Love is always rooted in freedom, and our relationship with God necessitates that God leave us free. Contemplation draws us a little closer to God, but the closer we get the more we realize the distance. "Contemplation is not the pleasant reaction to a celestial sunset, nor is it the perpetual twitter of heavenly birdsong. It is not even an emotion. It is the awareness of God, known and loved at the core of one's being."[7] The awareness of God deep within us is the best of apostolic activity. "The solitary, according to Isaac the Syrian, must first heal his own soul and only then care for the souls of others. Inner life in God is more important than any philosophic or missionary activity."[8] And according to Meister Eckhart, "The noblest attainment in this life is to be silent and let God work and speak within."[9]

---

5. Richard Rohr, *Breathing under Water: Spirituality and the Twelve Steps* (Cincinnati, OH: St. Anthony Messenger Press, 2011), 95.

6. This image comes from Ronald Moore as cited in Ronald Rolheiser, *Sacred Fire*, 172.

7. Carmen Acevedo Butcher, trans., *The Cloud of Unknowing and the Book of Privy Counseling. A New Translation* (Boston: Shambhala, 2009), epigraph.

8. Hilarion Alfeyev, *The Spiritual World of Isaac the Syrian*, Cistercian Studies 175 (Trappist, KY: Cistercian Publications, 2000), 70.

9. Martin Laird, O.S.A., *Into the Silent Land: A Guide to the Practice of Christian Contemplation* (New York: Oxford University Press, 2006), 23.

One of the most fascinating apostles for the long haul is former Jesuit Fr. John Dear, a prophetically dedicated peace activist priest. For decades John has traveled the world and written over two dozen books, all calling our war-weary and strife-stricken world to heed the gospel's constant call for peace. His work for peace flows forth from his graced life of prayer. In his book *Transfiguration*, Dear writes:

> Simply put, prayer is right relationship with God. Although God created us and loves us, we reject God, ignore God, resent God, fear God, pretend God does not exist, and hate God. But the spiritual life of daily meditation and fidelity leads us to friendship with God, even intimacy with God. Prayer is attention to and ongoing development of our individual, communal, and global relationship with God.[10]

Dear knows prayer is not easy. Yet he knows we need to pray and dedicate ourselves to the change prayer works in us:

> Prayer is at once the easiest and most difficult thing we can do. What could be easier than sitting alone with oneself and God in perfect peace and silence? Yet it is precisely this close-up encounter with ourselves and the great unknown that makes prayer so uncomfortable. In prayer we face ourselves as we are, in our poverty and brokenness, alone with our illusions and delusions, helpless before the universe and our inevitable deaths. From our need, we turn to God for help. Real prayer is humiliating. It is like a child sitting in a puddle of mud, calling out for help. Prayer means coming before God as we really are—broken, helpless, powerless, sinful, vulnerable, fragile and weak. But if we dare remain in the truth of our humanity and beg the God of mercy to have mercy on us, inevitably a new spirit of peace and mercy comes over us.[11]

Pastor Barbara Taylor realized the need to connect to brokenness and pain in order to grow. "I had been teaching world religions for several years before I realized how many of them grew out of great suffering."[12] And she realized her need for prayer.

---

10. John Dear, *Transfiguration: A Meditation on Transforming Us and Our World* (New York: Image Books, 2007), 56.

11. Ibid., 71.

12. Barbara Taylor, *An Altar in the World: A Geography of Faith* (New York: HarperOne, 2009), 155.

All of these visits have aided my sense that there are real things I can do, both in my body and my mind, to put myself in the presence of God. God is not obliged to show up, but if God does, then I will be ready. At the same time, I am aware that prayer is more than something that I do. The longer I practice prayer, the more I think it is something that is always happening, like a radio wave that carries music through the air whether I tune into it or not. This is hard to talk about, which is why prayer is a practice and not a discussion topic. The best I can do is tell you how it works for me. Since I am a failure at prayer, I keep an altar in my room. . . . At best, I think of it as a portal that stays open whether I go through it or not.[13]

But even if we are not naturally or easily silent and "prayerful," God can get to us. The portal often opens in ways unpredictable and mysterious. And we end up laying flowers on the altar of death and life. Mary Karr, an accomplished poet and superlative memoirist, shares her journey to faith in evocative and sparkling imagery from daily life. Her life as a mother of a small child and a wife in a marriage troubled by her dangerous drinking led her to attend a talk on getting sober, given by a young intern at a local hospital. Afterward, Mary seeks out the doctor. They sit "outside on the hospital steps under a mist-drenched moon."[14] The doctor, in a less than orthodox fashion, provides spiritual direction for Mary.

The doctor herself had been in deep trouble with addiction as a young teen, "giving blow jobs at the bus terminal for dope" (215). The young doctor credits her fourteen years of sobriety to a God in whom Mary cannot believe. The doctor informs Mary that she must make drastic changes in relation to booze. Mary needs to go to ninety meetings in ninety days. And, she tells Mary, "You have to start giving the higher-power thing a try" (217). Mary says she knows a Jenny who is sober but doesn't pray. The doctor asks what Jenny is like. Mary replies, "Mean as a snake" (217). The doctor responds, "You might find sober people who don't pray, but all the happy ones have some kind of regular meditative or spiritual practice" (217). Mary argues that she's never felt anything like faith. The doctor patiently replies, "Faith is not a feeling. . . . It's a set of actions. By taking the actions, you demonstrate more faith than somebody who actually has experienced the rewards of prayer and so feels hope" (217).

---

13. Ibid., 190.

14. Mary Karr, *Lit: A Memoir* (New York: Harper Perennial, 2009), 215. The numbers in parentheses on the following pages refer to page numbers in Karr's book.

Mary Karr and the doctor continue to discuss God. Mary worries that God won't be happy with someone like her showing up with "machine gun fire on my ass"(217). The doctor asks about Mary's image of God, as someone "pissed at you," and gently suggests that she see God in a new way. The doctor tells Mary that drinking is like the bad boyfriend who is beating you and you need to break up with him so you can notice the nice guy who "has a crush on you."

As Mary begins to imagine a God-for-her, a God who wants good for her, a God who does not judge and condemn her, the doctor asks what Mary wants out of life. What are her dreams? Mary would like to patch things up with her husband and get her writing going again. The doctor looks at her and asks, "Nothing else? That's it?" Mary says her "innards are roiling. The smoke in my mouth tastes like creosote. . . . Money, I say. I'd like some more money. It sounds shallow, but hell. . . . Still we need some fucking money." The doctor asks, "How much would seem like a gift from God?" Mary had only made nine thousand dollars the year before, and says maybe nine grand a year and a tenure-track job with health care. The doctor suggests, "Then pray for it. Just pray every day for ninety days and see if your life gets better. . . . What do you have to lose?" (219).

Mary goes home. When her husband and little boy are asleep, she goes to the living room. "I take a small cushion down and get on my knees for the first time in my life—prayer number one. Higher power, I say snidely. Where the fuck have you been?" (219). She feels more God's absence than presence. She doesn't know if God exists, but she thanks God for keeping her sober that day. And then she gets up. "Wait, the sober mind says—that's trying? You could've died last night. I flop back on my knees. And help me. Help. Me. Help me feel better so I can believe in you, you subtle bastard. Such is my first prayer—a peevish start, tight-lipped and mean of spirit, but a prayer nonetheless" (220). She makes it a regular thing. Praying for God to keep her sober. And at night she prays a simpler prayer: Thanks.

Like Anne Lamott, who says the two best prayers are "Help" and "Thanks," and she later adds, "Wow," Mary Karr takes her battered and bruised life, body and soul, to the living room to meet a God in whom she scarcely believes. And her life changes. The first week of her newfound sobriety, she is challenged by another alcoholic to just list the things for which she is grateful. Feeling her "chewing insides," a woman whose skin feels like a "too-tight sausage casing," she reluctantly and unexpectedly begins to list the small things for which she is grateful. From small things like the red leather chair in which she sits to the fact that her husband has not left her and taken her little boy away from her, she simply prays thanks.

> Enumerating these small things actually pierces me with a sliver of feeling fortunate. Then from that one moonlit meeting, the young doctor's face rises up in me, and I think of what she'd said about asking for my dream, so I add, While you're at it, I'd like some money. Not a handout. I'm willing to work for it. It takes a full five minutes to shut up begging, and it sounds crazy to say, but for the first time in a week, I don't want a drink at all. It's an odd sensation, since the craving's shadowed me every waking instant for the past few years. (224–25)

Mary experiences a quite dramatic turn as a result of her conversation with the doctor on the hospital steps. Her praying and reaching out to a higher power quickly frees her from the craving for alcohol. And even more, "the process of listing my good fortune stopped my scrambling fear, and in relinquishing that, some solid platform slid under me" (225). The solid platform manifests itself in a very dramatic and tangible manner: money is provided.

> I know people needier and way more deserving have prayed for harder stuff they needed more: to feed starving children, say, to get a negative biopsy result. Nonetheless, it's a stone fact—that within a week or so of my starting to pray—a man I don't know calls me from the Whiting Foundation to give me a thirty-five-thousand-dollar prize I hadn't applied for. Some anonymous angel had nominated me and sent in both my poems and a hunk of crappy autobiographical novel about my kidhood—maybe pinched from a writing group I'd once been in. (225)

Mary's journey continues on, and she is led to investigate churches. Her little eight-year-old boy, Dev, wants to go to church. "If you'd told me even a year before I start taking Dev to church regular that I'd wind up whispering my sins in the confessional or on my knees saying the rosary, I would've laughed myself cockeyed. More likely pastime? Pole dancer. Drug mule. Assassin" (330). She and Dev try several Sunday morning churches. Mary carries a paperback to read. "It's a year before we follow Toby and his wife Catherine, to their Catholic parish, maybe because I associate their church with the shame of my lapsed pals or the

Inquisition's torture devices" (333). She is drawn to the little Irish priest, Fr. Kane, who celebrates Mass in an "unvarnished way" and who "seems humble without being bent or cowed." For the first time, she doesn't open her paperback in church. Gradually, the communal Catholic experience of God draws her in. "Catholics aren't who I thought they'd be, not even close. It isn't the ritual of the high Mass that impresses me, but the people—their collective surrender. If I can't do reverence to that, how dead are my innards? Within a week or two, it's turning out that I forget to bring a paperback to Mass, so obviously, I'm not just coming for Dev anymore" (335).

Fr. Kane and the experience of the living Catholic faith works on her. Little Dev begins to prepare for baptism. Fr. Kane asks Mary where she is with all this. Mary has long and deep conversations with him. She finally confesses, "Maybe I don't belong here."

> "But you are here," he says. "What's keeping you from joining us? You come to Mass, but you're denying yourself the sacraments. Those are the consolations of the church." In Mass the next week, I enter and get on my knees like everybody else, saying the prayer I usually say at home. Opening my eyes, I actually tear up. There's something different about praying in company—I can't deny it—once you get over the feeling of being a poser. (337)

She may have felt like a poser, but I find Mary Karr's description of prayer and her spiritual journey one of the most honest and real I've ever encountered. Her reflection on her baptism amazes me.

> In the end, no white light shines out from the wounds of Christ that bathe me in his glory. Faith is a choice like any other. . . . Thinking it through is—at the final hour—horse dookey. You can only try it out. Not choosing Baptism would make me feel half-assed somehow, like a dilettante—scared to commit to praising a force I do feel is divine—a reluctance grown from pride or because the mysteries are too unfathomable.
>
> In the back of the church on Holy Saturday, I sit between Dev and Toby. In the pews, everybody holds an unlit candle, and the priest comes in with the altar's mega-candle. Stopping at the back row, he touches its taper to the charcoal filament on either side of the aisle. The flames passed one to another until *we're all holding fire in our hands*. (351, my emphasis)

I love that image. We are those who hold fire in our hands, and in our hearts. Little Dev says after the baptism: "*We belong to a great big family*" (354). That family is made up of innumerable Marys and Devs, people on the way. Mary Karr eventually enters into the Spiritual Exercises of St. Ignatius with Franciscan Sr. Margaret as her director. Among other lessons, Mary realizes that God loves her and God has a dream for her life (368–69, 384).

Fifteen years after her baptism, Mary visits Fr. Kane, who is near death.[15] She visits the stroke-stricken and cancer-ridden priest in his hospital room. She asks if he is mad at God. "'Not yet,'" he replies. "Maybe only that blue-eyed Irishman was a fit enough theological ninja to convert me. He'd met my doubts with his trademark delight and none of the stern piety my lapsed Catholic friends often railed against from pre–Vatican II catechisms." Mary had brought Fr. Kane a poinsettia, and they wheel him down to the chapel on the Feast of the Immaculate Conception. "'I hate that God lets you suffer like this,' I said. 'Oh,' he said, taken aback, 'God suffers more.' Then he bid me place the flower—first to one side of the statue, then the other. 'Looks good there,' he finally said, grinning up at me. Behind wire rims, his pale eyes crinkled; his cheeks flushed as if he'd just finished a fast polka." Mary wonders if "his face really did radiate the blue nimbus that saints in certain Renaissance paintings give off." Mary found in that doctor, in a Franciscan sister, in Fr. Kane, the spiritual directors she needed.[16] Mary Karr and Fr. Kane together took the flowers to the altar of death and of life.

The Best Prayer for the Long Haul: Liturgical Prayer. One of the strange permutations of our times is the split between spirituality and religion, between forms of personal prayer and communal, liturgical prayer. Spiritual direction in the Ignatian tradition recognizes the power of the unification of personal and communal prayer in our lives. To meet the difficulties of our age, we need to pray alone and with others. To know love, we must know others, and know others in God. That is what liturgical prayer can so powerfully provide. Thomas Merton relates liturgical prayer to one of the dominant problems of our times.

The whole problem of our time is the problem of love: how are we going to recover the ability to love ourselves and to love one another?

---

15. Mary Karr, "The End," op-ed article in the *New York Times*, December 27, 2009.
16. Ibid.

The reason why we hate one another and fear one another is that we secretly or openly hate and fear our own selves. And we hate ourselves because the depths of our being are a chaos of frustration and spiritual misery. Lonely and helpless, we cannot be at peace with others because we are not at peace with ourselves, and we cannot be at peace with ourselves because we are not at peace with God.[17]

Merton invites us to immerse ourselves in the power of liturgical prayer. The way out of our loneliness and spiritual misery, the way that necessarily unites us and brings us together is communal prayer, and the apex of such prayer, the Eucharist. "Precisely the great means which the Church has given us for entering into the Mystery of the Holy Trinity is the Sacrament of the Eucharist. . . . We enter into the mystery of the Holy Trinity not so much by thinking and imagining, as by loving."[18] This kind of prayer, regular and repetitive, done over and over, seeps into our souls and helps us love and discover our deepest, truest self. "We experience the things of God in much the same way as we experience our own intimate reality, we discover Him in much the same way as we discover the unsuspected depths of our own deep self. . . . [T]his means that if we would find our God we must first find our own true selves."[19]

We find our true selves and God's true self in the total donation of ourselves and God's self in the celebration of the Eucharist. "In other words, by our union with Christ in the Eucharist we find our true selves. The false self, the 'old man' is burned away by the fervor of charity generated by His intimate presence within our soul. And the 'new man' comes into full possession of himself as we 'live, now not we, but Christ liveth in us.'"[20]

The Eucharist is, in the felicitous phrasing of Ignatius of Antioch, "the medicine of immortality, the antidote for death, and the food that makes us live forever in Christ."[21] Liturgical expert Jesuit John Baldovin is one who has always urged the merging and relating of personal and liturgical

---

17. Thomas Merton, *The Living Bread* (New York: Farrar, Straus & Cudahy, 1956), xii.

18. Ibid., 50–51.

19. Ibid., 90–91, 93.

20. Ibid., 119.

21. Ignatius, *To the Ephesians* 20.2, cited in John Baldovin, S.J., *Bread of Life, Cup of Salvation: Understanding the Mass* (London: Sheed & Ward; Lanham, MD: Rowman & Littlefield, 2003), 180.

prayer. And the Eucharist brings all together. "Celebrating the Mass is central to our identity and mission as Christians because it means participating in a ritual way in the self-offering of Christ for the life of the world. . . . Why bother with Mass? We bother with the Mass because we 'bother with Jesus.'"[22] Baldovin explains that what is happening at Eucharist is much more than we can realize or imagine. "When we offer the gifts [at Mass] . . . the only gift we can really offer is Christ himself, who is transforming not only bread and wine, but all of us into the Body of Christ for the salvation of the World."[23]

Protestant scripture scholar Walter Brueggemann also attests to the power of communal worship and praise. In his book on the Psalms, he writes:

> Such praise is indeed our duty and our delight, the ultimate vocation of the human community, indeed of all creation. Yes, all life is aimed at God and finally exists for the sake of God. Praise articulates and embodies our capacity to yield, to submit, and abandon ourselves in trust and gratitude to the One whose we are. Praise is not only a human requirement and a human need, it is also a human delight. We have a resilient hunger to move beyond self, to return our energy and worth to the One from whom it has been granted. In our return to the One, we find our deepest joy. That is what it means to "glorify God and enjoy God forever."[24]

Ultimately, like Karr, Merton, Baldovin, and Brueggemann, we must give ourselves over to what God is doing with our lives. Spiritual direction eventually leads most people to a deeper practice of and desire for contemplative prayer, and it is in such prayer that we receive the graces we need to persevere over the long haul. Few describe or call for contemplative prayer better than Carmen Acevedo Butcher in her introduction to her presentation of *The Cloud of Unknowing*.

> Why has contemplation endured over the centuries? . . . because it builds bridges and works for social justice. It teaches us how to love, grow, be fully human. We need contemplation because . . . [i]t

---

22. Baldovin, *Bread of Life, Cup of Salvation*, 10.

23. Ibid., 169–70.

24. Walter Brueggemann, *Israel's Praise: Doxology against Idolatry and Ideology* (Philadelphia: Fortress Press, 1988), 1.

reconnects us to ourselves, to God, and to others. It helps us learn to forgive and heal our souls, . . . "an antidote to the mind's vulnerability to toxic emotions." Simply put, we need a way to generate joy.[25]

---

25. Carmen Acevedo Butcher, trans., *The Cloud of Unknowing and the Book of Privy Counseling: A New Translation* (Boston: Shambhala, 2009), xxiv–xxv. She quotes Daniel Goleman, *Destructive Emotions: A Scientific Dialogue with the Dalai Lama* (New York: Bantam, 2003), 3–4.

CHAPTER 8

Spiritual Direction as Accompanying Processes of Discernment

How long had he stood there, paralyzed, mortified by his clumsy incompetence, wave after wave leaping past him into the shore? Do something, he thought panicked, but what? How many times as a boy had he watched his father seize up in the middle of a room, a portrait of indecision, with no idea which way to turn, an angry wife tugging in one direction, a pretty grad student who'd confused him with the romantic hero of some novel they'd been studying pulling him in the opposite? It was as if he'd concluded that if he remained where he was long enough, whatever he wanted most would come to him of its own volition. Griffin remembered willing him to act, to do something, because it frightened him to see somebody stand frozen in one place for so long, unable to take that first step, the one that implied a destination.

—Richard Russo, *That Old Cape Magic*

But I knew that I needed to go through the Ignatian decision-making process of discernment. Meaning to sift or to sort, discernment is akin to gold panning, where the gravel has to be shaken through a sieve to reveal the nuggets of precious metal. Essentially it's separating the gold from the dross, the light from the dark, the good from the bad, in human experience. So, I put myself to discerning what the best thing to do was—asking what God was really wanting of me here and praying for freedom.

—Brendan McManus, S.J., *Redemption Road*

The first quote is from a wonderful novel, *That Old Cape Magic* by Richard Russo. The protagonist describes in delicious detail the paralysis that can descend on one who fails to discern. More often, a lack of discernment is revealed in the lack of direction, purpose, and clear cut choices characterizing the lives of those who just drift through life, or a period of their lives. This is all too common in the lives of young adults during their college years. Especially for young men, video games, beer, and hanging out fill the days when they could be studying, learning, and consciously forming themselves into the men they will be for the rest of their lives and all eternity.

The second quote is from *Redemption Road*, a fascinating book by an Irish Jesuit describing his walking Spain's pilgrimage route El Camino de Santiago de Compostelo. Brendan McManus reveals in intimate detail both the large and small discernments of that journey he undertook in memory of, and to honor, his brother Donal, who died of suicide. McManus follows and teaches the method of discernment discovered and given to the world by St. Ignatius of Loyola: "What was the secret of his [Ignatius'] effectiveness? It was his power of discernment of the action of the Holy Spirit within consciousness and his ability to coach others in the art of discernment; these endowments surely explain his enduring influence in the lives of Christians."[1]

Discernment happens in many venues and in many ways. Discernment is the process by which we discover our deepest, truest selves, and then we choose and act from that center of our hearts. The Catholic Catechism has a wonderful description of the heart.

The heart is the dwelling-place where I am, where I live; according to the Semitic or Biblical expression, the heart is the place "to which I withdraw." The heart is our hidden center, beyond the grasp of our reason and of others; only the Spirit of God can fathom the human heart and know it fully. The heart is the place of decision, deeper than our psychic drives. It is the place of truth, where we choose life or death. It is the place of encounter, because as image of God we live in relation: it is the place of covenant.[2] (CCC §2563)

1. James Connor, S.J., and the Fellows of the Woodstock Theological Center, *The Dynamism of Desire: Bernard J. F. Lonergan on the Spiritual Exercises of St. Ignatius of Loyola* (St. Louis, MO: Institute of Jesuit Sources, 2006), 321.
2. *Catechism of the Catholic Church* (New York: Doubleday, 1995), §2563.

Aaron Sorkin's movie *A Few Good Men* presents a good example of discernment. Lt. Danny Kaffee (Tom Cruise) is constantly challenged by Lt. Commander Jo Galloway (Demi Moore) to accept his responsibility to serve authentically, making full use of his talents, as lawyer for two young Marines accused of murder. Kaffee's analysis of the case is that his clients have no chance of winning acquittal. He has a reputation for taking the easy way out and plea bargaining cases. Galloway fervently believes the accused Marines deserve a real defense. She wants Danny to step up and do his job. He's ready to quit. She challenges him: "Why are you so afraid to be a lawyer?" Danny replies, "Dawson and Downey will have their day in court, they'll just have it with another lawyer." Jo replies, "Another lawyer won't be good enough. They need you. You know how to win. You know they have a case. You walk away from this now, you have sealed their fate." Danny says, "Their fate was sealed the moment Santiago died." He goes on to say that Jo lives in a dreamland. It doesn't matter what they think; it only matters what they can prove. Jo angrily confronts Danny and cuts him to the quick: "You know nothing about the law. You're a used car salesman, Daniel. You're an ambulance chaser with a rank. You're nothing. [beat] Live with that."

In the next scene, we see Danny in a bar listening to a slick lawyer bragging about some legal maneuver he's pulled off to benefit his corporate clients. The film cuts to Danny sitting on a bench at night, reflecting. Dare we say, discerning.

Next, we see the day starting as a military band is playing in Washington, DC. Soon we see the courtroom. Dawson and Downey are awaiting the start of their trial. Jo Galloway and Sam Weinberg (Kevin Pollack) are present for the defense, and Capt. Jack Ross (Kevin Bacon [isn't he in every movie?]) is there for the prosecution. Danny Kaffee walks in. He defiantly enters a plea of not guilty for his clients: "They're not guilty." The courtroom empties after the judge gavels the day's proceedings closed. Jo and Sam look at Kaffee, expressing extreme surprise. Kaffee looks at them and asks, "Why does a junior grade with six months' experience and a track record for plea bargaining get assigned a murder case? [beat] Would it be so that it never sees the inside of a courtroom?" He then launches into a series of instructions on how they will tackle the case. Jo Galloway can hardly believe what she's hearing. Kaffee pauses and looks around: "So this is what courtroom looks like."

Kaffee discerned. He was stung by Galloway's accusations, realizing there was more than a grain of truth in her criticism of him. He spends the night before the opening of the trial reflecting. He suspects that something more is going on than he has suspected. Why would a low-ranking lawyer "with a reputation for plea bargaining," for taking the easy way out, be assigned a murder case? Could it be that someone, some powers, want this case to go away quietly? Kaffee senses a call to respond to the desires of his heart to be a better lawyer, to be authentic and true to his calling. He decides to defend those who need his skills and expertise. The movie's climax is the thunderous confrontation between Lt. Kaffee (Cruise) and Col. Nathan R. Jessup (Jack Nicholson) with the famous lines "I want the truth!" "You can't handle the truth!" Discernment enabled Danny Kaffee to move toward and confront the truth, not only of the situation, but of himself.

Discernment is often helped by the help of another as we try to wend our ways to God. To discover, hold on to, and live out of the truth of our being, the viewpoint and wisdom of someone who has trod the path before usually is of great assistance to our journey. When someone comes to me and asks if I would be their spiritual director, I usually say, "Well, spiritual direction can do one, or all, of three things. (1) It can help us with our prayer, and develop and deepen our relationship with God. (2) It can help us live a more committed and vibrant life of discipleship with Jesus. And (3) spiritual direction can help us make choices— consciously informed, prayerfully reflected upon choices. That is discernment."

David Lonsdale, S.J., notes, "Christian discernment is not just any process of decision making that takes place in a vaguely prayerful setting. Good discernment . . . has to do with allowing our deepest attitudes, aspirations, values and relationships to come to the surface, so that it is they which give shape and direction to our choices."[3] Usually, especially with young adults, they want to concentrate on the third aspect, life choices. And young adults are often pondering the options before them as they make life choices. But the real meat and potatoes of discernment is the striving to place all of our gifts and talents, our hopes and dreams, our choices and challenges in relation to the kingdom of God. Lonsdale again: "Fundamentally, the Reign of God means a way of living both

---

3. David Lonsdale, *Listening to the Music of the Spirit: The Art of Discernment* (Notre Dame, IN: Ave Maria Press, 1993), 49–50.

communally and individually, in which we allow God to be at the center, so that 'God Reigns' in every dimension of our life."[4]

Much of the help a spiritual director can provide to a directee is listening and hearing how and where the directee may be resisting the nudges and pulls toward the values and practices of God's reign in his or her life. Some of the hesitancies and resistances may be immediately obvious. The ubiquitous struggles with addictions great and small hamper many of us. The battles between various ideologies and ecclesiological styles can constrict the freedom of a man or woman sincerely trying to hear and follow the lead of the Lord. Deeper, more problematic issues distressful to destructive images of God (God as judge and punisher) can be addressed as a director gently suggests that what is going on in the directee's head is not the Spirit of the God of love and mercy present in that person's heart. Some who try to enter into a relationship with God need to allow their relationship with themselves to ripen and mature. Those who, on the one hand, have a hard time loving and appreciating themselves, and those who, on the other, harbor grandiose visions of inflated self-worth are greatly helped by spiritual directors who skillfully and delicately help directees hear the challenge Jesus extends to them to both love themselves and realize they are not the be all and end all of existence. Spiritual direction in the context of living and loving for the kingdom of God means we gradually open to an ongoing awareness of the ways God is loping off large chunks of marble and shaping us into the statue beautifully emerging from our lives with the church and the Lord. Final stages of the perfecting of the statue involves a great deal of time sanding the rock and allowing the beauty to emerge.

Discernment presupposes the effort to pray and live life as a disciple. To use an analogy, to play football meant when I was younger keeping in shape; not getting in trouble with school authorities (always a bit of a struggle for me as a kid!); practicing with the team; and paying attention to the instructions, admonitions, and encouragement of the coaches. The days of big games were highlights. Discernment is much like playing a team sport. The disciple prays, lives life, pays attention to God in prayer and in the liturgical prayer of the church. But then there are "big games," discernment of life choices or large directional shifts in one's life. The choice of vocation; the decision to propose marriage to someone; the

---

4. Ibid., 50.

midlife discernment over whether to make major job changes; the careful choice and planning of retirement years—all call for major and longtime discernment.

Many in the Ignatian tradition, and St. Ignatius himself, often recommend that we carefully monitor our interior states of being, noting when we are in consolation and when in desolation. Consolation is when we are energized, enthused, and engaged, ready to do whatever God asks as we realize that the faith is flowing, hope is healing, and love is lasting. We are ready to say yes to anything in order to serve God's reign. In the words of David Fleming, "we find ourselves so on fire with the love of God . . . we begin to see everything and everyone in the context of God."[5] Desolation is the opposite. We find ourselves discouraged, despondent, in a word, "down." What we believed we were supposed to do is questioned. What we hoped for seems to recede beyond the murky horizon. Love is frustrating, fearful, and seemingly false. Nothing is worth the effort. Desolation is "when we find ourselves enmeshed in a certain turmoil of spirit or weighed down by a heavy darkness. . . . A lack of faith or hope or love in the distaste for prayer . . . when we experience the opposite of what has been described as consolation."[6]

Desolation is not depression. And consolation is not always a spiritual high. Desolation moves us away from the goal for which we were created, away from being our deepest, truest selves. Consolation strengthens and inspires us to stay the course and move resolutely toward our purpose for being. The classic gospel text is Luke 9:51: "When the days drew near for him to be taken up, he set his face to go to Jerusalem" (NRSV). Jesus was in consolation. He "set his face," knowing the danger involved, much the way Martin Luther King, Jr., or Archbishop Oscar Romero knew the danger involved in the stances they took in their times. Consolation is not always comfortable, and desolation is not always disagreeable. My tertian director Pat O'Sullivan, teaching us about discernment, once said, "Sailors heading to the whorehouse may seem happy, but they are not in consolation."

Personally, I've never found the sifting and sorting of this or that interior state as helpful with discernment as this one nugget I heard George

---

5. David Fleming, S.J., *Draw Me into Your Friendship: A Literal Translation and a Contemporary Reading of the Spiritual Exercises*, #316 (St. Louis, MO: Institute of Jesuit Sources, 1996), 251.

6. Ibid.

Driscoll, S.J., share in a homily. An accomplished and much sought-after spiritual director, George said that discerning from where some idea, hope, choice, possible course of action, originates is often murky and difficult. Much more helpful is to analyze and discern where one will end up if this or that direction is followed. George said, "If you sail from Los Angeles and are off one degree in your direction, it won't seem you're that far off course. But you'll miss Hawaii by miles." Discernment is as much about staying on course as it is about knowing from where the impulse to travel originates.

Spiritual Direction Rooted in Bernard Lonergan's Thought

As much as learning how God works with us individually in our personal histories is a key aspect of spiritual direction, there is also the wisdom of realizing the outlines of spiritual development articulated by arguably the most perceptive Jesuit who ever lived: Bernard Lonergan.

A highly esteemed contemporary Jesuit philosopher / theologian, Lonergan laid out a schema for realizing our potential as those who are being fashioned to live with God forever. He discerned a trans-temporal, trans-cultural pattern that exists in all human persons. We all experience, strive to understand our experience, form judgments based on our understanding, and make decisions and choices based on those judgments. Deep within this pattern of experiencing—understanding—judging—deciding exist inherent norms. To experience, we must be attentive. To understand, we must be intelligent. To judge, we must be reasonable. To decide, we must be responsible. I would add we are called to be creative, and to do so we must be loving. Spiritual direction aids us in monitoring and charting how well we are adhering to the inherent norms, the "Be-Attitudes," of Lonergan's system.[7] For we can fool ourselves, ignore our experience, muddle our understanding with bias, both personal and social. Lonergan developed a comprehensible schema, a normative pattern, describing the interior patterns of our minds, hearts, and souls. All human persons experience, in all times and places, in all communities and cultures; they strive to understand their experience, make judgments based on those understandings, and make choices and decide courses of action based on those judgments.

---

7. Tad Dunne, *Lonergan and Spirituality: Towards Spiritual Integration* (Chicago: Loyola University Press, 1985), 115–16.

LONERGAN'S TRANSCENDENTAL PRECEPTS
(i.e., "BE-ATTITUDES")

EXPERIENCE	BE ATTENTIVE
↓↑	
UNDERSTANDING	BE INTELLIGENT
↓↑	
JUDGMENT	BE REASONABLE
↓↑	
DECISION	BE RESPONSIBLE
↓↑	
CREATIVE ACTION	BE LOVING

The practice of the transcendental precepts—being attentive, intelligent, reasonable, responsible, and loving—moves us to conversion on the intellectual, moral, and religious levels of our being. Conversion, that is, meeting the demands of the "Be-Attitudes,"[8] leads to our becoming more and more authentic persons. Refusal or avoidance of the demands or the precepts sees us becoming inauthentic. Retreating from the demands of the "Be-Attitudes" results in our decline and the decline of our communities, on the personal, communal, societal, and global levels of our living together. Think of World War I and World War II as obvious examples. Think of global climate change today. Living authentically means progress is more probable on the personal, communal, societal, and global levels of our existence. Living unauthentically stalls progress or moves us and our communities and societies backward.

As a philosopher and theologian who prized and privileged the power of the intellect, Lonergan later in life learned a great deal as he battled alcoholism. His deepening realization of the power of the Holy Spirit to convert and change us (Rom 5:5), our communities, and our world led him to preach that being in love with God is the point and meaning of our existence as human persons.

Being in love with God is the basic fulfillment of our conscious intentionality. That fulfillment brings a deep-set joy that can remain

---

8. Ibid.

despite humiliation, failure, privation, pain, betrayal, desertion. That fulfillment brings a radical peace, the peace the world cannot give. *That fulfillment bears fruit in a love of one's neighbor that strives mightily to bring about the kingdom of God on this earth.* On the other hand, the absence of that fulfillment opens the way to the trivialization of human life in the pursuit of fun, to the harshness of human life arising from the ruthless exercise of power, to despair about human welfare springing from the conviction that the universe is absurd.[9]

Spiritual direction and paying attention to desolations and consolations, combined with the work of monitoring our adherence to the Be-Attitudes, charts our conversions. The ultimate goal of spiritual direction is making choices, daily choices and life choices, decisions that adhere to, and move us toward, the purpose of our existence: transcending where and what we are so we can be able to live with God in love and justice forever. Converted communities, consoled and consoling communities, change our world. Converted communities, consoled and consoling communities, can transform our violent age. Desolate and desolating people will take us in the wrong direction. The good news is that small communities and saints can have profound effects on the whole. Anthropologist Margaret Mead said it best: "Never doubt that a small group of thoughtful, committed citizens can change the world. Indeed, it is the only thing that ever has."[10]

What groups are authentic and moving history in the direction of the Reign of God? Which choices on the personal and communal level are on target and holding to the course of direction in tune with God's designs? God communicates with us through our desires and consolations. As groups and individuals we need to learn to listen to the silent sounds of consolation. God leads us by consoling us.

Ignatius instructs us to pay attention to these "touches [of consolation], more or less repeated, more or less certain." Learn to recognize them, treasure them, foster them, amplify them, submit to them, because you recognize them as the voice of God, as God's touch, nudge, pull, push or shove. Submit, as iron filings submit to

---

9. Bernard J. F. Lonergan, S.J., *Method in Theology* (New York: Seabury Press, 1972), 105 (my italics).

10. Margaret Mead Quotes, http//: www.thoughtco.com.

the pull of the magnet. When these touches disappear, or when they are absent, wait in patience for the return of the consolation of the Lord.[11]

The great Jesuit Dean Brackley wrote, "Sustaining a life of generous service requires a spirituality," and "Rightly understood, spirituality is the opposite of escaping from reality. We encounter ultimate reality not by leaving the world, but by plunging into it."[12] Discernment is all about analyzing relationships between the cultural and social matrices of our lives, and our desires to serve God in ways that transform both our times, our communities, and ourselves. Our choices from the daily and mundane to lifetime commitments are the seeds of change. The personal choices of young adults like John Lewis, Bernard Lafayette, Diane Nash, and James Bevel, young and idealistic and certainly not perfect human beings, joined with the gospel-inspired choices of Martin Luther King and the other ministers of the Southern Christian Leadership Conference, and thus was born the profoundly transformative Civil Rights movement of the 1960s. Segregation went from being legal, lethal, and largely unquestioned in 1955 to being abolished by the Civil Rights Act of 1964, signed by Lyndon B. Johnson, who had become president when John Kennedy was assassinated. Those young people found a way of sustaining their generous sacrifice and service. Their choices made the world in which we live better and more just. Their authenticity and courage changed the world.[13]

Discernment isn't just a way to "get our acts together," although that will often hopefully be a byproduct, or goal, of the process. Discernment is much more about attuning our attitudes, desires, and dreams to the dreams and desires of God for all the children, women, and men of the earth. We are all children of God. Discernment is done personally in spiritual direction, but such delicate attention to choosing can affect and effect not just us, but all of the world and all of reality. The cosmic dimensions of the practice of our faith can come to consciousness when we realize the whole of reality is in the perpetual, providential now. The

---

11. Connor et al., *The Dynamism of Desire*, 383.

12. Dean Brackley, S.J., *The Call to Discernment in Troubled Times: New Perspectives on the Transformative Wisdom of Ignatius of Loyola* (New York: Crossroad, 2004), 3, 23.

13. David Halberstam, *The Children* (New York, NY: Fawcett Books, 1998). Halberstam was a twenty-five-year-old reporter for the *New York Times* and accompanied many of the young heroes of the Civil Rights movement.

kingdom of God is within us, trying to bust out into our lives through the choices we discern, make, and commit ourselves to.

In reflecting on God's Revolution, the meaning of the Reign of God, and discernment, Brackley writes:

> The Reign of God is a banquet, a party, that all are invited to join (Matt 8:11; 22:2; Luke 15:23). . . . The Reign of God means new human beings, new communities, a new transfigured world (Rev 21:5). This is the cause to which Jesus calls. . . . This sounds wonderful, but can we take it seriously? Aside from the problem of faith itself, it seems a little too late to be talking about a great project for history. Hasn't history shown itself to be a story without a great plot? . . . Today none of those trains seem headed to the Promised Land. . . . [I]s love even possible? . . . But wait, moral goodness also grows and develops. We have raised our standards and sometimes our behavior in modern times. . . . Faith affirms that God's Reign irrupts into this world and advances in the heart of history. . . . The experience of this quiet assurance—that it makes sense to struggle and celebrate—is our solid grounds for hope. It is experience of such a kind (consolation) that we cannot give a full account of it. And yet it furnishes sufficient reason to believe in God's Reign, reason enough to trump the evidence to the contrary.[14]

Discernment is about realizing and relishing the consolations of our lives and times, and withstanding and surviving the desolation that inevitably clouds our sense of God's ever present mercy, joy, and love. To be discerning disciples means training ourselves to examine and sift the many moods, thoughts, hopes, fears, dreams, and so on, that twist and turn their way through our minds and hearts. Discernment also calls on us personally and as a community to sort and separate the many movements, institutional processes, and social and political currents that contour and channel the possibilities of our and others' lives. This social discernment names and claims social sin (e.g., racism) but also social grace (e.g., the Civil Rights movement of the 1960s in the U.S.).

The process and point of discernment is freedom. Michael Walzer in his deep meditation on Exodus and Revolution realized, "There is a kind of freedom in bondage." A slave or subject is free from some degree of responsibilities, "and there is a kind of bondage in freedom: the bond-

---

14. Brackley, *Call to Discernment*, 70–71.

age of law, obligation, and responsibility. . . . Israelite slaves could become free only insofar as they accepted the discipline of freedom, the obligation to live up to a common standard and to take responsibility for their own actions."[15] It's easier to just go with the flow and follow the dictates of a dictator. It relieves us from taking responsibility for our choices. But the God of Jesus Christ is not a dictator; God the Father is a persuader. General Dwight Eisenhower once said leadership is persuasion. You have to get people to want to do what you want them to do.[16] Jesuit Tom Green writes: "[F]or every good spiritual director, the director's role is not to mold souls according to some preconceived pattern but to help them interpret *their own* experience. The good director helps people to be free to follow the Lord in whatever way *he* chooses to lead them.[17]

The Christian God transforms us not by beating us over the head and making us do "x," "y", or "z." God's spirit works by planting desires in our minds and hearts. We find ourselves wanting what God wants. The best example of this is parenthood. Many people have shared with me how everything changes when they first hold a newborn. Being a mother or father makes you want to do everything for your child, from changing thousands of smelly diapers to putting up with teenage insanity, to supporting young adults emotionally and financially. The older I get, the more I stand in awe of good parents and all they do for their children. And the more I appreciate the overwhelming meaning of Jesus revealing God to be a good and loving parent.

In my *Being on Fire*, I shared these stories about parenting.[18] They are worth repeating here. In the old TV series *The West Wing*, Toby Ziegler, the dour speech writer who never smiles, admits to Leo McGarry, President Bartlet's chief of staff, that he is fearful that he will not love his soon-to-be-born twins the way he has heard others speak of love for their children. Toby has heard that after the birth of a child all is different, nothing else matters, the child becomes the most important thing in life. Toby honestly realizes he has things he wants to do, and children may not fit

15. Michael Walzer, *Exodus and Revolution* (New York: Basic Books, 1985), 52–53.

16. Bill Byron, S.J., *Next Generation Leadership: A Toolkit for Those in Their Teens, Twenties & Thirties Who Want to Be Successful Leaders* (Scranton, PA: Scranton University Press, 2010), 9.

17. Thomas H. Green, S.J., *Opening to God: A Guide to Prayer* (Notre Dame, IN: Ave Maria Press, 1977), 20 (his italics).

18. Richard G. Malloy, S.J., *Being on Fire: Top Ten Essentials of Catholic Faith* (Maryknoll, NY: Orbis Books, 2014), 15–16.

into that schema. Later, the nurse presents him with two six-pound three-ounce beautiful, beanied babies, one in blue and the other in pink. He informs them that their names are Huck and Molly, after his wife's father and a young secret service agent who died in the line of duty. He tells them, "We're going to have to get you food and dentists and clothing. And whatever else you need. And no one told me you come with hats." Toby is filled with an overwhelming love for his children. Toby gets it.

Most parents "get it" in one way or another. I have a friend whose teenage son wasn't doing very well in high school Spanish class. One Friday afternoon, my buddy picked up his son after school and asked how it was going with Spanish. "Just fine," the unloquacious son replied. Next week the report card came. His son had flunked Spanish. That evening the Dad was yelling at his son, "I asked you just last Friday how you were doing in Spanish, and you said fine. And now your report card comes home telling me you flunked! Why'd you tell me you were doing fine?" The kid replied, "Dad, I only wanted to get yelled at once." My friend had to laugh. It's all about challenging his son while still loving him no matter what. My friend gets it.

God gets it. In *Jesus of Nazareth*, Pope Benedict movingly reveals his view of God who exists like a parent in loving relationship, a God who can be understood as a good mother, a good father. Parental love, the care, concern, the love and service lavished on babies and kids, reveals the love of God.

> We see that to be God's child is not a matter of dependency, but rather of standing in the relation of love that sustains man's existence and gives it meaning and grandeur. One last question: Is God also Mother? The Bible does compare God's love with the love of a mother. . . . The mystery of God's maternal love is expressed with particular power in the Hebrew word *rahamim*, . . . "womb," later used to mean divine compassion, . . . God's mercy. The womb is the most concrete expression for the interrelatedness of two lives and of loving concern.[19]

The loving parental image of God consoles and challenges us. God's will is clear: that the Kingdom come. We pray that truth every time we pray the Our Father. The Reign of God comes to reign in our lives when

---

19. Pope Benedict XVI, *Jesus of Nazareth: From the Baptism in the Jordan to the Transfiguration* (New York: Doubleday, 2007), 139.

we freely choose to allow God to be God in all we think and do. The more we are free, the more we depend on God. Freedom and dependence on God are in direct, not inverse, proportion. Discernment monitors our free choices, always aiming toward our choosing the values of the kingdom. God's values are clear—the Beatitudes (Mt 5:3–11), the attitude of Zacchaeus (Lk 19:1–10), the loving service of the Good Samaritan (Lk 10:25–37), the truth of the parable of the talents (Mt 25:31–46)—that those who use their wealth to serve the poor and needy enter the kingdom; those who chose otherwise are lost. Discerning makes it more probable that we will accept and even chose the cross that leads to life rather than taking the easy road (Mt 7:13). Developing a discerning heart makes us better able to know how to apply the lessons of Catholic social teaching to the pragmatic choices placed before us by our political and social systems.

Ed Kinerk, S.J., reveals the crucial importance of desires in our evaluating, choosing, and living out our spiritual discernments. According to Kinerk and St. Ignatius, desires are to be understood as graces, or gifts from God. God places desires in us. So, too, desires can come from, or take us toward, that which is not God. Thus, discernment has to do with learning how to distinguish which desires move us to God and God's reigning in our lives, and which desires move us off track, toward a destination we don't deeply nor truly want.

> Our desires generate power, physical energy, and often peril, but they also galvanize our spirituality and our mission as Jesuits. If we hesitate too much, if we are timid about our stronger desires for God and his service, we will have failed to utilize the greatest source of human vitality and passion which God has given us. Likewise, if we vacillate because of an unwillingness to let go of desires which conflict with our mission and vocation, we will endlessly burn away our limited energies in needless frustration. In either case we rob ourselves of the wholesome happiness which God intends for his servants and which Ignatius envisioned for his companions.[20]

Kinerk goes on to say that there is power in our desires, power to make us happy in our apostolic service of the Lord. Our desires are deeply rooted in and originate from our imagination. The images and meanings

---

20. E. Edward Kinerk, S.J., "Eliciting Great Desires: Their Place in the Spirituality of the Society of Jesus," *Studies in the Spirituality of Jesuits* 16, no. 5 (November 1984): 2.

we carry within our souls make us want what we want and do what we do. Spiritual direction can be a wonderful gift that helps us know and own the images and meanings of our lives and commitments. The example of holy men and women, those recognized as saints, and the millions and millions of people who just live loving lives of service to others, are images of who and what we want to be.

The revelation of God in sacred Scripture is one privileged place and source of images and meanings informing our souls. The Bible is the quintessential mode we can utilize to set ourselves up for being discerning disciples. Cardinal Carlo Martini, S.J., a world-renowned biblical scholar, writes:

> The Bible is an extraordinary school for the discernment of feelings because reflecting on my daily feelings and on those of biblical characters helps me compare the emotive world of my passions and emotions with the clarity and order of God's mystery; I am invited to reflect on my feelings in and with Jesus.
>
> The Bible lets me understand why I am sometimes sad and other times cheerful; why I go from enthusiasm to indifference or even to disgust. There is a basic rule of evangelical feeling: to feel just as Jesus Christ.[21]

The Ignatian method of contemplating the gospels has informed my ways of being a Jesuit and my life discernments. In my early years, I closely identified with Peter and his enthusiastic, sometimes bombastic way of being wholeheartedly for Jesus. I would try and walk on water with him. I sometimes would deny Jesus in ways small to large, and sometimes destructive. But I would always find my way back to a forgiving and challenging God. In John 18:18, Peter is huddled around a charcoal fire "with the slaves and the police" (NRSV). Peter "was standing with them," not with Jesus. Peter wants to stay near the fire of warmth and comfort. He doesn't want to be crucified with Jesus. So, when challenged to declare his allegiance to Jesus, to support his Lord, Peter fails, bitterly and shamefully. The cock crows, and we can feel and hear Peter's pain and humiliation. Then, in John 21:9 we hear of another charcoal fire, a fire cooking fish and bread: fish, an early Christian symbol for Christ; bread, an allusion to Eucharist. Any writer will immediately recognize that the

---

21. Carlo Maria Martini, S.J., *A Prophetic Voice in the City: Meditations on the Prophet Jeremiah* (Collegeville, MN: Liturgical Press, 1997), 77.

image of two charcoal fires so close together in the story cannot be a coincidence. Jesus is cooking breakfast for the guys who are out fishing. Peter dives in and swims to Jesus. He can't wait for the boat to get to land. Jesus asks Peter, "Do you love me?" and makes a clear call and instruction to Peter: "Follow me."

As I've gotten older, I've become more and more mesmerized by Paul. The story not just of his startling conversion, but of his years in obscurity before he began writing the epistles that so revealed the deeper meanings and cosmic significance of Jesus the Christ, shows a person captivated by Christ and on fire to spread the good news of our salvation. As I've preached and taught in many venues and places, I more and more admire Paul's persistence and courageous commitment to the Lord and the church, in spite of hardship and difficulty. And I marvel at his ability to give up everything for Christ. Paul left a lucrative and esteemed position as a Pharisee to give all his talents and treasure to a fledging movement peopled by women, slaves, and others held in low regard in the world of the Roman Empire.

Trying to live and share Faith, Justice, and Reconciliation, the trinity making up the basic mission of the Society of Jesus, has led me from Philadelphia to Chile and back to Camden, New Jersey, and Scranton, Pennsylvania. My discernment has the graced assistance of the vow of obedience. The old joke among Jesuits goes: "You discern. They discern. They decide." Truly, I have found peace and energy in the missions given me by provincials and superiors. When I was in Chile, I found a great desire to get out of backwoods Osorno and up to Santiago. I wanted to get involved in "really serving the poor" and in all the "revolutionary," liberation theology–themed energies of Chile's capital under the Pinochet dictatorship in the mid-1980s. But after a year in Santiago, I learned that a gringo needed to patiently and intelligently follow the Chileans' lead, that I was certainly no savior, or even a key player, in anything. Instead, I spent a year doing simple and humble service in La Parroquia de La Santa Cruz and in two day-care centers run by Hogar de Cristo in Santiago, tutoring and playing guitar for the kids. The year was wonderful in many ways, and my relationships with parishioners taught me much about how to be a Jesuit and, eventually, a priest.

But when I left Chile after my three-year stay, I realized that maybe I'd been more apostolically effective in Osorno, teaching the boys. I learned from the poor in Santiago that there are many ways and venues to serve

God and the poor. One day, some thirty years later, I come into my office at the University of Scranton. The phone light is on, indicating a new message. I push some buttons and all of a sudden the speaker phone fills the room with the loud and wild sounds of adult men, who most likely were slightly inebriated on Chilean wine, laughing and singing "Take Me Home, Country Roads." In heavily accented English: "Helloo Meester Rick, this is your alumnos de Colegio San Mateo." It was the gang from my classes in Osorno calling me from their thirty-year high school reunion. They somehow found my phone number and wanted to contact me. They remembered me after all those years. What was God doing for those kids through me back in the 1980s? God knows . . .

After four years of theology studies and ordination, I was sent to Holy Name parish in Camden, where I lived and served from 1988 to 2003. Those fifteen years were filled with inner-city ministry to mostly Latino people living in what was then the poorest and most violent city in the United States. There the people of Holy Name made me a priest and a better man. Then the Society of Jesus moved me over to live at St. Joseph's University to run campus ministry, and to concentrate on teaching and writing. I wasn't wholly in favor of the move, and sat my first year at St. Joe's wondering what I was doing living the luxurious life of a university Jesuit. But I got my first book written and have lived my love-hate relationship with higher education these past sixteen years. The students are great, but today's higher education system too often makes rich kids poor with exorbitant interest on loans. It deeply troubles me that students are going into such deep debt to provide people like me with such comfortable lives.

Still, maybe I've touched the minds and hearts of some students who will eventually go and transform the Camdens of the world. And I was directly challenged by Dean Brackley, S.J. He was enthusiastic about my work at St. Joe's and told me, "Mugs (my nickname among Jesuits), the great challenge for us is the conversion of our own middle-class tribe." Even though Jesuit schools and universities are far from being filled with the middle-class and working-class kids that formed the student bodies of the 1940s–1970s, there are thousands of young people in our schools from various strata of society. Can we do something with them?

As I enter my sixties, I realize I have fewer years of active ministry left. A large part of me would love to get back to a Camden or the Wind River Indian reservation in Wyoming (the local bishop wanted me to take the parish there), but provincials' discernments do not concur. And if I'd stayed in better physical shape, maybe I'd be better suited for something strenuous and demanding. Still, as one provincial once challenged me, "You're standing in front of college students who have to take notes on everything you say. They actually like it when you preach and play your guitar. Don't you think you can do something for the Lord in a situation like that?"

The beauty and blessing of a long life in the Society of Jesus, or within any group in the church, is that eventually we learn the truth that even when we thought we were driving the car, Jesus was in the back seat navigating in ways we little understood or appreciated. As I grow older, on my good days I'm content to ride shotgun and let Jesus drive. Where it will get me is a never-ending continuous surprise and adventure.

An aboriginal woman in Australia once said about "missionaries," "If you have come to help me, you are wasting your time. But if you have come because your liberation is intimately bound up with mine, then let us walk together." The great Greg Boyle, S.J., often says that he and the gang members are more ministers to one another. He isn't there to save them. The homies and Greg save one another, kinship flourishes; those who stand on the margins together see the borders and boundaries erased in their minds and hearts. Discernment in my life has led me to root myself in the Society of Jesus and in the mission we live today. Some do it on the front lines of direct service to the poor. Many of us serve in areas and arenas less dramatically or directly connected to those suffering in poverty. But we all should strive to be mindful and aware of the poor in our midst or across town, and teach and preach in ways that call us all to respond to the needs of men and women mired in poverty.

Some things that are simple and obvious don't need to be discerned. My lunatic fantasy of leaving the Society of Jesus and marrying Julia Roberts is self-evidently insane (although, who knows, if she met me and realized my charms . . .). On bad days, when the kids aren't listening, and university life here is too soft and comfortable, or too stressed and frustrating, filled with "battles so bitter for stakes so small," I daydream of going back and working directly with the poor. But is that really for the poor, or more for me? People will think I'm a "better" and "more authentic" Jesuit if I'm back in Camden! Or will they? And, let's be honest, not that many people are thinking all that much about who I am and what I do anyway. Maybe someday I'll get over myself.

Good discernment is marked by consolation and confirmation. Joy should mark our basic disposition as companions of Jesus. We who seek

God should do so with a smile on our faces, rather than with a scowl at the world God has given us, and within which God is bursting through like sunlit beams on cloudy days. When we have made a choice, lived it out for a while, and find ourselves deeply consoled, we can trust the choice discerned. If we sincerely try to do something we think God wants us to do, but find ourselves constantly and consistently distressed and desolate, it's time to redo the discernment. God doesn't want us to be miserable. God desires good for us.

> Although discernment is concerned with choices, it reaches beyond the level of action. As we have seen, is allows the Spirit of God to shape not only our actions but also our hearts, the center from which those actions flow. By responding in daily life to the call of the Spirit, we are allowing God's will to be done in us, and thus allowing the Spirit to transform us and re-create us in the image and likeness of God. We are on a journey toward being what God would have us to be, toward the fullness of life.[22]

On the better days, which I gratefully can say are the vast majority of my days, I know that I am supposed to be a Jesuit, and do the Jesuit thing, wherever I am and whatever I am doing. God is the ultimate arbiter and evaluator of my life. I trust the Society of Jesus and the vow of obedience to get me where I am supposed to be and doing what I am supposed to be doing.

---

22. Lonsdale, *Listening to the Music of the Spirit*, 137.

CHAPTER 9

Spiritual Direction to Challenge, Transform, and Re-create Our World

So here is my question plain and simple: What happened to the church that once gave the empire fits, and now fits right in with the empire?
—Robin Meyers, *Spiritual Defiance*

The great danger in today's world, pervaded as it is by consumerism, is the desolation and anguish born of a complacent yet covetous heart, the feverish pursuit of frivolous pleasures, and a blunted conscience. Whenever our interior life becomes caught up in its own interests and concerns, there is no longer room for others, no place for the poor. God's voice is no longer heard, the quiet joy of his love is no longer felt, and the desire to do good fades. This is a very real danger for believers too. Many fall prey to it, and end up resentful, angry and listless.
—Pope Francis, *The Joy of the Gospel*, #2

Today's consumerist cultures do not foster passion and zeal but rather addiction and compulsion. They demand resistance. A compassionate response to these cultural malaises will be necessary and unavoidable if we are to share in the lives of our contemporaries.
—"A Fire That Kindles Other Fires," GC 35, Decree #2.

Prayer is not meant to make us into a world unto ourselves. We do not pray in order to escape the world around us. We pray with one eye on the world so that we can come to understand what is really being asked of us here and now, at times like this, as co-creators of the universe.
—Sr. Joan Chittister, O.S.B., *The Breath of the Soul*

The saintly bishop of Recife Brazil, Dom Helder Camara (1909–1999), was often accused of being too ideological with his pastoral practices, calling for justice and care of the poor. He replied, "Let the one without an ideology be the first to cast an ideology." He also cogently noted, "When I give food to the poor they call me a saint. When I ask why they are poor, they call me a communist." Spiritual direction helps us know and live our relationship with Jesus. And Jesus sends us to heal and help our brothers and sisters.

Spiritual direction is best done when social conditions of the Body of Christ are examined as closely and astutely as interior movements of heart and head. Spiritual direction in the Ignatian tradition is not navel gazing, or a self-centered self-improvement program. Spiritual direction aims to help and encourage those committed to the gospel to discern how to live their personal lives and their communal commitments in ways that transform themselves and our world. Spiritual direction at its best is rooted in and flourishes forth in love. The poet Willam Blake evocatively saw, "And we are put on earth a little space / That we might learn to bear the beams of love." To be those who realize our relation to the light of God is a gift of spiritual direction. Thomas Merton observes: "We do not become fully human until we give ourselves to each other in love. And this must not be confined only to sexual fulfillment: it embraces everything in the human person—the capacity for self-giving, for sharing, for creativity, for mutual care, for spiritual concern."[1]

Merton grew to realize that we give ourselves to each other on many levels beyond the personal level of our being. He was writing on the issues of the relation between personal holiness, spirituality, and social concerns in his 1963 book *Life and Holiness*. We do not just give ourselves to one another in love only on the personal or familial level; we are called by the gospel also to give ourselves to one another in love on the societal and global levels. The political economy is as much, if not much more, an arena within which we must discern and spiritually direct the graced energies of our human being. Merton preaches: "There is no charity without justice. . . . True charity is love, and love implies a deep concern for the needs of another. It is not a matter of moral self-indulgence, but of strict obligation. I am obliged by the law of Christ and of the Spirit to be

---

1. Thomas Merton, *Love and Learning* (New York: Harcourt, Inc., 1965–1979), 27.

concerned with my brother's need. . . . How many terrible problems in relations between classes, nations, and races in the modern world arise from the sad deficiency of love!"[2]

Learning how to choose and love wisely and well, on many levels and in and through many relationships, is one of the gifts of spiritual direction. IgnatianSpirituality.com provides a brief and cogent description of spiritual direction.

> Spiritual direction is "help given by one Christian to another which enables that person to pay attention to God's personal communication to him or her, to respond to this personally communicating God, to grow in intimacy with this God, and to live out the consequences of the relationship." (William A. Barry and William J. Connolly, *The Practice of Spiritual Direction*)
>
> • **Spiritual direction focuses on religious experience.** It is concerned with a person's actual experience of a relationship with God.
>
> • **Spiritual direction is about a relationship.** The religious experience is not isolated, nor does it consist of extraordinary events. It is what happens in an ongoing relationship between the person and God. Most often this is a relationship that is experienced in prayer.
>
> • **Spiritual direction is a relationship that is going somewhere.** God is leading the person to deeper faith and more generous service. The spiritual director asks not just "what is happening?" but "what is moving forward?"
>
> • **The real spiritual director is God. God touches the human heart directly.** The human spiritual director does not "direct" in the sense of giving advice and solving problems. Rather, the director helps a person respond to God's invitation to a deeper relationship.

Spiritual direction is about a relationship that is going somewhere. That somewhere is the transformation of our world. Those who seriously commit to the Lord Jesus and his reign do so realizing what we are up against. Still, faith empowers us to strive to ameliorate our world. Jesuits, and all who follow Jesus, are called to be servants of Christ's mission.

---

2. Thomas Merton, *Life and Holiness* (New York: Herder and Herder, 1963), 114–15.

We recognize, along with many others, that without faith, without the eye of love, the human world seems too evil for God to be good, for a good God to exist. But faith recognizes that God is acting through Christ's love and the power of the Holy Spirit, to destroy the structures of sin which afflict the bodies and hearts of his children. Our Jesuit mission touches something fundamental in the human heart: the desire to find God in a world scarred by sin, and then to live the Gospel in all its implications.[3]

Pennsylvania senator Bob Casey attended Scranton Prep and the College of the Holy Cross, graduating in 1982. He then spent a year as a Jesuit volunteer, teaching at the Gesu School, 17th and Thompson Streets, in the heart of North Philadelphia. He has never forgotten his time with the children of Philadelphia. Speaking to a group of administrators of service programs, he said that his time as a Jesuit volunteer made him walk the halls of Congress always thinking of "the last and the least, the lonely and the lost." In 1928, Lyndon Johnson taught poor Mexican children in Cotulla, Texas. LBJ never forgot the sight of kids rummaging through garbage looking for food to eat, "shaking the coffee grounds off the grapefruit rinds and sucking the rinds for the juice that was left." He would spend his own money on materials for the Mexican children. He never forgot those little kids, and, as president, strove to make their lives better. As president, he returned to Cotulla and proclaimed, "The children of Mexican-Americans have been taught that the end of life is a beet row, or a spinach field, or a cotton patch. So to their parents throughout the land this afternoon, we say, help us lift the eyes of our children to a greater vision of what they can do with their lives."[4] Casey and LBJ evidence that spiritual desires for justice can influence and make better our society. Politicians, business leaders, hedge fund managers, celebrities: these folks may need spiritual direction more than religious types!

Robin Meyers, whom I quoted earlier, is a college professor and minister in Oklahoma City, where he has pastors the Mayflower Congregational United Church of Christ. He passionately preaches that churches

---

3. From "Servants of Christ's Mission," #36/11, Decree #2 of General Congregation 34 of the Society of Jesus, in John W. Padberg, S.J., ed., *Jesuit Life and Mission Today: The Decrees & Accompanying Documents of the 31st—35th General Congregations of the Society of Jesus* (St. Louis, MO: Institute of Jesuit Sources, 2009), 526.

4. Melissa Block, "LBJ Carried Poor Texas Town with Him in Civil Rights Fight," *National Public Radio*, April 11, 2014.

professing to follow Jesus Christ must be active in resisting anti-gospel currents in our world. The gospel calls us to transform our society and world.

> In America, the Bible has been used primarily to preserve the status quo, rather than to challenge or change it. People still argue over the term "social gospel"—*as if there's any other kind.* We continue to make distinctions between individual sin and collective sin; between salvation of the soul and salvation of the system. This separation of private piety from public engagement has been toxic for the church. It conjures the cartoon of people praying inside a sanctuary while the people outside are starving, homeless, and persecuted.[5]

Too many of us read the gospels as instructions for personal salvation in the life to come. The truth is that the gospels are talking about salvation now, the times in which we live now, in the world we make for one another now. The word "salvation" comes from the Latin *salus.* The Roman goddess *Salus* was patroness of safety and well-being of both the individual and the state. It is also associated with "health." The name "Jesus" means "God saves." Jesus saves us now, and calls us to save one another in this life even as we prepare for the next.

Bishop N. T. Wright argues that we too often miss the point of the gospels because we don't realize the social implications of the story of Israel and its relation to the good news of Jesus presented in the gospels. Matthew, Mark, Luke, and John are all telling us about Jesus because Jesus is the fulfillment of the history of Israel. The Hebrew Scriptures teach that every seventh day is a Sabbath, every seven years a sabbatical year, and every forty-ninth year (7x7) was to be a Jubilee year, "when slaves were freed, when land sold off by the family was to be restored to its original owner, when things should be put back as they should be."[6] According to Wright, Jesus is the new Moses, David, and Elijah all rolled into one. It's as if a politician in our day could combine the courage and prudence of Washington, the wisdom and fortitude of Lincoln, and the vision and justice of Franklin D. Roosevelt. Everyone reading the gospels in the years they were written would have been very aware of who and what Jesus is in relation to Israel's history.

---

5. Robin Meyers, *Spiritual Defiance: Building a Beloved Community of Resistance* (New Haven, CT: Yale University Press, 2015), 90.

6. N. T. Wright, *How God Became King: The Forgotten Story of the Gospels* (New York: HarperOne, 2012), 70.

Israel's story is thus the microcosm and beating heart of the world's story, but also its ultimate saving energy. What God does for Israel is what God is doing in relation to the whole world. That is what it means to be Israel, to be the people who, for better or worse, carried the destiny of the whole world on their shoulders. *Grasp that, and you have a pathway into the heart of the New Testament.*[7]

For Wright, the gospels are all "about God in public, about the kingdom of God coming on earth, as in heaven through the public career and death and resurrection of Jesus. . . . The central message of all four canonical gospels . . . is that the creator God . . . is at last reclaiming the world as his own."[8] The kingdom of God is what the world would be like if God was really in charge of our political, social, and cultural systems.

Pastor Barbara Taylor calls attention to what happens when we get to the heart of the gospels. We begin the hard work of loving one another. "The wisdom of the Desert Fathers includes the wisdom that the hardest spiritual work in the world is to love the neighbor as the self—to encounter another human being not as someone you can use, change, fix, help, save, enroll, convince, or control but simply as someone who can spring from the prison of yourself, if you will allow it."[9] Freed of an overdose of overly self-centered concern, we realize that God directs us to pay attention to others, those in need. "All you have to do is recognize another you 'out there'—your other self in the world—for whom you may care as instinctively as you care for yourself. To become that person, even for a moment, is to understand what it means to die to yourself. This can be as frightening as it is liberating. It may be the only real spiritual discipline there is."[10]

What would our society, our world, our global political economy be like if Christians, over two billon people on earth, practiced kingdom economics instead of crony capitalism's machinations, policies of the powerful that leave billions in poverty? What if we really cared for the other in need? But will those in power ever choose differently?

---

7. Ibid., 73 (italics added).

8. N. T. Wright, *Surprised by Scripture: Engaging Contemporary Issues* (New York: HarperOne, 2014), 165–66.

9. Barbara Taylor, *An Altar in the World: A Geography of Faith* (New York: HarperOne, 2009), 93.

10. Ibid.

Professor Robert Reich, former Secretary of Labor, notes that from 1978 to 2013, CEO pay rose 937 percent; the wages of a typical worker rose only 10.2 percent.[11] The old song goes, "The rich get rich and the poor they lose, so the Bible says and it still is news." The rich also increasingly control political power and the ways the market game is structured. In 2012, the billionaire Koch brothers' political network blew more than $400 million to get their chosen candidates elected. Preparing for the 2016 elections, the Kochs, along with their super-rich friends, amassed a "war chest" of almost $1 billion. This means their power almost equals that of the two major political parties.[12]

Unbelievable amounts of corporate welfare, stagnant wages for the middle class since 1973, and an overall sense that the "system" simply is not working in any way equitably and fairly for the vast majority of people in the United States has unleashed a vicious backlash. In 2015, long before Donald Trump captured the presidency in 2016, Reich predicted: "It is likely that in the coming years the major fault lines in American politics will shift from Democrat versus Republican to anti-establishment versus establishment—that is, to the middle class, working class, and poor who see the game as rigged versus the executives of large corporations, the inhabitants of Wall Street, and the billionaires who do the rigging."[13]

But will the rich choose heaven? "How hard it is for those who have wealth to enter the kingdom of God!" (Lk 18:24; RSV). Two years ago, I replied to an email from Legatus, a Catholic business organization: "Thanks for your invitation. I'm flattered that you ask me to speak before your group. One thing though, are you sure I'm the kind of speaker you want? By anyone's calculus, I'm what many would categorize as a 'liberal' Jesuit, quite in the mold of Pope Francis who also questions the assumptions and outcomes of an unbridled, predatory capitalism (cf. *The Joy of the Gospel*). Rush Limbaugh would call us both 'Marxists,' although we don't follow Marx but the one who said 'you cannot serve both God and Mammon,' i.e., illegitimate wealth. I'm not the kind of priest or thinker with whom, I imagine, members of Legatus would agree. My take on Catholic Social Teaching, and my readings of social reality, may not be all that welcome among your group. Although I clearly recognize the cru-

11. Robert Reich, *Saving Capitalism for the Many, Not the Few* (New York: Alfred A. Knopf, 2015), 97.

12. Ibid., 173, 178.

13. Ibid., 187–88.

cial role business leaders play in operationalizing our Catholic faith in the real world, I usually find some business folk less than open to some of my views on social justice, and the need for society to radically change social structures in order to create a world of love and peace and justice for all (e.g., providing health care to all members of society; raising the minimum wage; stopping the spending of 57 percent of the federal budget on the military; and, yes, redistributing wealth more equitably so that the one percent don't have it all while the bottom 40 percent have almost nothing[14]). Again, thanks for the invitation, but I wouldn't want you to find you had invited someone you didn't want to hear."

The representative of this group of Catholic business CEOs and leaders dedicated "to study, spread and live the Catholic faith in our business, professional and personal lives" (http://www.legatus.org/) replied, "Even if our group was less than open to your way of thinking, wouldn't it be that type of group to which you really would want to speak? When the self-canonized saint of capitalism [Limbaugh] accuses the Pope of being a Marxist, it just may be the opportune time to make your point with conservative Catholics. What fun is there in preaching to the converted? Easy, I guess, for me to say as I do not have to stand at the lectern and speak to a potential[ly] hostile audience." Well, as it turned out, they weren't exactly hostile, more just very, very annoyed with me. Let's just say, as civil as our exchange was, we ended up agreeing to disagree, and go home early. To get to my speaking venue, I drove south from Scranton for ninety minutes in torrential rainstorms, an omen to which maybe I should have paid more attention. We had a quiet Mass, and the first reading that day was from the prophet Amos. The Gospel was Matthew's healing of the demoniacs, which ends with Jesus being asked to leave town. Rarely have the daily readings and my experience of the day dovetailed so completely.

After a wonderful meal at a lavish country club, I was introduced. Things started off well as the audience laughed at my opening joke. But from there it was pretty much downhill. Everything I said was quickly countered by a question based on a Fox News view of the world. After about twenty-five minutes of what was to be a forty-five-minute presentation, one CEO type stood, paused to allow all to see the sour look on his face, and pointedly pronounced that I was preaching to the wrong choir,

---

14. UpWorthy.com, "Nine out of ten Americans are completely wrong about this mind-blowing fact."

and we might as well call it a night. Some were a little taken aback at the guy's rude dismissal (after all I am a priest, albeit a Jesuit, and this group is Catholic!). Some asked if I had anything else to speak on. I wondered if they'd like to hear what the pope had to say. Most said no, but a few, trying to save the situation, said yes. I went on for two or three minutes noting a bit of what the pope presents in #53–59 of *The Joy of the Gospel*, but saw I was making no converts. My few supporters were uncomfortable. One of the annoyed-to-angry men frankly commented, "The pope, I'm afraid, is a communist."

I had begun my presentation by saying I think business is part of the solution to societal problems such as poverty, a crumbling infrastructure, the need to ameliorate our health and educational systems. But when I began to question beliefs about predatory capitalism, you'd think I'd blasphemed.

Facts don't help these folks call into question the machinations of our political economy. They had little problem with one out of four children in the United States, under the age of six, living in poverty, while overall, 22 percent of children in our country are poor (the poverty line for a family of four at that time was $23,492). In the developed world, only Mexico (26 percent), Chile (24 percent), and Turkey (23 percent) have higher child poverty rates than the United States.[15] The Dow was 6,626 points in 2008 and hit an all-time high of 17,000 the day I gave this talk in July 2014. In early 2017, the Dow went above 20,000. My suggestion that the $750 billion bailout of Wall Street is corporate welfare was, to be honest, not well received at all, and I never even got to the analysis of how much government subsidizes pro sports teams' stadiums, Walmart, and other corporate giants. Recent reports that "nearly all the gains" of the past forty years have gone to people in the top 20 percent of the income brackets (those making over $100,000 a year) were disbelieved.[16] That the 400 richest people in the United States have more wealth than the bottom 50 percent of Americans didn't faze my audience.[17]

---

15. Frontline, "By the Numbers: Poor Kids in the U.S." (November 20, 2012), http://www.pbs.org.

16. Adam Davidson, "It's Official: The Boomerang Kids Won't Leave," *New York Times Magazine*, June 20, 2014.

17. See Robert Reich's documentary *Inequality for All*, http://inequalityforall.com; also, Julie Polter, "Rigged," cover story for *Sojourners*, August 2014.

The group readily dismissed the fact that workers are getting 10 to 15 percent less than ten years ago, the first such decline in U.S. history.[18] They had no problem with the top one percent and even 0.01 percent reaping huge rewards while the U.S. middle class is disappearing. And increase taxes? They scoffed, "How could you expect rich people to work if they were taxed as they were in the 1960s, or 1980s?" George W. Bush's tax cuts are gospel. The Gospels and Catholic social teaching are, in their view, sinful socialism. One voiced the most memorized scripture among the rich: Jesus said, "The poor you shall always have with you." I didn't have the chance to point out Jesus said that to Judas (Jn 12:8): "Judas, the poor you will always have with *you*." Jesus didn't say, "Keep people poor and, in my name, make them even more impoverished."

The group firmly believed that the ones who make money can do with it whatever they will. Those who have less should not envy those who do well. How the rich get rich, and stay rich, is not to be questioned. Wages are self-evidently fair, since the omniscient, magic, and magnificent Market determines everything. The minimum wage is only for teenagers; no need to raise it. David Letterman's making $43 million while the average school teacher makes $43,000 is no problem. Letterman is worth it. Judge Judy's making $25 million to Chief Justice Roberts's $217,000 is just the way the market determines things. And CEOs making hundreds times more than the average worker is just fine.[19]

Questions of justice didn't seem to trouble the minds or hearts of this group. Suggestions that they view Robert Reich's documentary *Inequality for All* were met with stony stares. My reference to the second economic bill of rights championed by FDR in January of 1944 was put down with, "FDR: That's when government got involved and ruined everything." The idea that the government sets the rules is fine, as long as the rules favor the rich. But government helping the poor or the middle class? Anathema! On the other hand, Pope Francis clearly states:

> While the earnings of a minority are growing exponentially, so too is the gap separating the majority from the prosperity enjoyed by those happy few. This imbalance is the result of ideologies which defend the absolute autonomy of the marketplace and financial

---

18. David Peterson, "Can Free Market Principles Reverse America's Decline?" Review of Samuel Gregg's *Becoming Europe, New Oxford Review* (May 2014): 36.

19. Michael J. Sandel, *Justice: What's the Right Thing to Do?* (New York: Farrar, Straus and Giroux, 2009), 18, 162.

speculation. Consequently, they reject the right of states, charged with vigilance for the common good, to exercise any form of control. A new tyranny is thus born, invisible and often virtual, which unilaterally and relentlessly imposes its own laws and rules. (*The Joy of the Gospel,* #56)

It was a nice stipend, which, considering the time in preparation, travel costs, and presentation, probably paid me about $10 an hour. That wouldn't get me anywhere near the U.S. median family income of $50,217 a year in 2013 ($53,718 in 2015),[20] but it is much more than what the 47 million Americans living in poverty get, or what 80 percent of our planet's population, who live on less than $10 a day, survives on.[21]

The reading from Amos that day proclaimed, "I hate, I despise your feasts. . . . But let justice roll down like waters, and righteousness like an ever-flowing stream" (5:21, 24; RSV). Later, as I was driving home in the darkness and rain, I wondered, what will happen when these people get to the gates of heaven? I've often preached that the problem with the sin of racism is that the racist will choose not to enter heaven when it is apparent that heaven is a place of racial diversity and harmony. The problem with riches is that our clinging to them may mean we cannot grasp what is of true and eternal value. Rich persons may not want to enter heaven when they see that it is a place where justice reigns, where God "has filled the hungry with good things, and the rich he has sent empty away" (Lk 1:53; RSV). Will the rich want to enter heaven where there will be no rich and no poor? Will they choose heaven, when they realize that there those who were wealthy in this life will have only as much as everyone else in God's reign?

The stakes in our choosing are high. We really will receive what we deeply desire. If we desire a world of justice and peace, someday, some way, we will get there. But if heaven is a place of justice and peace, and we are too wedded to the ways of war making and inequality, will we choose heaven?

When I read a reflection on authenticity by Sr. Joan Chittister, O.S.B., I was reminded of those folks at the Legatus dinner. She writes, "False Gods are easy to come by in life. They seduce us with power and money and fame. They are the things I can't give up, the things I can't do without, the things that shout my identity to the world so that the world can

20. See http://www.census.gov.
21. See http://www.globalissues.org.

know how important I am."[22] Associating ourselves in religious groups that tell us how great we are, how religious we are, how good we are for God and the world is not authenticity. It's not transformative nor pleasing to God. It's the blindness of the Pharisee praying before the tax collector, a Roman lackey and despised enemy of the oppressed Jewish people (cf. Lk 18:9–14). Sr. Joan continues, "We make Gods out of the social system we have cultivated. . . . We make gods out of the baubles and trinkets of our lives. We learn to even make gods out of the very religious practices and spiritual disciplines that are meant to lead us beyond ourselves to God."[23] We cannot go to God from a position of strength, power, and self-sufficiency. "We must learn to pray out of our weakness so that God can become our strength"[24] (cf. 2 Cor 12:9).

The Jewish prophets knew the truth of the covenant; we are dependent on God. Jesus lived the prophetic tradition of the Jewish people. The Hebrew prophets didn't predict the future so much as they proclaimed how the present ought to be structured socially based on the realities and demands of the future, wherein God's reign would be firmly established and the covenant honored. Ronald Rolheiser notes that the Jewish prophets clearly taught that God favors the poor.

> Jesus took this even further. He endorsed the idea that God favors the poor, but added the notion that God is in the poor, that we meet God in the poor, and that how we treat the poor is (with no escape clauses) how we treat him. In effect, Jesus told us that no one gets into heaven without a letter of reference from the poor. This, although clear in the Gospels and in the Jewish scriptures, is often rather misunderstood or rejected by many sincere Christians.[25]

When I preach on Matthew 25:31–46, the parable of the Judgment of the Nations, in which those who care for and serve the poor and needy are gifted with heaven while those who don't are sent away, or on Mary's Magnificat, where the rich are sent "empty away" (Lk 1:53; RSV), someone will often approach me and say, "Well, Father, you have to remember that Jesus said, 'the poor you will have with you always.'" I respond (I

---

22. Joan Chittister, O.S.B., *The Breath of the Soul: Reflections on Prayer* (New London, CT: Twenty-Third Publications, 2009), 29.

23. Ibid., 29–30.

24. Ibid., 31.

25. Ronald Rolheiser, *Sacred Fire: A Vision for a Deeper Human and Christian Maturity* (New York: Image Books, 2014), 48–49.

hope not "react," and I hope kindly) that Jesus said that to Judas: Judas, you who are all overly worried about money, the poor you will always have with *"You, Judas"* (Jn 12:8). Jesus didn't say, "Keep the poor always destitute. I want my followers to be good capitalists, practicing the perverted idea that God wants the few to have so much and the many to have so little." The Eucharist shows that God wants us to share the goods of this earth. There's no institution of the Eucharist, "this is my body, this is my blood," in John's Gospel. Instead, Jesus takes off his tunic at the Last Supper and washes the feet of his disciples. Jesus says that is how we are to serve one another. The washing of the feet was a shocking sign. That is why Peter reacts to the idea so negatively. The equivalent today would be Jesus taking his disciples to a nursing home and cleaning up the urine and excrement of the helpless patients, and telling his followers to do the same.

Pastor Barbara Taylor recounts her experience as a volunteer at a homeless shelter:

> It is unclear how I ended up with the job of cleaning toilets. Was it a clergy thing? Or was it because I showed up once a season? Whatever it was, the toilets were mine—all three of them—all smelling of vomit, all splattered with diarrhea, all slick with urine. Short of falling head first into the septic tank, I could not imagine anything worse, which made it the perfect job for me. Scrubbing the bowls one by one, I thought of St. Francis kissing the lepers. I thought of Jesus washing feet. I thought of Mother Teresa bathing the dying of Calcutta. By the time I reached the third bowl I was entirely out of spiritual fantasies, which left me free to remember that I too used toilets, occasionally as these toilets had been used. I was made of the same stuff as other humans. What came out of me smelled no better than what came out of everyone else. Welcome back to earth, you earthling. Welcome home, you beloved dirt-person of God.[26]

Those who desire to find God through the practice of spiritual direction will necessarily be encouraged to ponder and pray over the social systems of our lives as much as on our personal journeys. We need to prayerfully pray through social sin as much as we pray through our personal peccadillos. We need to listen for how God is calling us to cooperate with social grace as much as for how God is calling us to resist social

---

26. Taylor, *An Altar in the World*, 153.

sin. Prayer and spiritual direction, discernment and decisions, in the light of God's desire that the Kingdom come, are about social as much as personal transformation. Pastor Robin Meyers writes:

> It was Bruggemann who said "Sabbath, in the first instance, is not about worship. It is about work stoppage. It is about withdrawal from the anxiety of the system of Pharaoh, the refusal to let one's life be defined by production and consumption and the endless pursuit of private well-being." Just imagine the power of millions of Christians who refuse to shop when we are supposed to be resting and grateful.[27]

There are endless ruminations over why mainstream Christian churches are seeing the young look elsewhere for spiritual sustenance, or worse, not even search for spiritual meaning at all. Thirty-five percent of millennials claim no religious affiliation.[28] The alarming increase of various addictions and eating disorders, as well as the ever-increasing need for counselors among the affluent young in the United States, evidences a lack of institutional connection with young adults' lives. Those in their twenties and thirties are not only showing their alienation from churches, political parties, and other institutions of society. They are also showing an alarming proclivity to drift through life. An arresting and challenging message may be more what they need to hear than endless affirmations of how special they are.

> People are not fleeing churches today because they have lost their deep hunger for spiritual connection and participation in authentic spiritual communities. Rather they are fleeing because so many churches now seem bereft of the very spirit that birthed them in the first place. If the clergy want to find their people, they might try looking in coffee shops, in homeless shelters, among the young who have pitched their tents in parks to dramatize economic injustice. While we shop, salute and worship celebrities and athletes, the

---

27. Robin Meyers, *Spiritual Defiance: Building a Beloved Community of Resistance* (New Haven, CT: Yale University Press, 2015), 114. He quotes from Walter Brueggemann, *Journey to the Common Good* (Louisville, KY: Westminster John Knox, 2010), 26.

28. Tony Compolo and Shane Claiborne, "The Evangelicalism of Old White Men Is Dead," *New York Times*, op-ed page, November 29, 2016.

world is falling apart. What we need today is a move to *Occupy Religion*.[29]

Pastor Robin Meyers, speaking from the heartland of the America, not some effete, elite site located deep in the universities and East Coast outlets of the often unfairly maligned main stream media, trumpets the need for us to do something new, something alarming and challenging. As N. T. Wright puts it, "Somehow, if we are to speak wisely of God as King and Jesus as Lord, we have to speak of something radically new. . . . All Kingdom work is rooted in worship. Or to put it the other way around, worshipping the God we see at work in Jesus is the most politically charged act we can ever perform. Christian worship declares that Jesus is Lord, and that therefore, by strong implication, nobody else is."[30]

My own religious tradition in the Society of Jesus, the Jesuits, makes much the same plea and call as Pastor Meyers. This will not be easy and will not necessarily feel good. This will hurt before it heals. This will cost all we have. But when we've lost what we don't need, we will know freedom and truth and love. Many will not go along with this true and real gospel program.

> We need to recognize that the Gospel of Christ will always provoke resistance; it challenges men and women and requires of them a conversion of mind, heart and behavior. . . . [T]he call of Christ is always radically opposed to values which refuse spiritual transcendence and promote a pattern of selfish life. Sin is social in its expression, as is the counter witness offered by grace: unless a Christian life distinctly differs from the values of secular modernity, it will have nothing special to offer. One of the most important contributions we can make to critical contemporary culture is to show that the structural injustice in the world is rooted in a value system promoted by a powerful modern culture which is becoming global in its impact.[31]

---

29. Meyers, *Spiritual Defiance*, 115.

30. N. T. Wright, *Simply Jesus: A New Vision of Who He Was, What He Did, and Why He Matters* (New York: HarperOne, 2011), 207.

31. From "Our Mission and Culture," #108/24, Decree #4 of General Congregation 34 of the Society of Jesus. In John W. Padberg, S.J., ed., *Jesuit Life and Mission Today: The Decrees & Accompanying Documents of the 31st–35th General Congregations of the Society of Jesus* (St. Louis, MO: The Institute of Jesuit Sources, 2009), 543.

Jesuits in our times are calling us to the transformative hope preached in the gospel of Jesus. They want us to respond to the poverties of our world, both the spiritual poverty of our age and also the economic and material poverty suffered by billions of our brothers and sisters.

> To follow Christ bearing his Cross means announcing his Gospel of hope to the many poor who inhabit our world today. The world's many 'poverties' represent thirsts that, ultimately, only he who is living water can assuage. Working for his Reign will often mean meeting material needs, but it will always mean much more, because human beings thirst at many levels; and Christ's mission is directed to human beings. Faith *and* Justice; it is never one without the other. Human beings need food, shelter, love, relationship, truth, meaning, promise, and hope. Human beings need a future in which they can take hold of their full dignity; indeed they need an absolute future, a 'great hope' that exceeds every particular hope.[32]

Jesuits see our mission not just as Faith and Justice but also as a call to reconciliation. Back in 1975, when the mission of Faith and Justice was articulated for our times, the text read "The mission of the Society of Jesus today is the service of faith, of which the promotion of justice is an absolute requirement." But the next sentence seemed to drop out of extensive awareness among many of us who focused on faith and justice. "For reconciliation with God demands the reconciliation of people with one another."[33] In 2008, some thirty-three years later, the Society of Jesus called for a mission that concentrates on reconciliation and dialogue. In a section entitled "Call to Establish Right Relationships: A Mission of Reconciliation," Jesuits said: "In this global world marked by such profound changes, we now want to deepen our understanding of the call to serve faith, promote justice, and dialogue with culture and other religions in the light of the apostolic mandate to establish right relationships with God, with one another, and with creation."[34]

---

32. From "A Fire That Kindles Other Fires," #30/13, Decree #2 of General Congregation 35 of the Society of Jesus, in Padberg, *Jesuit Life and Mission Today*, 738 (italics in original).

33. From "Jesuits Today," #48/2, Decree #4 of General Congregation 32 of the Society of Jesus, in Padberg, *Jesuit Life and Mission Today*, 298.

34. From "Challenges to our Mission Today," Decree #3 of General Congregation 35 of the Society of Jesus, in Padberg, *Jesuit Life and Mission Today*, 746.

Spiritual direction aids those who pray. And those who pray in the prophetic words of Mons. Oscar Romero are those who truly move history in the direction of the Reign of God.

> The true protagonists of history are those who are most united with God, because with God's viewpoint they can best attend to the signs of the times, the ways [*caminos*] of Providence, the building of history. Oh, if we only had persons of prayer among those who oversee the fate of the nation and the fate of the economy! If, instead of relying on human devices, people would rely on God and on his devices, we would have a world like the one the church dreams of, a world without injustices, a world with respect for rights, a world with generous participation by all, a world without repression, a world without torture. (July 17, 1977)[35]

"Faith isn't where your head is. Faith isn't where your heart is. Faith is where your ass is." —Dan Berrigan, S.J.

---

35. Oscar Romero, *The Violence of Love*, comp. and trans. James R. Brockman, S.J. (Maryknoll, NY: Orbis Books, 2004), 5.

Conclusion

There is a crack, a crack in everything. That's how the light gets in.
— Leonard Cohen, "Anthem"

Why do so few see the star? Only because so few are looking for it.
— Alfred Delp, S.J. (Nazi victim),
The Prison Meditations of Father Delp

I think joy and sweetness and affection are a spiritual path. We're here to know God, to love and serve God, and to be blown away by the beauty and miracle of nature. You just have to get rid of so much baggage to be light enough to dance, to sing, to play. You don't have time to carry grudges; you don't have time to cling to the need to be right.
— Anne Lamott

Joy is the best makeup.
— Anne Lamott

Freedom from, freedom for, freedom to be with
— Thumbnail sketch of the goals of the Spiritual Exercises of St. Ignatius

In all things, to love and to serve (en todo amar y servir).
— The motto of St. Ignatius

When I was a small boy, my mother would take us up from Philly to her sister's home in Gerritsen Beach, New York, near Sheepshead Bay, Brooklyn, where they were born and raised. The family joked that my Aunt Gertrude had married "outside the faith." She was an Irish girl who had married an Italian guy. I loved visiting the Colombos. The back door of their house opened onto a small dock on an industrial canal filled with boats. I had never ventured into the deep area of any pool or pond. Now, my cousin Joe Colombo was ten years older than I. One day—I was five at the time—he picked me up and flipped me into the water. I splashed around screaming, "It's too deep! It's too deep!" Joe just looked at me and said, "Ricky, relax. You only have to stay on top of the water." That all of a sudden made so much sense to me. If I could swim in three feet of water, I could swim in thirty. Then my mother came out of the house, whopped Joe on the head, and yelled at him for almost drowning her kid.

Spiritual direction is like that insight into the depth of water. We are continually told we need to float and let God's current take us where it will; swimming against the tide will get us nowhere. We just need to remain on the water and not sink.

Joe Colombo lived a good life. He was a professional musician, a superb guitarist. He married a wonderful woman. They enjoyed the 1960s, and would proudly show off their tickets to Woodstock. After their second child arrived, Joe settled down and got a master's degree in physics so he could have a more regular life and provide for his family. He was one of the smartest guys I'd ever met. But religion and Joe parted ways when he was young. His mother's daily Mass, daily rosary routine, didn't fit his way of life. Science and music filled his heart and imagination.

Until, at fifty-eight, he was diagnosed with cancer. He called me up, and asked me to come and see him. "I don't have a good feeling about this." He was appropriately angry. "I know people get cancer. But I've spent years teaching. In a few years I could retire. The next twenty years were going to be mine. We were going to move to Hawaii. Great skies for my telescopes!" I was sitting there listening to a guy I'd always admired and loved. I was wondering why he'd called me up to see him, since I knew he wasn't a believer. Then, surprise.

"Ricky. I gotta tell you something. They took me into the operating room a few weeks ago. I was lying there looking up at the ceiling. I couldn't believe it. The act of contrition came back to me. That stuff is still all in there. I haven't paid attention to it in years."

At first, we read the words of Gerard Hughes, S.J.: "The treasure is hidden within you ... within the field of our inner experience."[1] Through music and science, Joe had paid a great deal of attention to his inner experience, and at the end of his days, he reconnected with the spiritual aspects of the mystery of his life and loves in ways that led him to hope and trust in a God he had not, for a long time, "hung out with" (Joe's words). It was a grace and privilege for me to grow closer to my cousin

1. Gerard W. Hughes, S.J., *God of Surprise* (New York & Mahwah, NJ: Paulist Press, 1985), 1, 26. Cf. epigraph in Preface to this book.

as he prepared for death. It was a consolation to preside and preach at his funeral knowing where he was in relation to God. It wasn't like I was his formal "spiritual director." The Holy Spirit was doing that. I was just along for the ride. In Joe, I witnessed how our relationship with God can make us larger, more connected to peace and joy and hope and love, even as we undergo death.

There was a man named John Bigger. He and his wife had a baby. Who was bigger, John Bigger or the baby? Well, actually the baby, because the baby is—wait for it—a "little Bigger"! Da, dum . . . drum roll please! Corny joke, but it makes the point: Spiritual direction is always making us a little bigger, more open, more willing and able to encompass those we meet with the love, compassion, and mercy of God. The point of our being women and men of prayer is that we become not just people who pray, but those who live our lives attuned to and clicked into what God is doing in our lives and world. French Jesuit Francois Roustang writes in his seminal *Growth in the Spirit*: "To become, day by day, as a traveler who awakens to landscapes he has not even imagined or a stranger who journeys through an unknown land for the first time, is to make ourselves capable of understanding the order of the universe and situating our own action within the work of God."[2] Or, in the more earthy articulation of an elderly Jesuit to a younger Jesuit: "One, know and realize that you are not God. Two, this is not heaven. Three, don't be an asshole" (a bit of advice on how to live in the Society of Jesus).

Growing in the practice of prayer, and connecting our prayer to our personal and social lives, will help us grow bigger and get us out of running in circles. Martin Laird shares a story of what he observed when he would go for long walks to clear his head. A man would often be out in the fields letting his four Kerry blue terriers out for a run. Three of the dogs would bound happily about, working off excess energy, but the one would run around in tight circles. "One day I was bold enough to ask the owner, 'Why does your dog do that? Why does it run in little circles instead of running with the others?' The man explained that before he acquired the dog, it had lived practically all its life in a cage and could only exercise by running in circles."[3] All this poor, little dog knew was

---

2. Francois Roustang, *Growth in the* Spirit, trans. Kathleen Pond (New York: Sheed and Ward, 1966), 217.

3. Martin Laird, O.S.A., *Into the Silent Land: A Guide to the Practice of Christian Contemplation* (New York: Oxford University Press, 2006), 19–20.

running in circles. Prayer, spiritual direction, and living as disciples of Jesus disciplined in freedom will unbind us and send us traveling far beyond anything we can hope or imagine.

Life lived open to the Spirit is God's work in us. The great news of the good news is that God is God! This means we don't have to be God. We can rest assured that we don't have to be God. We don't need to judge, compete to be "Number One," or prove ourselves to God or anyone else. The great freedom of Ignatian spirituality, often learned in the processes and dialogues of spiritual direction, allows us to be filled with the joy of the sons and daughters of God. Knowing how we have been gifted, and how we are called to share those gifts with others, means we can take our place in graced creation and rest in peace. Sr. Joan Chittister, O.S.B., writes:

> The greatest obstacle to the spiritual life is the temptation to make ourselves our own God. It is one thing to know my own gifts and to nurture them. But it is entirely another to presume I have them all. . . . We have been given natural talents in order to develop them for the sake of others. Each of us has been given something that is meant to make the world a better place for the rest of us. . . . We are here to give our gifts to the world. . . . If I don't know my own gifts, if I don't develop my gifts, I cannot possibly fulfill the purpose of creation in me.[4]

To fulfill the purpose for which we are created is the challenge and promise of spiritual direction and the following of Christ. And so it goes. As Tolkien, one of Joe Colombo's favorite authors, writes in *The Fellowship of the Ring*, "The Road goes ever on and on / Down from the door where it began. / Now far ahead the Road has gone, / And I must follow, if I can / Pursuing it with eager feet, / Until it joins some larger way / Where many paths and errands meet / And whither then? I cannot say." Spiritual direction ultimately prepares us for final journeys.

At some point, all spiritual writing must yield to poetry. Allow Robert Frost to have the final word:

---

4. Joan Chittister, *The Breath of the Soul: Reflections on Prayer* (New London, CT: Twenty-Third Publicatons, 2009), 26–27.

Away!

Now I out walking
The world desert,
And my shoe and my stocking
Do me no hurt.

I leave behind
Good friends in town.
Let them get well-wined
And go lie down.

Don't think I leave
For the outer dark
Like Adam and Eve
Put out of the Park.

Forget the myth
There is no one I
Am put out with
Or put out by.

Unless I'm wrong
I but obey
The urge of song
I'm—bound—away!

And I may return
If dissatisfied
With what I learn
From having died.

Acknowledgments

I t is quite impossible to thank and acknowledge all who made this book possible. Over forty years, so many spiritual directors have sat and listened, encouraged and challenged me. Many are the Jesuits who have formed me and graced me with their gifts as spiritual directors. They are all exemplary companions of Jesus and servants of Christ's mission. To name a few: Henry Haske, S.J.; George Aschenbrenner, S.J.; William Sudzina, S.J.; Dennis Ryan, S.J.; Willie Walsh, S.J.; John Schwantes, S.J.; Brian McDermott, S.J.; Joe Grady, S.J.; Fernando Salas, S.J.; Gap LoBiondo, S.J.; Bill Sneck, S.J.; John Kavanaugh, S.J.; John Dear, S.J.; Gene Garcia, S.J.; Mark Aita, S.J.; Tom Roach, S.J.; and Bob Hamm, S.J. The Jesuits at St. Joe's Prep in Philadelphia, especially Vince Taggert, S.J., deserve special mention and thanks for not throwing me out of the school.

Many of my grade school teachers, especially from my earliest days with Sr. Grace Marian, R.S.M., and Sr. Marie Michael, R.S.M., and the teachers through my teen years at St. Joe's Prep, taught me how to read and write and, most importantly, think. Many excellent teachers at the old Weston Jesuit School of Theology inform much of the theological background to the ideas of this book. Thanks to Stanley Marrow, S.J.; Dan Harrington, S.J.; Ed Falherty, S.J.; Brian Daley, S.J.; Peter Fink, S.J.; Sharon Parks Daloz and the folks at St. Patrick's at Blue Hill and Dudley in Roxbury, Massachusetts.

Many religious women have taught me much about spirituality and spiritual direction: Linda Stilling, S.S.N.D.; Catherine Quinn, S.H.C.J.; Joan Jungermann, S.S.N.D.; Mary Mitchell, O.P.; Dottie Aprich, S.S.J.; Rosemarie Kolmer, O.S.F. The sisters should be always cherished. No need for investigations.

Married couples and families such as the Ryans, Muraskis, McGraths, Bradfords, Gerrauthys, Nicolas, Connells, Hills, Vazquezes, Morrises, and many others have taught me much about how God works in families, especially in the mysteries of raising children.

The whole team at Orbis books, especially Mike Leach, Jim Keane, and Maria Angelini, make the whole process of producing a book professional, pleasant, and peaceful. Muchas Gracias.

Index

DATE DUE

IL 18712163		
		PRINTED IN U.S.A.

US$20.00

RELIGION/SPIRITUALITY
RELIGION/CHRISTIAN LIFE/SPIRITUAL GROWTH
RELIGION/CHRISTIANITY/CATHOLIC

SPIRITUAL DIRECTION
A Beginner's Guide
Richard G. Malloy, SJ

In a lively and personal style that responds especially to millennials' questions and concerns, Richard Malloy introduces readers to the art and practice of Spiritual Direction in the Jesuit tradition.

"This exceedingly wise book, steeped in experience and filled with real-life examples, is destined to help many people understand the essential practice of spiritual direction. Father Malloy is known for his inviting, accessible, and often lighthearted style, and his new book will be a great blessing to all those who seek to deepen their relationships with God."
—James Martin, SJ, author, *Jesus: A Pilgrimage*

"*Spiritual Direction* is a suspension bridge, uniting Ignatian spirituality and this great longing within us all to find our way. This most helpful book is chock-full of humor and humanity, a huge heart, and a humble invitation into the spiritual life." —Greg Boyle, SJ, author, *Tattoos on the Heart*

"We finally have the *freedom* and the *skill* to tell people that they can trust their own inner experience because of the rediscovered gift of spiritual direction. This gives Christianity a strong opportunity for both depth and actual change of consciousness. Richard Malloy's book is a major contribution in this direction."
—Richard Rohr, OFM., Center for Action and Contemplation

"What nobler calling than helping people discover how they have been uniquely touched by God and how to fulfill God's will by each becoming a better, freer, more inviting me? . . . Here is a down-to-earth handbook from someone who really knows how—and as important—how not to proceed, how to assess the materials each has . . . and how best to incorporate those elements into the small cathedral each of us is called upon to create."
—William J. O'Malley, SJ, author, *Holiness*

Richard G. Malloy, SJ, is the university chaplain at the University of Scranton and has served as a professor and university chaplain at St. Joseph's University in Philadelphia. He is the author of *A Faith That Frees* and *Being on Fire*, both Catholic Press Association award winners from Orbis Books.

Cover design: John F. Levine
Photograph: Archways at the Qutub Shahi Tombs, Hyderabad, India. ©2009 McKay Savage

ORBIS BOOKS
Maryknoll, New York 10545
OrbisBooks.com

ISBN 978-1-62698-253-6
52000
9 781626 982536